McGraw-Hill's

500
U.S. History
Questions

Volume 1: Colonial to 1865

Also in McGraw-Hill's 500 Questions Series

McGraw-Hill's

500

U.S. History

Questions

Volume 1: Colonial to 1865

Ace Your College Exams

Stephanie Muntone

New York Chicago San Francisco Lisbon London Madrid Mexico City
Milan New Delhi San Juan Seoul Singapore Sydney Toronto

1 2 3 4 5 6 7 8 9 10 11 12 13 14 15   QFR/QFR   1 9 8 7 6 5 4 3 2

ISBN   978-0-07-178060-5
MHID   0-07-178060-2

e-ISBN 978-0-07-178061-2
e-MHID   0-07-178061-0

Library of Congress Control Number 2011944607

Series interior design by Jane Tenenbaum

McGraw-Hill products are available at special quantity discounts to use as premiums and sales promotions or for use in corporate training programs. To contact a representative, please e-mail us at bulksales@mcgraw-hill.com.

This book is printed on acid-free paper.

CONTENTS

INTRODUCTION

Congratulations! You've taken a big step toward achieving your best grade by purchasing *McGraw-Hill's 500 U.S. History Questions, Volume 1: Ace Your College Exams*. We are here to help you improve your grades on classroom, midterm, and final exams. These 500 questions will help you study more effectively, use your preparation time wisely, and get the final grade you want.

This book gives you 500 multiple-choice questions that cover the most essential course material. Each question has a detailed answer explanation. These questions give you valuable independent practice to supplement your regular textbook and the groundwork you are already doing in the classroom.

You might be the kind of student who needs to study extra questions a few weeks before a big exam for a final review. Or you might be the kind of student who puts off preparing until right before a midterm or final. No matter what your preparation style, you will surely benefit from reviewing these 500 questions that closely parallel the content, format, and degree of difficulty of the questions found in typical college-level exams. These questions and their answer explanations are the ideal last-minute study tool for those final days before the test.

Remember the old saying "Practice makes perfect." If you practice with all the questions and answers in this book, we are certain that you will build the skills and confidence that are needed to ace your exams. Good luck!

—*Editors of McGraw-Hill Education*

AUTHOR'S NOTE

The terms *American Indians* and *Native Americans*, used to describe the first settlers of the Americas, are both misnomers. *Indians* reflects the geographical ignorance of the earliest European explorers, who thought when they arrived in the Caribbean that they had reached "the Indies." *Native Americans* is a misnomer because, according to current archaeological knowledge, human beings are not native to the Americas but came here from elsewhere.

During the period of time covered in this book, the U.S. government consistently referred to these first peoples as Indians. This term appears in the U.S. Constitution and in all other official government treaties and documents. Literature written throughout the period uses the term *Indians*. The government established a Permanent Indian Frontier, and Congress passed an Indian Removal Act during the presidency of Andrew Jackson. The term was never used pejoratively; it was as neutral as words like *French* or *African*. It was used until the 1990s, when the term *Native Americans* first appeared.

For the sake of historical appropriateness and to avoid stylistic awkwardness, this book uses the term *Indians* throughout when referring to peoples of more than one Indian nation. When possible, specific names such as Iroquois or Shawnee are used.

CHAPTER 1

Beginnings

The Settlement and Colonization of North America

1. Which was NOT one motive for the European exploration and colonization of the New World?
(A) desire for religious and political freedom
(B) expansion of European-based empires
(C) discovery of the Northwest Passage
(D) greed for gold, treasures, and natural resources
(E) assimilation into the cultures of the West

2. Native Americans, or American Indians, originally came from
(A) Africa
(B) Asia
(C) Europe
(D) North America
(E) South America

3. Which was the first European nation to sponsor a transatlantic voyage of exploration?
(A) England
(B) France
(C) Italy
(D) Portugal
(E) Spain

4. The relatively swift conquest of the North American tribes was mainly due to the European explorers'
(A) sophisticated weapons
(B) superior intelligence
(C) numerical strength
(D) religious faith
(E) literacy

5. What was the primary French activity in North America during the 16th century?
   (A) founding and expanding large, permanent French settlements
   (B) fighting battles with the Indian population
   (C) fighting a war against the British over colonial territory
   (D) establishing a new fur-trading industry
   (E) drawing up plans for a canal in the Great Lakes region

6. The tribal societies of the first North Americans were generally characterized by all of the following EXCEPT
   (A) respect for the land and environment
   (B) hostile relations with other tribes
   (C) democratic political structures
   (D) clearly defined gender roles
   (E) lack of a conquering or expansionist mentality

7. Christopher Columbus's first voyage to the Caribbean (1492) is historically important because
   (A) he was the first European to explore mainland North America
   (B) he was the first European to stake a claim to mainland North America
   (C) he realized that he had found a large landmass of which Europeans had previously been ignorant
   (D) it marked the beginning of the cultural exchange between Europe and the Americas
   (E) it proved that it was possible to reach Asia by sailing west from Europe

8. Which was the only large city in the future United States to be established by the French?
   (A) Baltimore
   (B) Boston
   (C) New Orleans
   (D) Philadelphia
   (E) Washington

9. John Cabot's 1496 voyage to the North American mainland is historically significant because
   (A) it was the first contact between the peoples of the two hemispheres
   (B) it proved that a ship could reach Asia by sailing west from Europe
   (C) it demonstrated that the northern reaches of North America were uninhabitable, confining later exploratory voyages to the southern regions
   (D) it proved that North America was not Asia but an intervening continent previously unknown to Europeans
   (E) it encouraged the European powers to continue searching for the Northwest Passage

10. Which best describes the Iroquois Confederacy?
   (A) an intertribal peacekeeping organization
   (B) an organization that oversaw warfare between Iroquois and non-Iroquois tribes
   (C) a series of violent Iroquois raids on colonial settlements
   (D) a group of linguistically and culturally related tribes
   (E) territory that belonged to the Iroquois according to agreement with the European colonists

11. Notable Spanish explorers of the future United States include all of the following EXCEPT
   (A) Pedro Menendez de Áviles
   (B) Hernando de Soto
   (C) Alvar Nuñez Cabeza de Vaca
   (D) Francisco Vásquez de Coronado
   (E) Francisco Pizarro

12. Which was the first North American colony claimed by Great Britain?
   (A) Massachusetts
   (B) Plymouth
   (C) Virginia
   (D) Florida
   (E) Carolina

13. Relations between the Indians and the early Spanish explorers were generally characterized by
   (A) cooperation
   (B) friendship
   (C) neutrality
   (D) hostility
   (E) tolerance

14. Which man did NOT play a major role in England's early exploration of the New World?
    (A) William Byrd
    (B) Henry Hudson
    (C) Walter Raleigh
    (D) John Smith
    (E) John White

15. Spanish and Spanish-sponsored parties explored and/or settled all the following areas of North America EXCEPT
    (A) the Pacific coast
    (B) the northern Atlantic coast
    (C) the Gulf of Mexico
    (D) the Southwest
    (E) the Mississippi valley

16. The first inhabitants of North America developed such a wide variety of cultures because
    (A) they came to North America from many different lands
    (B) they came from distinctly different home cultures
    (C) their religious beliefs were different
    (D) they were not ethnically related to one another
    (E) they settled in different physical environments

17. Which is NOT an important figure in the European discovery, exploration, and settlement of Spanish California?
    (A) Simón Bolivar
    (B) Juan Rodríguez Cabrillo
    (C) Bartolomé Ferrelo
    (D) Junípero Serra
    (E) Sebastián Vizcaíno

The Development and Settlement of the British Colonies

18. Which colony was founded in order to provide a fresh start for debtors?
    (A) Florida
    (B) Georgia
    (C) North Carolina
    (D) South Carolina
    (E) Virginia

19. Which best describes the Fundamental Orders of Connecticut (1639)?
  (A) a set of strict religious guidelines and the criteria for church membership
  (B) a charter for a college of theology and liberal arts in New Haven
  (C) a royal charter that established ownership of the land
  (D) a peace treaty with the local Penobscot tribes
  (E) a written constitution that established the structure of the government

20. What was the most important effect of the Salem witch trials of the 1690s?
  (A) The era of theocracy in New England was ended.
  (B) The entire population of Salem abandoned the town.
  (C) The leaders amended the royal charter of Massachusetts Bay.
  (D) The accusers of Salem were tried and executed in their turn.
  (E) Puritan worship was banned throughout New England.

21. Which of the following was NOT a major motive for 17th-century New Englanders to move south and found new colonies such as Connecticut?
  (A) They wanted to live in a less restrictive society.
  (B) They sought good land for farming.
  (C) They did not believe in many of the tenets of Puritanism.
  (D) They opposed chattel slavery.
  (E) They believed in at least some separation between church and state.

22. Anne Hutchinson is a significant figure in early colonial history because
  (A) she was the first woman in the colonies to preach from a pulpit
  (B) she played a leading role in the founding of the colony of Rhode Island
  (C) she was an unofficial religious leader and an outspoken critic of the church establishment
  (D) she founded the first antislavery society in the British colonies
  (E) she was accused of witchcraft and executed during the Salem trials

23. What was the significance of Bacon's Rebellion?
  (A) It denied colonists the right to settle on Indian lands.
  (B) It made large-scale planters realize that a system of indentured servitude worked against their economic interests.
  (C) It made the legislatures legalize slavery throughout the colonies.
  (D) It resulted in the division of the colony of Carolina into two sections.
  (E) It established a system of paid labor for large-scale farms.

24. Which of the following does NOT accurately describe the colony
of Pennsylvania?
(A) It was founded as an experiment in religious tolerance.
(B) Its capital, Philadelphia, was the largest city in the British colonies.
(C) It expressly established full civil and legal rights for Indian
inhabitants.
(D) It was given as a land grant to a prominent English Quaker.
(E) It never recognized the legality of chattel slavery.

25. Why is William Bradford an important figure in early colonial history?
(A) He was appointed the governor of the Jamestown colony in 1607.
(B) As the leader of the company of Pilgrims, he established the colony
of Plymouth in 1620.
(C) He received a royal land grant to found the colony of Pennsylvania
in 1681.
(D) He claimed the colony of Virginia for England in the mid-1580s.
(E) He seized the colony of New Amsterdam from the Dutch in 1664.

26. What was the most common form of government in early 18th-century
New England?
(A) popular democracy
(B) republic
(C) constitutional monarchy
(D) theocracy
(E) dictatorship

27. The present-day state of Maine originally formed a part of the colony of
(A) Connecticut
(B) Massachusetts
(C) New Hampshire
(D) Rhode Island
(E) Vermont

28. Why did the Puritan authorities banish Roger Williams from
Massachusetts Bay?
(A) He believed that the colonists should sever their ties to Great Britain.
(B) He argued for the abolition of chattel slavery.
(C) He advocated strict separation of church and state.
(D) He was considered unfit for leadership in the colony.
(E) He preached against peace with the local Indians.

29. Which does NOT accurately describe one aspect of society in New England and the mid-Atlantic colonies during the 18th century?
    (A) a mercantile and trading economy
    (B) the growth of sophisticated large cities
    (C) trained, skilled labor with work done by hand
    (D) subsistence farming except in the most urban locations
    (E) the rise of manufacturing

30. Which is NOT one reason why Benjamin Rush is a notable figure in colonial history?
    (A) He was the first professor of chemistry in North America.
    (B) He cofounded the first antislavery society in North America.
    (C) He was a pioneer and reformer in the treatment of mental illnesses.
    (D) He championed higher education, including women's education.
    (E) He perfected a safer technique of delivering babies.

31. The term *overseer* refers to
    (A) a minister of a Puritan or Congregational church in New England
    (B) a white man who supervised the fieldwork of slaves on a southern plantation
    (C) a mistress of a "dame school" who taught the youngest children to read and write
    (D) a royal governor who had executive powers over a colonial legislature
    (E) a customs inspector who checked the cargo brought in by merchant ships

32. The colony of Maryland was originally founded as
    (A) a refuge for Catholics fleeing persecution in Britain
    (B) a refuge for Anglicans fleeing persecution in Britain
    (C) a Protestant colony with less restrictive rules and customs than those in New England
    (D) the center of the British tobacco-growing and trading industry
    (E) a Quaker colony that would practice religious tolerance and political equality

33. Why was the passage of the English Bill of Rights important to the history of the colonies?
    (A) It became part of the British Constitution.
    (B) It included a long list of individual rights of the citizens.
    (C) It was the result of a peaceful revolution against a monarch.
    (D) It was an example of legislative supremacy in government.
    (E) It altered the colonies' relationship to Great Britain.

34. Which of the following did NOT characterize the role of the church in 17th-century Massachusetts?
    (A) Both men and women were allowed to preach from the pulpit.
    (B) Only church members could run for political office.
    (C) Only church members had the right to vote.
    (D) Religious dissenters were ostracized or banished.
    (E) Moral offenses were treated as civil crimes.

35. Which of the following was NOT one of the 13 original British colonies?
    (A) Delaware
    (B) Georgia
    (C) New Hampshire
    (D) Rhode Island
    (E) Vermont

36. King Philip's War had all the following effects on the New England region EXCEPT
    (A) halting the peacetime economic activities of fishing and trading
    (B) destroying or seriously damaging many towns and settlements, both Indian and colonial
    (C) bankrupting the colonial treasuries
    (D) substantially reducing the Indian and colonial population, especially men of fighting age
    (E) ending the hostilities between the Indian tribes and the colonists

37. Why did the South NOT develop as a mercantile society?
    (A) Each plantation was largely self-sufficient.
    (B) People lived too far apart from one another.
    (C) There were no cities in the South.
    (D) The South was economically very poor.
    (E) The southern climate did not encourage the development of trade.

38. Which best describes the Mayflower Compact?
    (A) a royal charter
    (B) a set of religious commandments
    (C) a deed to property
    (D) a constitution
    (E) a declaration of war

39. Which of the following was the first permanent British settlement
   in the future United States?
   (A) Boston
   (B) Jamestown
   (C) Plymouth
   (D) Richmond
   (E) Roanoke

40. Which best describes the colonists' reaction to the Navigation Acts
   of the mid-1600s?
   (A) They petitioned Parliament to repeal the acts.
   (B) They ignored the acts, maintaining a thriving smuggling industry.
   (C) They imposed heavy fines on shipowners who flouted the acts.
   (D) They suffered economic hardship by obeying the acts to the letter.
   (E) They boycotted British imported goods until the acts were
       overturned.

41. What happened during the Salem witch trials?
   (A) Several people were accused of witchcraft, but no one was convicted
       because there was no eyewitness evidence.
   (B) Several people were accused of witchcraft and were heavily fined
       when they confessed.
   (C) Several people brought lawsuits against the town of Salem after
       they were falsely accused of witchcraft.
   (D) Several people were convicted of witchcraft and banished from
       the colony.
   (E) Several people were executed for practicing witchcraft
       on unsupported accusations.

42. Which best explains why the Indian tribes and the European settlers
   never assimilated into one society?
   (A) They could not learn one another's languages.
   (B) Their physical characteristics were too different.
   (C) Their worldviews were irreconcilable.
   (D) They were unable to communicate.
   (E) They disliked one another on a personal, individual level.

43. The term *middle passage* refers to
- (A) the flatboat journey up or down the Mississippi River
- (B) the organization of the Middle Atlantic region into colonies
- (C) the role of the colonial assemblies in passing or vetoing legislation proposed by the royal governors
- (D) the treaties between colonial assemblies and Indian leaders regarding land rights
- (E) the transport of kidnapped Africans across the Atlantic to the Americas

44. New York is the only colony that the British
- (A) purchased outright from the Lenape and Delaware tribes
- (B) seized from its Dutch founders and governors
- (C) founded inland rather than on the Atlantic coast
- (D) established as a penal colony
- (E) offered as a land grant to a highly placed Englishman

45. What was the purpose of the Navigation Acts of the mid-17th century?
- (A) to force Catholics to convert to Anglicanism or leave Britain
- (B) to encourage trade between the Netherlands and the British colonies
- (C) to encourage free trade among the colonies
- (D) to restrict trade between the British colonies and all nations except Great Britain
- (E) to ensure that the colonies imported more goods than they exported

46. Pocahontas's friendship with the Jamestown colonists was historically important because she
- (A) set an example of friendship and mutual aid between the Algonquin tribes and colonists
- (B) served as an interpreter between the colonists and the Algonquin leaders
- (C) made it possible for the Algonquin tribes and the people of Jamestown to trade with one another
- (D) ensured that the colonists granted the Algonquin people equal legal rights
- (E) permanently ended hostilities between the Algonquin tribes and colonists

47. By the end of the 17th century, African chattel slavery had become much more prevalent in the South than the North because
(A) the South was a region of large-scale, labor-intensive farming
(B) the North had a much colder climate
(C) northerners did not share white southern racial prejudice
(D) northern colonies outlawed the slave trade on religious grounds
(E) most African immigrants chose to travel south

48. Northeastern Indian tribes with whom the colonists interacted throughout the 17th century, both in friendship and in conflict, included all of the following EXCEPT
(A) Algonquin
(B) Delaware
(C) Huron
(D) Iroquois
(E) Shoshone

49. King Philip's War is best described as
(A) an all-out war between the Wampanoag and Narragansett tribes
(B) a series of Indian raids on settlements in Massachusetts
(C) armed skirmishes between French and English settlements
(D) an uprising of French colonists against the French government
(E) an armed African slave rebellion in the British colonies

50. The Maryland Toleration Act of 1649 established all of the following EXCEPT
(A) freedom of worship for all Christians who believed in the Holy Trinity
(B) the death penalty for those who denied or spoke disrespectfully of the Holy Trinity
(C) banishment from the colony for those who did not observe the Christian Sabbath
(D) severe criminal penalties for those who spoke disrespectfully of Christian doctrines
(E) minor criminal penalties for those who insulted Christians for their religious faith

Culture, Society, and Everyday Life in the British Colonies

51. Which best describes the Great Awakening of the mid-18th century?
  (A) a movement to reform education
  (B) a crackdown on smuggling
  (C) a temperance movement
  (D) a revival of Protestant religious fervor
  (E) an upsurge in literacy throughout the colonies

52. A *captive narrative* is best described as
  (A) a historical novel about the recent past, with plenty of action and adventure
  (B) the story of the author's experiences as a slave and his or her escape
  (C) the story of the author's experience of being kidnapped by Indians and his or her escape or release
  (D) a book-length poem about a heroic figure of the distant past
  (E) a traditional Indian story told and retold orally down the generations

53. Which best describes the 18th-century method colonial doctors used to protect patients from smallpox?
  (A) infecting a person with a very mild case of smallpox to build up an immunity
  (B) vaccinating a person with cowpox to build up an immunity
  (C) isolating a sick patient until he or she got better
  (D) encouraging people to avoid fresh air, especially at night
  (E) warning people not to drink too much coffee or tea

54. Why was the abolitionist movement so limited in scope in the early colonial period?
  (A) African slaves were contented with their status at that time.
  (B) Quakers spoke out strongly in favor of abolition.
  (C) It was relatively easy for enslaved Africans to escape from their owners.
  (D) Most northerners were ignorant of the reality of slavery in the South.
  (E) Parliament passed laws against the abolitionist movement.

55. Harvard College was founded in 1636 as a center for the study of
  (A) the liberal arts
  (B) humanism
  (C) theology
  (D) history and philosophy
  (E) science and technology

56. The Great Awakening of the mid-1700s emphasized individual salvation by
   (A) separation of church and state
   (B) faith in God
   (C) predestination
   (D) good works
   (E) sincere repentance for sins

57. The Pilgrims were also called Separatists because they had broken all ties to
   (A) the king of England
   (B) the Catholic Church
   (C) the Anglican Church
   (D) the Mayflower Compact
   (E) the royal colonial charter

58. Which best describes the precedent of a free press as established in New York in 1735?
   (A) There were no limits on the freedom of the press.
   (B) Writers were free to publish true facts.
   (C) Freedom of the press was subject to political censorship.
   (D) Freedom of the press was subject to religious censorship.
   (E) Freedom of the press was subject to legal censorship.

59. Which of the following was NOT a significant 18th-century American painter?
   (A) John Singleton Copley
   (B) Thomas Eakins
   (C) Charles Willson Peale
   (D) Gilbert Stuart
   (E) Benjamin West

60. Which was NOT a popular literary genre for colonial American writers?
   (A) autobiography
   (B) history
   (C) poetry
   (D) prose fiction
   (E) theology

61. A slave might take on any of these responsibilities on a large southern plantation EXCEPT
(A) blacksmith
(B) cook
(C) coachman
(D) nanny
(E) tutor or governess

62. Which is NOT one reason why Benjamin Franklin was such a notable figure in colonial Philadelphia?
(A) He was the printer and author of the popular periodical *Poor Richard's Almanack.*
(B) He redesigned the streetlights, making them burn more cleanly and brightly.
(C) He invented the lightning rod, which protected city buildings from being struck and set on fire during storms.
(D) He helped to establish the city's first mint and designed its coins.
(E) He founded the city's first subscription library and its first club for philosophical and scientific research.

63. All of the following wrote significant works of literature during the colonial era, EXCEPT
(A) Anne Bradstreet
(B) Ralph Waldo Emerson
(C) Increase Mather
(D) Mary Rowlandson
(E) Samuel Sewall

64. Which region of the colonies outlawed theatrical performances altogether?
(A) New England
(B) New York and New Jersey
(C) Pennsylvania and Delaware
(D) Virginia and Maryland
(E) the Carolinas and Georgia

65. Phillis Wheatley is significant in American history as
(A) the first runaway slave to write a narrative of her experiences
(B) the first African-American to write and publish a book
(C) the first American woman to sue successfully in court for full political equality
(D) the only woman known to have served as a soldier (disguised) in the French and Indian War
(E) the first biographer of George Washington

66. The typical colonial childhood after age 10 or 11 was a time of
    (A) earning wages
    (B) playing games
    (C) learning a specific trade or skill by working with an adult
    (D) attending school five days a week for six hours a day
    (E) studying at home with a tutor or governess in preparation for college

67. Which does NOT describe one aspect of community and family life
    in a small colonial town or village?
    (A) It was very common for a woman to marry two, three, or even four
        times in her life.
    (B) Young people frequently married in their mid- to late teens and
        promptly began to have families.
    (C) Community social activities were not segregated by age or gender;
        everyone participated.
    (D) All family members ate their meals together, almost always in their
        own home.
    (E) Everyone in the household contributed his or her wages and efforts
        to the expenses of the whole family.

68. Which of the following is NOT one aspect of musical life embraced
    by the British colonists?
    (A) Individuals studied singing or learned to play instruments
        to entertain friends and family at home.
    (B) Independent professional musicians, sometimes joined by talented
        amateurs, gave concerts in such cities as Philadelphia and Boston.
    (C) People sang in church choirs throughout the colonies, sometimes
        accompanied by an organ or other instruments.
    (D) Major colonial cities established professional opera companies
        and symphony orchestras.
    (E) Composers wrote and published new hymns and anthems to be sung
        during religious services of various denominations.

69. Jonathan Edwards and George Whitefield are significant figures associated
    with
    (A) architecture
    (B) journalism
    (C) literature
    (D) music
    (E) preaching

70. Which field of endeavor was NOT open to women in the British colonies?
    (A) author
    (B) judge
    (C) midwife
    (D) religious leader
    (E) teacher

CHAPTER 2

The War for Independence

The French and Indian War, 1747–1763

71. What was the purpose of the Proclamation of 1763?
    (A) to settle the peace terms after the French and Indian War
    (B) to create a permanent border between the British colonies and Indian territory
    (C) to state that Britain controlled all of North America east of the Mississippi River
    (D) to require that France give up its North American colonies to Britain
    (E) to require that Spain give up its North American colonies to Britain

72. Benjamin Franklin based the Albany Plan of Union on
    (A) the English Bill of Rights
    (B) the Mayflower Compact
    (C) the Iroquois Confederacy
    (D) Penn's Charter of Liberty
    (E) the Fundamental Orders of Connecticut

73. Which was NOT one result of the French and Indian War?
    (A) The colonists gained their first experience of organized military action.
    (B) France ceded all territory east of the Mississippi River, except New Orleans, to Britain.
    (C) Mutual distrust and resentment flourished between the British Army and the colonial troops.
    (D) Britain accumulated an enormous war debt.
    (E) The colonists lost interest in creating any kind of national union.

74. In the Treaty of Paris of 1763, France ceded all its North American territory to
   (A) Britain and Spain
   (B) Spain and Austria
   (C) Austria and Britain
   (D) Prussia and Britain
   (E) Spain and Prussia

75. The French and Indian War came about because of a dispute over
   (A) treaties with the Indians
   (B) religious faith
   (C) territorial expansion
   (D) individual rights and freedoms
   (E) chattel slavery

76. The Albany Plan of Union is best described as
   (A) a national constitution for the 13 British colonies
   (B) a constitution for the colony of New York
   (C) a freely elected legislature that would govern all the colonies
   (D) a loose association for the mutual security of all the colonies
   (E) a strong central legislative assembly and executive that would share governing powers with the individual colonies

77. What was Canada's status at the end of the French and Indian War?
   (A) controlled by Britain
   (B) controlled by France
   (C) controlled by the Indians
   (D) controlled by Spain
   (E) independent

78. Which best describes the role played by Indians during the French and Indian War?
   (A) They sided with France against Britain.
   (B) They sided with Britain against France.
   (C) They sided first with France, then with Britain.
   (D) They remained neutral throughout the war.
   (E) They opposed both Britain and France throughout the war.

79. Why did Britain decide that the colonies must assume a share of the British war debt?
(A) The colonial troops were very poor soldiers.
(B) The war had been fought to benefit the colonies.
(C) Britain gained no territory from the war.
(D) The colonies were responsible for Britain losing the war.
(E) Colonial soldiers had deserted so often and so regularly.

80. What was the main reason why the British forces won the Battle of Quebec?
(A) The British had abler commanders.
(B) The British had help from the Indians.
(C) The British outnumbered the French.
(D) The British were more familiar with the terrain.
(E) The British had superior weapons.

81. Why did the colonial leaders reject the Albany Plan of Union?
(A) They did not trust one another.
(B) They preferred to be governed by the British Parliament.
(C) They did not agree on the details of the plan.
(D) They did not want Albany to be the new national capital.
(E) They were not ready to declare American independence from Britain.

82. The 1748 Treaty of Logstown was an agreement of mutual support between
(A) the French and the Indians
(B) the British and the Indians
(C) the Iroquois and Ohio tribes
(D) the French and the Spaniards
(E) the British and the Spaniards

83. Which best describes the territory disputed during the French and Indian War?
(A) the settled British colonies on the Atlantic coast
(B) the land between the settled British colonies and the Mississippi River
(C) the land between the Atlantic and Pacific Oceans, and between the Canadian and Mexican borders
(D) the land west of the Mississippi River and north and east of Mexico
(E) the land immediately surrounding the Great Lakes, including water rights to the lakes themselves

84. What was the key French concern at the outbreak of the French and Indian War?
(A) acquiring land on which to build permanent French settlements
(B) fighting an all-out war against the powerful British Army
(C) Indian invasion of settled French territory
(D) continued access to the Ohio and Mississippi Rivers shipping route
(E) British invasion of settled French territory

85. George Washington was sent into the western territory in 1753 under orders to
(A) launch a full-scale military attack on French forts
(B) work with the French to establish British-French territorial boundaries
(C) warn the French to leave the territory, as it was claimed by Britain
(D) sign treaties with the local Seneca, Iroquois, and Huron tribes
(E) deliver a formal declaration of war to the French commanders

86. France signed a treaty with Spain in 1762 in order to
(A) prevent further British expansion to the west
(B) maintain its claims to its own North American territory
(C) bring Spain into the French and Indian War as a French ally
(D) retain French control over the port of New Orleans
(E) protect its economic interests in North America

87. The Albany Plan of Union and the U.S. Constitution both reflect which important principle of American government?
(A) the separation of powers
(B) the establishment of a national capital
(C) independent sovereignty of the individual states
(D) popular democracy
(E) equality for all citizens under the law

88. Which best describes the North American territory controlled by Britain at the end of the French and Indian War?
(A) the 13 colonies on the Atlantic coast and most of Canada
(B) the 13 colonies on the Atlantic coast plus the Great Lakes region and most of Canada
(C) everything east of the Mississippi River except New Orleans, plus most of Canada
(D) everything east of the Mississippi River except New Orleans and Spanish Florida, plus most of Canada
(E) everything east of the Mississippi River and south of the Canadian border

89. Which best describes the relations between the regular British Army and the colonial soldiers?
    (A) The British regulars provided the colonists with valuable training and discipline.
    (B) The British regulars refused to serve with the colonial soldiers.
    (C) The British regulars learned valuable lessons from the colonists' experience of fighting the Indians.
    (D) The British commanders helped to establish the first regular army in the colonies.
    (E) The British regulars largely ignored and scorned the colonists.

90. What was the outcome of the 1754 military skirmish at Fort Necessity?
    (A) The French permanently drove the Virginians out of the region.
    (B) The Indians came to the rescue of the outnumbered Virginians.
    (C) The Virginian troops won the skirmish by luck and superior strategy.
    (D) The French forces massacred the Virginian troops.
    (E) The French laid siege to the fort and forced the Virginians to surrender.

91. Which is NOT one provision of the Albany Plan of Union?
    (A) that the colonies establish a general government to administer all of them as a unit
    (B) that Parliament would maintain its authority over the general government
    (C) that the monarch would maintain his or her authority over the general government
    (D) that the monarch should appoint an executive officer for the general government
    (E) that the legislature for the general government should meet at least once a year

92. Which was NOT a reason why the colonists opposed the Proclamation of 1763?
    (A) They had already begun to settle the western territory.
    (B) Many of them had received official land grants in the western territory.
    (C) The proclamation was illegal according to the terms of several colonies' royal charters.
    (D) They did not believe that the king had the authority to issue the proclamation.
    (E) They wanted to drive the Indians farther away from the settled coastal region.

93. Which best describes the colonial military forces as of the outbreak of war in 1747?
(A) an organized, well-trained national militia on call at all times
(B) an organized, well-trained militia in each colony; no national militia
(C) an unorganized, poorly trained militia in each individual colony; no national militia
(D) well-trained militias in some colonies but no organized militias in others; no national militia
(E) a regular standing army of the colonies, with trained officers

94. Which colony did NOT enlarge its size by expanding westward after the French and Indian War?
(A) Georgia
(B) New York
(C) Pennsylvania
(D) South Carolina
(E) Virginia

95. Which was NOT a result of the Battle of the Wilderness?
(A) Roughly two-thirds of the British and colonial troops were killed.
(B) The troops constructed what would become the first leg of the Cumberland (National) Road.
(C) Washington led the retreat of the survivors to eastern Virginia.
(D) The Seneca and other local tribes decided to transfer their support from the French to the British.
(E) The French defeated the British and colonial forces.

The Road to Revolution

96. The Boston Massacre was a direct result of the
(A) Boston Tea Party
(B) installation of troops in peacetime
(C) passage of the Stamp Act
(D) passage of the Sugar Act
(E) revocation of the Massachusetts charter

97. How did the colonists react to the passage of the Intolerable Acts?
(A) They tarred and feathered the stamp inspectors.
(B) They drank only tea that had been smuggled in from the Netherlands.
(C) They called for the revocation of the royal charter of Massachusetts.
(D) They began cultivating coffee since they could no longer drink tea.
(E) They sent leaders from all the colonies to a general meeting to discuss a united response.

98. What was the purpose of the colonial committees of correspondence?
- (A) to keep one another informed of recent British legislation so that all could present a united response
- (B) to establish and maintain a postal service among the 13 colonies
- (C) to communicate with Britain about specific colonial objections to parliamentary legislation
- (D) to circulate anonymous letters accusing specific British officials of crimes
- (E) to urge the public to take up arms against the redcoats

99. Which was NOT among the parliamentary measures that the American colonists referred to as the Intolerable Acts?
- (A) Administration of Justice Act
- (B) Boston Port Act
- (C) Massachusetts Government Act
- (D) Quartering Act
- (E) Stamp Act

100. Which was NOT an immediate and direct effect of the Boston Massacre?
- (A) John Adams agreed to defend the redcoats arrested after the riot.
- (B) Samuel Adams demanded that the redcoats be ordered out of Boston.
- (C) John Hancock commissioned a portrait of Samuel Adams, which was used for propaganda purposes.
- (D) Thomas Hutchinson disbanded the Massachusetts legislature.
- (E) Paul Revere distributed an engraving of the riot that was circulated throughout the colonies.

101. Which of the following colonial actions provoked Parliament into passing the Intolerable Acts?
- (A) signing the Declaration of Independence
- (B) harassing the British stamp inspectors
- (C) dumping chests of East India tea into Boston Harbor
- (D) convening the Constitutional Convention
- (E) demanding that the Massachusetts governor order the army to leave Boston

102. What happened during the Boston Massacre?
- (A) A mob of colonists threw stones at a group of redcoats, who retaliated by firing on them.
- (B) A group of redcoats fired on colonists who were staging a peaceful demonstration.
- (C) A group of Indians stormed into Boston and tried to take the city by force.
- (D) Colonists and redcoats fired on one another from opposite sides of a city plaza.
- (E) A redcoat accidentally killed a colonist, provoking a brawl in which more people were killed.

103. The colonists protested the Sugar Act of 1764 for all these reasons EXCEPT
- (A) it would cut heavily into the profits of the colonial merchants
- (B) it was a tax imposed on the colonists without their consent
- (C) it would deprive merchant captains accused of smuggling of their right to a trial by jury
- (D) it enforced an existing import duty that had rarely if ever been enforced
- (E) it was an illegal attempt to regulate colonial trade

104. The delegates to the First Continental Congress agreed on all of the following responses to Britain EXCEPT
- (A) to declare independence from Britain
- (B) to suspend all trade with Britain
- (C) to establish and train a militia in each colony
- (D) to demand the repeal of the Intolerable Acts
- (E) to call for the removal of the army of occupation

105. Which best describes the overarching principle behind all the colonial protests against Parliament?
- (A) the divine right of kings
- (B) government by the consent of the governed
- (C) full social equality for all
- (D) freedom of religious worship
- (E) a free-market economy

106. The First Continental Congress was convened specifically in order to
- (A) appoint a delegation to lay the colonial case before Parliament in London
- (B) formally unite the colonies and establish a central government
- (C) declare independence from Great Britain
- (D) discuss responses to the Intolerable Acts
- (E) raise a standing army and appoint a commander in chief

107. The Intolerable Acts included all of the following measures EXCEPT
- (A) stating that Massachusetts legislators would be royally appointed
- (B) closing the port of Boston temporarily
- (C) establishing a standing army in the city of Boston
- (D) denying Massachusetts the right to try royal officials accused of crimes
- (E) stating that colonists must feed and house soldiers on demand

108. What became of the redcoats involved in the Boston Massacre?
- (A) They were immediately sent back to Great Britain for their own safety.
- (B) They were immediately sent back to Great Britain for punishment.
- (C) They were killed in the Boston Massacre.
- (D) They were dishonorably discharged from the British army.
- (E) They received a fair trial in which they were acquitted of murder.

109. All of the following wrote famous pamphlets protesting the various acts of Parliament during the pre-Revolutionary period EXCEPT
- (A) John Dickinson
- (B) Daniel Dulaney
- (C) Nathan Hale
- (D) Thomas Jefferson
- (E) James Otis

110. In support of their claim that Parliament did not represent them, the colonists used all the following arguments EXCEPT
- (A) They were not British citizens.
- (B) They were not allowed to vote for even one member of Parliament.
- (C) No members of Parliament lived in the American colonies.
- (D) A representative was bound to support the interests of his particular constituents, not the interests of an entire nation or empire.
- (E) No members of Parliament were familiar enough with American interests and concerns to represent them adequately or fairly.

111. Colonial responses to the Stamp Act included all of the following EXCEPT
- (A) convening a meeting of leaders from several colonies to discuss the situation
- (B) organizing militias within each colony in case the need arose to defend the colonies against the redcoats
- (C) publishing essays and pamphlets outlining and discussing objections to the act
- (D) harassing the stamp inspectors and destroying their property
- (E) forming activist groups to organize popular resistance

112. The Quartering Act of 1774 stated that
- (A) colonists must allow redcoats to lodge in their houses, when requested to by the army
- (B) each colony would be divided into four sections, each section administered by a royal official who would report directly to the royal governor
- (C) farmers and planters throughout the colonies must pay new taxes based on the number of quarter-acres of land they used for growing crops
- (D) Parliament would reduce the tax on East India tea to one-quarter of the amount they had suggested in the Tea Act
- (E) any colonist convicted of treason against Britain could be punished by being hanged, drawn, and quartered

113. What was the most important overall effect of the Intolerable Acts?
- (A) to inspire the colonists to create a new national government
- (B) to persuade the colonists to take up arms against Britain
- (C) to overturn the government of the Canadian colony
- (D) to unite the colonies against a common enemy
- (E) to destroy the prosperous colonial economy

114. The immediate priority of the Second Continental Congress was to discuss the colonial response to the
- (A) Declaratory Act
- (B) Proclamation of 1763
- (C) Olive Branch Petition
- (D) Battles of Breed's Hill and Bunker Hill
- (E) Battles of Lexington and Concord

115. How did the leaders in Parliament respond to colonial protests against
the Sugar Act?
(A) They repealed the Sugar Act.
(B) They lowered the tax assessed by the Sugar Act.
(C) They disbanded the colonial legislatures.
(D) They closed the colonial ports.
(E) They sent troops to maintain order in the colonies.

116. When customs inspectors attempted to enforce the Sugar Act in Rhode
Island, which was NOT among the people's responses?
(A) Officials would fail to appear at shipowners' trials, so judges would
dismiss cases on the pretext of lack of evidence.
(B) When a ship was seized and the owner convicted, the court would
often sell the ship back to him at a fraction of its worth.
(C) Dockworkers, sailors, and others would flatly refuse to assist
the customs inspectors in their efforts.
(D) Shipowners would order their crews to throw disputed goods
overboard so that they could not be seized by the customs inspector.
(E) When ships were about to be seized for smuggling, disguised men
boarded the ships and carried the cargo away to a place of safety.

117. In response to the passage of the Stamp Act, the Virginia House
of Burgesses passed all the following resolutions EXCEPT
(A) that until the passage of the Stamp Act, Great Britain had never
attempted to impose internal controls or taxes on the people
of Virginia
(B) that Englishmen could not be taxed without their own consent,
or the consent of their elected representatives
(C) that the 13 united colonies should declare their independence
from Great Britain
(D) that Virginians enjoyed the same rights and privileges as Englishmen
and had enjoyed these rights since the colony's founding
(E) that the royal charter of Virginia established Virginians' civil and legal
status as citizens of the British Empire

118. Which was NOT among the reasons why John Dickinson of Pennsylvania (among other patriots) opposed declaring independence in July 1776?
(A) The colonies did not have sufficient grounds for a rebellion against their king.
(B) The colonies had no firm foundation for unity, having never settled where they stood in relation to one another.
(C) No other nation had yet agreed to support the colonies in their conflict with Britain.
(D) Congress should wait to declare independence until it had designed a government and chosen its leaders.
(E) Britain might easily persuade France and Spain to oppose the united colonies in an all-out war.

119. The participants in the Boston Tea Party dressed up as Indians for all of the following reasons EXCEPT
(A) they knew that the actual Indians would never be blamed for storming the *Dartmouth*
(B) they hoped that the British officials would assume that Indians had committed the crime
(C) they knew they were committing treason and assumed the disguise for protection
(D) they wanted everyone to be able to deny recognizing any of the participants
(E) they did not want to be prosecuted for the destruction of valuable property

120. The burning of the *Gaspée* in 1772 was an example of the ongoing conflict between the
(A) colonial citizens and the standing army
(B) standing army and the navy
(C) navy and the colonial smugglers
(D) colonial smugglers and the merchants
(E) merchants and the ordinary citizens

121. The Galloway Plan of Union proposed that the colonies should
(A) establish a national assembly that would serve as an American branch of Parliament
(B) form a loose federation for their mutual security and protection
(C) establish a national standing army for their own self-defense
(D) declare their independence from Britain
(E) demand actual representation in Parliament

122. Which British political leader disagreed with the argument that Parliament had the right to tax the colonies?
(A) William Blackstone
(B) George Grenville
(C) Thomas Hutchinson
(D) William Pitt
(E) Charles Townshend

123. Why did Parliament repeal the Stamp Act?
(A) Parliament had raised enough revenue to pay off the French and Indian War debt.
(B) The leaders took the colonial protests seriously.
(C) Parliament intended to reorganize the administration of all the colonies.
(D) The king argued that the Stamp Act was doing far more harm than good.
(E) The leaders realized that the Stamp Act could not be enforced.

124. In response to the colonists' claims that Parliament did not represent them, parliamentary leaders argued that
(A) the monarch represented all citizens of the British Empire
(B) Parliament was too far away to represent the colonists
(C) the colonists were not British citizens
(D) the colonists were virtually represented in Parliament
(E) the colonists had no right to representation

125. Which colony did Parliament regard as the fount of all the American protests, violence, and rebellion?
(A) Massachusetts
(B) New York
(C) Pennsylvania
(D) Rhode Island
(E) Virginia

126. Thomas Jefferson's *Summary View of the Rights of British America* (1774) was the most radical discussion and assertion of colonial rights to that time because it
   (A) directly accused the king of abusing his power over the colonists
   (B) pointed out that the colonists were being taxed not for their own benefit, but for the benefit of the people of Great Britain
   (C) objected to the British argument that the colonists were virtually represented in Parliament
   (D) suggested that the leaders of the 13 colonies should meet and discuss their common grievances against Parliament
   (E) denied Parliament's right to regulate colonial imports and exports

127. Which is NOT a reason the Stamp Act Congress gave for its objections to the Stamp Act?
   (A) The Stamp Act violated the colonists' right to trial by jury.
   (B) The colonists were not, and for reasons of distance could not be, represented in Parliament.
   (C) The colonists did not owe allegiance to the king of Great Britain.
   (D) The people of Great Britain had no right to vote on taxes that applied not to themselves, but only to the colonists.
   (E) The taxes imposed by the Stamp Act and other recent parliamentary acts would cause grave economic hardship in the colonies.

128. John Adams served as the defense attorney for the redcoats involved in the Boston Massacre because he
   (A) was appointed by the courts and thus had no choice in the matter
   (B) insisted on the soldiers' right to representation and a jury trial
   (C) wanted to gain recognition throughout the colonies
   (D) supported the British side of the quarrel with the colonists
   (E) had witnessed the Boston Massacre and knew exactly what had happened

129. Why did the colonists oppose the Tea Act of 1773?
   (A) Obeying it would have forced them to buy and drink inferior tea.
   (B) Obeying it would have helped to resolve the tension between Britain and the colonies.
   (C) The provisions of the Tea Act made the Dutch threaten to break off colonial trade.
   (D) The Tea Act raised the price of tea beyond what the colonists considered fair.
   (E) The price of the tea included a tax the colonists did not want to pay.

130. The Stamp Act stated all of the following EXCEPT
  (A) that a variety of documents must be printed on stamped paper, at a tax determined by the type of document
  (B) that the colonial assemblies had three months to determine appropriate taxes for the different types of stamped documents
  (C) that legal cases dealing with enforcement of the Stamp Act could be tried in the admiralty courts
  (D) that revenue raised by the Stamp Act would be used to pay the expenses of maintaining the standing (British) army in the colonies
  (E) that both civil and ecclesiastical courts throughout the colonies must use stamped paper

131. Who organized the Boston Tea Party?
  (A) the First Continental Congress
  (B) the merchants of Boston
  (C) the royal governor of Massachusetts
  (D) the Sons and Daughters of Liberty
  (E) the Massachusetts Assembly

132. The Declaratory Act of 1766 stated that
  (A) Parliament had total legislative authority over the colonies
  (B) the elected colonial legislatures must disband
  (C) the colonies were in rebellion against Britain
  (D) Britain had the right to maintain a standing army in the colonies
  (E) the colonies must allow Britain to control and regulate trade

133. What important distinction did the colonists make between the amended Sugar Act and the subsequent acts of Parliament?
  (A) The Sugar Act was submitted to the colonial assemblies for a vote.
  (B) The Sugar Act applied equally to all the colonies, not just Massachusetts.
  (C) The Sugar Act was a legitimate attempt to regulate trade.
  (D) The Sugar Act did not have a negative impact on the colonial economy.
  (E) The Sugar Act was a direct tax.

134. Which best describes the system of government in the individual British colonies before the American Revolution?
  (A) constitutional monarchy
  (B) hereditary monarchy
  (C) popular democracy
  (D) republic
  (E) dictatorship

The American Revolution, 1775–1783

135. Which was NOT a consideration that led the Continental Army to invade Canada in 1775?
(A) the prospect of an alliance with Canada's French population
(B) the possibility of adding Canada to the new nation the colonists hoped to create
(C) the hope that Britain would abandon the Massachusetts campaign to defend Canada
(D) the desire to eliminate Canada as a base of operations for the British Army
(E) the fact that Canada appeared to be an easy target for conquest

136. Which of the following was NOT a provision of the 1783 Treaty of Paris?
(A) Britain recognized the United States as an independent nation.
(B) The United States owned all North American territory east of the Mississippi River.
(C) Britain would give up the right to colonize any part of North America.
(D) The United States would pay all its current debts to Britain.
(E) The United States gained fishing rights in the Gulf of St. Lawrence.

137. What was the most important reason for the American victory over the Hessian troops at the Battle of Trenton?
(A) The Hessians were caught completely off guard because it was Christmas.
(B) The Americans greatly outnumbered the Hessians.
(C) The Americans were better trained than the Hessians.
(D) The Hessians were less familiar with the terrain than the Americans.
(E) The Americans were better equipped and better armed than the Hessians.

138. Which is NOT one reason why so many American colonists remained loyal to Great Britain during the Revolutionary War?
(A) They believed that it was wrong to rebel against a hereditary monarch.
(B) They wanted to protect their status as British subjects.
(C) They felt direct personal loyalty to King George III.
(D) They were unwilling to risk the consequences of committing treason.
(E) They did not find the various acts of Parliament either onerous or oppressive.

139. The Olive Branch Petition is best described as a
- (A) trade agreement between Britain and the colonies
- (B) plea to the king to settle the conflict between Parliament and the colonies
- (C) declaration that the colonies were an independent nation
- (D) repudiation of hereditary monarchy as a viable form of government
- (E) justification of the colonial decision to take up arms against Britain

140. Which best describes the British strategy at the beginning of the war?
- (A) Capture Philadelphia and force the American leaders to surrender.
- (B) Capture New York, thus dividing the colonies in half.
- (C) Raise an army in Canada that would march against the Americans from the north.
- (D) Bribe or persuade the African slaves to rise up against the Continental Army.
- (E) Enlist the military aid of their French allies against the Continental Army.

141. Why did the final version of the Declaration of Independence eliminate a reference to slavery as "cruel war against human nature"?
- (A) The majority of the delegates in Congress supported the slave trade.
- (B) The delegates agreed that this was not the right time in history to free the slaves.
- (C) The delegates did not like the implication that they were slaves of the king.
- (D) The southern delegates would not otherwise vote in favor of the Declaration.
- (E) The delegates felt that the question of slavery was not relevant to the question of American independence.

142. *Common Sense* makes all of the following arguments EXCEPT
- (A) the colonies should maintain a close alliance with Britain
- (B) government in any form is, at best, a necessary evil
- (C) the colonies should create a national representative government of their own
- (D) hereditary monarchy is an inherently bad form of government
- (E) the colonies should declare their independence from Britain

143. Which of the following did NOT play a major military role
in the Revolutionary War?
(A) Benedict Arnold
(B) Benjamin Franklin
(C) Alexander Hamilton
(D) Israel Putnam
(E) George Washington

144. What happened immediately after the Battle of Concord?
(A) The colonies declared their independence from Britain.
(B) Britain declared war on the colonies.
(C) The redcoats retreated to Boston, followed by the colonial troops.
(D) The colonies decided to raise a national army.
(E) Congress ratified the Articles of Confederation.

145. During the Revolution, what important military lesson did the American
troops show that they had learned from the Indians?
(A) allowing women to serve as soldiers in battle
(B) switching sides depending on individual interest
(C) fighting across open fields
(D) making extensive use of cavalry troops
(E) attacking by stealth whenever possible

146. The major difficulties facing the Continental Army during the winter truce
of 1777–1778 included all of the following EXCEPT
(A) disagreements in Congress over how the war should be conducted
(B) loss of confidence in some civilian quarters over Washington's ability
to command
(C) massive desertion among the troops
(D) absence of funding for food, clothing, boots, or supplies
for the troops
(E) inability to call up necessary reinforcements

147. What was the purpose of Thomas Paine's *The American Crisis*?
(A) to rally support for the Continental Army among the civilian
population
(B) to argue for the abolition of chattel slavery as soon as the war
was won
(C) to articulate the reasons why the colonies desired independence
from Britain
(D) to criticize George Washington's conduct of the war
(E) to persuade powerful European nations to support the American
cause

148. Which of the following persuaded France to join the Revolutionary War?
- (A) the outcome of the Battle of Saratoga
- (B) the outcome of the Battle of Trenton
- (C) the outcome of the Battle of Charleston
- (D) the arguments against monarchy advanced in *Common Sense*
- (E) the list of grievances against the king in the Declaration of Independence

149. Why did the redcoats first march on Concord in 1775?
- (A) to surround the city of Boston and create a state of siege
- (B) to take charge of a cache of weapons hidden there
- (C) to stage a battle against the colonial minutemen on the village green
- (D) to capture the leaders of the Second Continental Congress
- (E) to prove to the colonists that they could not possibly win an all-out war

150. Which best describes John Paul Jones's contribution to the Revolutionary War?
- (A) fighting battles with British warships in New York Harbor
- (B) breaking the British naval blockade of Philadelphia
- (C) sinking British supply ships in the waters off Great Britain
- (D) supervising the buildup of the Continental Navy
- (E) winning an upset victory over a British warship off Great Britain

151. What was the typical fate of Tories who fell into the hands of patriots?
- (A) They were publicly executed.
- (B) They were tortured.
- (C) They were banished from the colonies.
- (D) They were imprisoned, robbed, and humiliated.
- (E) They were forced to enlist in the Continental Army.

152. Which is NOT one of the reasons Benedict Arnold decided to switch sides in the fall of 1780?
- (A) his belief that the colonies were committing treason against the British crown
- (B) his inability to meet his extravagant personal expenses
- (C) his belief that his military victories were unappreciated
- (D) his punishment for inappropriate conduct as military governor of Philadelphia
- (E) his marriage into a prominent Tory family

153. What was George Washington's most formidable asset as the commander of the Continental Army?
(A) He was more experienced than the British generals.
(B) He had the full confidence of all the American political leaders.
(C) He commanded the personal loyalty of his troops throughout the war.
(D) His commanding officers were more able than those on the British side.
(E) His troops were better equipped and better prepared than the redcoats.

154. Which was NOT one result of the Battle of Brooklyn?
(A) The Americans retreated from Brooklyn to Manhattan.
(B) The British began to move their ships out of New York Harbor.
(C) The Continental Army suffered more than 1,500 casualties.
(D) British General William Howe decided to cross the river and attack Manhattan.
(E) Hundreds of men deserted the Continental Army.

155. Which best describes the British military strategy at the start of the southern campaign in 1780?
(A) to persuade Spain to come into the war as a British ally
(B) to free the African slaves in exchange for their enlistment in the British Army
(C) to distract Washington's troops from their attempt to liberate Philadelphia
(D) to march north, conquering each southern colony en route
(E) to eliminate the Continental Navy as a major American weapon

156. The Declaration of Independence includes all of the following EXCEPT
(A) an official declaration of war against Great Britain
(B) a discussion of the natural rights of humankind
(C) a list of specific grievances against the British king
(D) a statement that the former British colonies were fully independent and self-governing
(E) an explanation of the reasons for the separation from Great Britain

157. Unlike the British troops, the American troops faced the constant handicap of
  (A) mass desertion
  (B) raids by hostile Indian tribes
  (C) slave rebellions
  (D) betrayal by their foreign allies
  (E) lack of reinforcements upon which to draw

158. The Battle of Saratoga had all these important effects EXCEPT
  (A) it ended the military campaign in the northern colonies
  (B) it persuaded France to increase its active support for the American side
  (C) it persuaded the leaders in Congress to issue an official declaration of independence from Britain
  (D) it marked the failure of the British strategy to divide the colonies
  (E) it renewed support for the war among the patriot civilian population

159. Which is NOT among the Enlightenment ideals that began to pervade all levels of American society during the Revolutionary period?
  (A) the importance of a national system of education
  (B) equal rights for men and women
  (C) the abolition of chattel slavery
  (D) separation of church and state, both locally and nationally
  (E) the perfectibility of human society under the American system

160. What was the most important effect of the Battle of Bunker Hill?
  (A) It made the delegates in Congress decide to declare the colonies' independence from Great Britain.
  (B) It brought the militias of all the colonies to Massachusetts to support the siege of Boston.
  (C) It persuaded Congress to appoint a commander in chief of the Continental Army.
  (D) It convinced the British that they would win a quick, easy victory over the Americans.
  (E) It gave the Americans confidence that they could hold their own against the British.

161. Which of the following events took place almost simultaneously with the outbreak of the Revolutionary War?
(A) Daniel Boone blazed the Wilderness Road into Kentucky.
(B) Benjamin Franklin spoke out against parliamentary legislation in London.
(C) Cinque led a mutiny of kidnapped Africans on board the ship *Amistad.*
(D) Thomas Paine published the pamphlet *Common Sense.*
(E) James Wilkinson and Aaron Burr plotted against the United States.

162. Which is NOT one role played by patriotic colonial women in the Revolutionary War?
(A) They enlisted in the Continental Army.
(B) They fired on the enemy in emergency situations.
(C) They marched and camped with the army as cooks, laundresses, and nurses.
(D) They commanded military brigades.
(E) They spied on Tories and British officials for both Congress and the Continental Army.

163. The constant wartime skirmishes and raids on the western frontier of the colonies were significant because of their effect on the
(A) Treaty of Paris
(B) Battle of Yorktown
(C) Articles of Confederation
(D) Indian alliance with the colonies
(E) French alliance with the colonies

164. Which of the following was NOT among the British military leaders during the American Revolution?
(A) John Burgoyne
(B) Guy Carleton
(C) Charles Cornwallis
(D) William Howe
(E) William Moultrie

165. Which is NOT among the grievances against King George III that form the central section of the Declaration of Independence?
   (A) He ordered the dismissal of colonial assemblies whenever those assemblies defended the rights of the colonists.
   (B) He kept a standing army in the colonies in peacetime without the consent of the colonial assemblies.
   (C) He imposed taxes on the colonists without their consent or the consent of their elected representatives.
   (D) He was attempting to instigate a rebellion of African slaves against the white colonists, especially in the South.
   (E) As the monarch, he was ultimately responsible for making war on his own subjects, beginning at Lexington in April 1775.

166. No one knows who fired the first shot of the Revolutionary War because
   (A) the Americans won the opening battle
   (B) the British won the opening battle
   (C) no one survived the opening battle
   (D) there are no surviving eyewitness accounts of the opening battle
   (E) the accounts of the participants in the opening battle contradict each other

167. Which was NOT stated in the 1778 treaty between France and the United States?
   (A) France recognized the United States as a sovereign nation.
   (B) Great Britain was the common enemy of France and the United States.
   (C) France permanently renounced all claims to North American territory controlled or recently controlled by Great Britain.
   (D) France and the United States were required to aid one another in future military conflicts with other nations.
   (E) France and the United States were responsible for their own expenses during the Revolutionary War.

168. As a result of the British attack on Charleston Harbor in the spring of 1776,
- (A) the British gave up any attempt to invade the South for more than two years
- (B) the British established a major power base from which to invade the Carolinas and Virginia
- (C) the British and the Americans found themselves in a military stalemate that would last for many months
- (D) the Americans suffered a serious defeat in which they lost hundreds of men
- (E) the Continental Army began to consider inviting slaves to enlist

169. The Shawnee and Cherokee tribes of the southern Appalachians sided with the British because the British
- (A) offered them a high price for the Kentucky territory
- (B) opposed American settlement of Kentucky
- (C) refused to recognize Kentucky as the 14th colony
- (D) offered them superior trade goods at lower prices than the American settlers
- (E) had repealed the Proclamation of 1763

170. All of the following were important victories for the Continental Army EXCEPT
- (A) the Battle of Germantown
- (B) the Battle of Princeton
- (C) the Battle of Saratoga
- (D) the Battle of Trenton
- (E) the siege of Yorktown

171. What was the purpose of William Dawes and Paul Revere's ride on April 18, 1775?
- (A) to spread the news of the Battles of Lexington and Concord
- (B) to summon the militia forth to besiege the redcoats in Boston
- (C) to recruit Sons of Liberty to participate in the Boston Tea Party
- (D) to warn the militia between Boston and Concord that the redcoats were on the march
- (E) to spread the news of the passage of the Intolerable Acts

172. Which of the following did NOT play a major role in the Second Continental Congress?
(A) John Adams
(B) John Dickinson
(C) John Hancock
(D) Richard Henry Lee
(E) William Pitt

173. Why did Connecticut and Massachusetts send Ethan Allen, Benedict Arnold, and their troops to Fort Ticonderoga?
(A) to take charge of a large number of cannons for the Continental Army
(B) to establish an official boundary between New York and Vermont
(C) to drive the redcoats over the border into Canada
(D) to take control of the main roads between Canada and the colonies
(E) to enlist the military aid of the Iroquois and other northern tribes

174. Which does NOT describe one important effect of the Battle of Trenton?
(A) The Continental Army gained a large quantity of cannons, arms, and ammunition.
(B) Hope of ultimate victory over the British was rekindled throughout the colonies.
(C) Washington's troops gained new confidence in their own strength and ability.
(D) The British forces remaining in New Jersey were now in retreat.
(E) The two armies agreed to a truce for the duration of the winter.

175. Both enslaved and free Africans participated in the Revolutionary War in all the following roles EXCEPT
(A) solider or sailor in both British and Continental forces
(B) cook or servant in both British and Continental forces
(C) political leader
(D) political spy
(E) military guide or scout

CHAPTER 3

Founding a New Nation

The United States Under the Articles of Confederation

176. Which best describes the Northwest Ordinance of 1787?
 (A) an order to survey the Northwest Territory and divide it into three to five sections that would become states once the population had grown to a sufficient number
 (B) a federal policy for the settlement, organization, and future statehood of the Northwest Territory
 (C) a bill of individual rights to apply only to the settlers of the Northwest Territory
 (D) an official statement of the boundary lines around and within the Northwest Territory
 (E) a treaty setting forth U.S. and Indian rights over various sections of the Northwest Territory

177. The Virginia Statute for Religious Freedom of 1786 established
 (A) support for a constitutional bill of individual rights
 (B) the official status of the Episcopal (Anglican) Church
 (C) the right to religious demonstration (such as prayer) at public assemblies
 (D) freedom from taxation for any official religious body or denomination
 (E) absolute freedom of religious worship with no civil penalty

178. What was the greatest weakness of the Articles of Confederation?
  (A) They gave the federal government no power to raise money from the states.
  (B) They established no legislative branch for the national government.
  (C) They put too much power into the hands of the federal judiciary.
  (D) They reserved no right of self-government to the states.
  (E) They required a unanimous vote of all the states to pass any legislation.

179. Shays's Rebellion was fought over the issue(s) of
  (A) conflict with Indians over ownership of land
  (B) state taxation and seizure of land for nonpayment
  (C) the establishment of a military draft
  (D) the right of the citizens to bear arms
  (E) voting rights for free adult citizens

180. Which was NOT one reason why James Madison argued for wholesale revision of the Articles of Confederation?
  (A) Congress was unable to compel the states to pay reasonable taxes.
  (B) The states were operating too independently and thus coming into conflict with one another.
  (C) The states were entering into illegal independent agreements with the Indians.
  (D) Each state was represented equally in Congress.
  (E) Congress could not compel the states to work together in their own economic interests.

181. The Articles of Confederation created a Congress that had all these governing powers EXCEPT
  (A) to convene each year in order to carry out its responsibilities
  (B) to oversee a national foreign policy
  (C) to raise revenue by taxing the states and the people
  (D) to settle all conflicts that arose between or among individual states
  (E) to fix weights and measures and to coin money

182. Which best describes the group that was given voting rights in most of the original 13 state constitutions?
  (A) all adult men
  (B) all adult men, except Indians
  (C) free adult men, except Indians
  (D) free adult men who owned a specified amount of property, except Indians
  (E) free adult men who owned a specified amount of property, except Indians and Africans

183. What provision was made for loyalists in the Treaty of Paris?
  (A) They must swear a loyalty oath to the United States.
  (B) They must move to Britain or any of its colonies.
  (C) Only Congress could determine their punishment or penalty.
  (D) Only their home state could determine their punishment or penalty.
  (E) They were to suffer no punishment or penalty.

184. The Northwest Territory included all of the following states EXCEPT
  (A) Illinois
  (B) Iowa
  (C) Michigan
  (D) Ohio
  (E) Wisconsin

185. Which was NOT a factor in the American economic crisis of 1784–1788?
  (A) a trade imbalance in which the United States imported much more than it exported
  (B) high taxes levied by the individual state legislatures
  (C) a scarcity of gold and silver throughout the United States
  (D) a steep drop in the price of American products
  (E) the refusal of foreign countries to permit American importers to buy on credit

186. Congress achieved its only real success during the Confederation period in the area of
  (A) international treaties and diplomacy
  (B) military supplies and support
  (C) territorial expansion
  (D) domestic economic policy
  (E) industrial development

187. The 13 former colonies began to write their new state constitutions immediately after the
(A) British surrender at Yorktown
(B) ratification of the Articles of Confederation
(C) signing of the Declaration of Independence
(D) signing of the Treaty of Paris
(E) ratification of the U.S. Constitution

188. Which was NOT one provision outlined in the Northwest Ordinance?
(A) Each section of the Northwest Territory could elect its own government once it had a large enough population.
(B) Each section of the Northwest Territory would be eligible for statehood once it had a large enough population.
(C) Congress would appoint a temporary government for each section of the Northwest Territory.
(D) Slavery was banned in the Northwest Territory.
(E) Any slave who escaped to the Northwest Territory would gain his or her freedom.

189. Under the Articles of Confederation, the individual states retained all the following rights EXCEPT
(A) to have between two and seven representatives in Congress
(B) to trade freely with all the other states
(C) to sign a peace treaty with any foreign nation
(D) to determine the amount of their annual federal tax
(E) to maintain a trained citizen militia and a store of arms

190. Which is NOT a major argument John Adams made in his influential pamphlet *Thoughts on Government* (1776)?
(A) Individual rights should form the foundation of the government.
(B) The purpose of government was to enable society to function peacefully, freely, and prosperously.
(C) A republic was the best possible form of government.
(D) The powers of the three branches of government must be kept separate.
(E) The legislative branch should itself be divided into branches, each able to check the power of the others.

191. In what respect did the Massachusetts Constitution represent a major step forward in political thought from the constitutions of the other states?
(A) It was written by a convention specifically called together for that purpose.
(B) It was submitted to the people of the state for their approval.
(C) It called for a governor and a bicameral legislature, each with checks on the powers of the other.
(D) It was the work of a small committee of experienced political leaders.
(E) It was written by the same legislature that had governed the state since before the Revolutionary War.

192. The Vermont Constitution, ratified in 1777 and again in 1786, includes a long list of specific grievances against
(A) Canada
(B) Great Britain
(C) Massachusetts
(D) New Hampshire
(E) New York

193. Under the Articles of Confederation, which of the following had the greatest governing powers?
(A) the chief executive
(B) the U.S. Congress
(C) the state legislatures
(D) the national court system
(E) the commander in chief of the army

194. What was the outcome of the Annapolis Convention of 1786?
(A) to devise a new set of regulations for interstate trade and commerce
(B) to call for a convention to revise and amend the Articles of Confederation
(C) to adjourn without taking any action because only five states were present
(D) to recommend the best location for the capital city of the United States
(E) to send out a report recommending specific changes to the Articles of Confederation

195. The Articles of Confederation state that every free person had the right to
- (A) travel freely into or out of any of the states, if not a fugitive or pauper
- (B) have his or her case heard by a jury if accused of a crime
- (C) vote if free, male, and age 21 or older
- (D) refuse room and board to troops in peacetime
- (E) speak and publish opinions and true facts without civil or criminal penalty

196. The Northwest Ordinance expressly granted settlers in the Northwest Territory all these individual rights and freedoms EXCEPT
- (A) freedom of religious worship
- (B) the right, if accused of a crime, to be tried by a jury
- (C) protection from cruel or unusual punishment
- (D) freedom to speak and publish without restraint
- (E) the right to be compensated for property confiscated by the state

197. Which describes one major obstacle to ratification of the Articles of Confederation?
- (A) They did not settle rival claims to land between the 13 colonies and the Mississippi River.
- (B) They made no mention of the Christian religion as a requirement for high national office.
- (C) They did not attempt to settle the controversy over chattel slavery of Africans.
- (D) They denied the individual states any independent self-governing powers.
- (E) They created a strong central executive branch.

198. The Virginia Declaration of Rights of 1776 established all of the following EXCEPT
- (A) that the freedom of the press must not be restrained
- (B) that only conscience could dictate the manner of any individual's religious worship
- (C) that a citizen militia was less dangerous to liberty than a standing army
- (D) that a state could not be compelled to obey any federal laws it regarded as unconstitutional
- (E) that no hereditary privileged class of people would be tolerated in society

199. Which is NOT one of the powers the Articles of Confederation granted to the individual states?
  (A) to determine the procedure of appointing or electing their own representatives to Congress
  (B) to appoint military officers to command their own militia
  (C) to expand into new territory or otherwise alter their own geographical borders
  (D) to determine the manner of raising taxes owed to the federal treasury
  (E) to make policy regarding Indian tribes within their own states, subject to overall federal policies

200. Which of the following is called for in both the Articles of Confederation and the Constitution?
  (A) a unicameral legislature
  (B) a bicameral legislature
  (C) a chief executive
  (D) a ban on the granting of titles of nobility
  (E) a ban on religious tests as a qualification for high government office

The Constitution and the Bill of Rights

201. Which is NOT one way in which a free press provides a check on the power of the government?
  (A) It provides a platform for discussion of government policies.
  (B) It provides a means for the leaders to communicate with the people.
  (C) Its reporters serve as the citizens' representatives in press conferences and interviews.
  (D) It informs the people about the actions and decisions of their representatives.
  (E) It makes questionable and/or criminal activities public knowledge.

202. A two-thirds majority in each house of Congress, or a national convention called by Congress at the request of two-thirds of the state legislatures, are the two ways of
  (A) proposing a constitutional amendment
  (B) impeaching the president
  (C) declaring a law unconstitutional
  (D) adding a new state to the United States
  (E) declaring war on a foreign power

203. The American system of government, with its powers divided among three branches, was first described in print by which Enlightenment *philosophe*?
- (A) Benjamin Franklin
- (B) Thomas Hobbes
- (C) John Locke
- (D) Charles-Louis de Secondat, Baron de Montesquieu
- (E) Voltaire

204. Article I of the Constitution assigns the vice president the duty of
- (A) succeeding the president in office if he or she dies or becomes incapacitated
- (B) traveling abroad to negotiate treaties with foreign powers
- (C) signing congressional legislation
- (D) presiding over the Senate and casting the tiebreaking vote when called upon
- (E) introducing legislation to the Congress

205. What check does the Constitution place on the president's power to sign a treaty with another country?
- (A) The Supreme Court must determine that the treaty is constitutional.
- (B) Both houses of Congress must approve the treaty by majority vote.
- (C) The Senate must approve the treaty by a two-thirds vote.
- (D) Two-thirds of the state legislatures must ratify the treaty.
- (E) The citizens must approve the treaty by direct popular vote.

206. The *Federalist Papers* were written to persuade people to support the ratification of the
- (A) Bill of Rights
- (B) Constitution
- (C) Declaration of Independence
- (D) Northwest Ordinance
- (E) Treaty of Paris

207. The Preamble to the Constitution embodies the framers' respect for the principle of
- (A) federalism
- (B) majority rule
- (C) the separation of powers in the government
- (D) equal rights for all citizens under the law
- (E) government by the consent of the governed

208. As described in the Constitution, the United States is
   (A) a federal republic
   (B) a popular democracy
   (C) a loose association of independent sovereign states
   (D) a constitutional monarchy
   (E) an expanding empire

209. The Great Compromise combined earlier ideas for the structure
of the legislature in requiring that Congress
   (A) consist of a unicameral legislature
   (B) consist of a bicameral legislature
   (C) represent all the states by population in both houses
   (D) represent all the states equally in both houses
   (E) represent the states equally in one house and by population
       in the other

210. James Madison was the single most important influence on the shaping
of the U.S. government for all these reasons EXCEPT
   (A) his articulate authorship of nearly half of the *Federalist Papers*
   (B) the leading role he played in the debates in the Constitutional
       Convention
   (C) his arguments in the Virginia convention on ratification
       of the Constitution
   (D) his authorship of the text of the Constitution of the United States
   (E) the comprehensive notes he took during the debates in Philadelphia

211. Which was NOT one reason why the framers guaranteed freedom
of religious worship in the Constitution?
   (A) The results of the Salem witch trials proved the importance
       of the separation of church and state.
   (B) Few of the framers of the Constitution were religiously orthodox
       or observant.
   (C) All of the states already had religiously diverse populations.
   (D) The desire for individual rights and independence was very strong
       throughout the United States.
   (E) The nation's founders believed that open participation in religious
       worship was incompatible with good government.

212. The Constitution defines treason against the United States as
(A) committing serious crimes while holding high government office
(B) making war against the United States or aiding its enemies
(C) falsifying or rigging votes to change the results of a national election
(D) bribing high government officials to pass or veto certain bills
(E) lying under oath in a grand jury proceeding

213. Which of the following was NOT among the major influences
on the delegates to the Constitutional Convention?
(A) the English Bill of Rights
(B) the Roman Republic
(C) the Magna Carta
(D) the Declaration of the Rights of Man and of the Citizen
(E) the ideas of the Enlightenment

214. Which best explains the check ordinary citizens of the United States
have on the power of the government?
(A) Citizens can communicate directly with their representatives.
(B) Citizens can vote for candidates who represent their interests.
(C) Citizens can sue the government for damages.
(D) Citizens can refuse to exercise their right to vote.
(E) Citizens can impeach a high government official for committing
crimes.

215. If the Senate votes to convict an impeached president, it has the power to
(A) remove the president from office and ban him or her from holding
office in the future
(B) fine the president his or her full salary for the year
(C) banish the president from the United States for life
(D) order the president's trial in the appropriate civil or criminal court
(E) have the president tried for high treason against the United States

216. According to the Preamble, the Constitution has all of the following
purposes EXCEPT
(A) to secure individual liberties for all citizens and their descendants
(B) to maintain domestic peace
(C) to establish the permanent borders of the nation
(D) to provide for the defense of the nation
(E) to ensure justice for all citizens

217. Why did the framers of the Constitution include a clause permanently banning the establishment of a titled American aristocracy?
- (A) to pave the way for the eventual abolition of African chattel slavery
- (B) to protect the traditional British and American right to a trial by jury for anyone accused of a crime
- (C) to prevent the creation of a standing army that would endanger individual liberty and safety
- (D) to ensure that freedom of religious worship would remain the law of the land
- (E) to avoid creating a class that would enjoy privileges because of birth rather than merit

218. Which three men wrote the *Federalist Papers* under the signature "Publius"?
- (A) John Adams, Alexander Hamilton, and John Jay
- (B) John Adams, Thomas Jefferson, and James Madison
- (C) Benjamin Franklin, Alexander Hamilton, and James Madison
- (D) Alexander Hamilton, John Jay, and James Madison
- (E) George Washington, John Adams, and Thomas Jefferson

219. As of 1787, the Constitution included all of the following EXCEPT
- (A) a list of the civil liberties and legal rights of U.S. citizens
- (B) an explanation of how the chief executive was to be chosen
- (C) a procedure for amending the Constitution
- (D) a description of the federal legislature and its responsibilities
- (E) a list of the types of legal cases over which the Supreme Court would have jurisdiction

220. What was the result of the Three-Fifths Compromise?
- (A) Each Indian was counted in the Constitution as three-fifths of a person in determining a state's total population.
- (B) Each African slave was counted in the Constitution as three-fifths of a person in determining a state's total population.
- (C) Three-fifths of the states would have to ratify any proposed constitutional amendment for it to become law.
- (D) Three-fifths of the members of both houses of Congress would have to vote against an impeached president for him or her to be forced out of office.
- (E) Three-fifths of the Senate would have to vote in favor of a nominee for him or her to be confirmed as a Supreme Court justice.

221. Which right is NOT guaranteed in the Fifth Amendment?
  (A) A person cannot be tried twice for the same crime.
  (B) No one can be compelled to testify against himself or herself.
  (C) The government may not take over private property without the owner's consent.
  (D) Only a grand jury can decide to indict a person for a capital crime.
  (E) No one can be imprisoned or executed except by due process of law.

222. How did the *Federalist Papers* respond to the Antifederalist concern about the dangers of a small group of like-minded people tyrannizing over the central government?
  (A) The majority would always be able to outvote such a small group.
  (B) Such a small group could easily be overpowered by the force of arms.
  (C) Small political interest groups always disbanded of their own accord after a short time.
  (D) The interests of all Americans were identical; therefore, no such small groups would ever be created.
  (E) Small groups of this type did not have a place in the national government.

223. The constitutional rights of citizens who are accused of crimes include all of the following EXCEPT
  (A) the right to a speedy and public trial
  (B) the right to a trial by a jury of his or her peers
  (C) the right to reasonable bail and, if convicted, reasonable fines or penalties
  (D) the right to be informed, upon arrest, of his or her constitutional rights
  (E) protection from searches without probable cause or a search warrant

224. Most of the original state constitutions were substantially reworked after widespread complaints over
  (A) an inadequate balance of powers
  (B) the lack of any reference to individual rights and freedoms
  (C) the failure to establish judicial systems
  (D) the lack of uniformity among the constitutions of the different states
  (E) the haste with which they had been written, without input from the citizens

225. What was one of the most effective arguments the Antifederalists made against the governmental structure set forth in the Constitution?
   (A) Republican government could only succeed in countries much smaller than the United States.
   (B) The individual states had far too much power over the central government.
   (C) The American aristocracy would soon have all the national power in its hands.
   (D) The Constitution did not settle the issues of Indian policy or chattel slavery.
   (E) Southerners were overrepresented in the legislature because of the way the slave population was counted.

226. Half of the amendments in the Bill of Rights deal with issues related to
   (A) the natural and inalienable rights of humankind
   (B) freedom of religious worship
   (C) the rights of accused criminals
   (D) rights that the individual states maintain under the Constitution
   (E) rights to ownership of personal property

227. According to the Constitution as originally written, how did a candidate become vice president of the United States?
   (A) by being the running mate of the successful presidential candidate
   (B) by coming in second in the electoral college vote for president
   (C) by receiving a majority in the electoral college vote for vice president
   (D) by majority vote in the House of Representatives
   (E) by majority vote in the Senate

228. The bestselling American autobiography *The Interesting Narrative of the Life of Olaudah Equiano* (1789) emphasizes which legal or social anomaly?
   (A) the constant insistence on states' rights in a nation of states that were entirely dependent on one another for prosperity and security
   (B) women's constitutional right to run for office in a nation where they were not allowed to vote
   (C) legal barriers to immigration in a nation entirely populated by immigrants and their descendants
   (D) treatment of the Indians as a hostile foreign population when they were the original settlers of the continent
   (E) the existence of chattel slavery in a nation founded on liberty and equality

229. Which accounts for the fact that white southerners were disproportionately represented in Congress as of the ratification of the Constitution?
(A) Their slaves had no civil or political rights but were still counted as part of the total population.
(B) Their states were larger and more densely populated than the northern states.
(C) The most important political leaders of the Revolutionary era were from the South.
(D) The commander in chief of the Continental Army was a Virginian.
(E) Southerners believed that they had more of a stake in the national government than northerners.

230. Which is NOT one of the major political themes championed in the *Federalist Papers*?
(A) the principle of federalism
(B) the importance of security over liberty
(C) the danger of factions
(D) the separation of powers
(E) the need for representation

231. What was the response of the Virginia Antifederalists when the Constitution was sent to their legislature for ratification in 1788?
(A) They refused to call a ratifying convention.
(B) They called a convention that refused to ratify the Constitution.
(C) They ratified the Constitution but submitted a suggested bill of rights to add to it.
(D) They agreed to ratify the Constitution only if their suggested bill of rights was adopted.
(E) They ratified the Constitution without further argument.

232. The Constitution grants Congress the power to do all of the following EXCEPT
(A) declare war
(B) supervise military policy and decisions during a war
(C) override a presidential veto of any bill by a two-thirds majority vote
(D) convene at least once every year
(E) regulate international trade

233. According to the Constitution as originally written, which of the following would be chosen by direct popular vote?
(A) governors of the individual states
(B) Supreme Court justices
(C) the president of the United States
(D) members of the Senate
(E) members of the House of Representatives

234. Why did the delegates to the Constitutional Convention vote to keep their proceedings secret until the debate was ended?
(A) They knew that their work would be unpopular among the citizens.
(B) They were afraid of provoking an armed popular uprising.
(C) They wanted to protect themselves from all outside political pressure.
(D) They were concerned that foreign spies might report their activities to other governments.
(E) They knew that some high officials might regard their proceedings as high treason.

235. Which of the following describes a check of the executive branch of the government on the judicial branch?
(A) The president can veto legislation.
(B) The president can declare a law unconstitutional.
(C) The president can dismiss justices if they commit crimes.
(D) The president can nominate justices.
(E) The president can appoint justices.

236. The First Amendment guarantees all of the following freedoms EXCEPT
(A) freedom of the press
(B) freedom to stage peaceful gatherings and demonstrations
(C) freedom to vote in all elections
(D) freedom of speech
(E) freedom of religious worship

237. The executive power to veto a bill is checked by the legislative power to
(A) override the veto by a two-thirds majority vote
(B) stage a filibuster
(C) call for a referendum
(D) petition the states
(E) impeach the president

238. Which of the following is NOT guaranteed in the Bill of Rights?
   (A) freedom from cruel and unusual punishment for crimes
   (B) possession of rights other than those listed in the Constitution
   (C) protection against search and seizure of property without a warrant
   (D) protection from being compelled to testify against oneself in court
   (E) the right to vote for all free men age 21 or older

239. The Constitution states that the president of the United States is to be chosen by
   (A) popular vote
   (B) the Supreme Court
   (C) the Congress
   (D) the electors of all the states
   (E) the governors of all the states

240. On what grounds did the Antifederalists oppose ratification of the Constitution as originally written?
   (A) They opposed the secrecy under which the Constitutional Convention had been conducted.
   (B) They believed that a weak central government would give too much power to the individual states.
   (C) They objected to the monarchical powers given to the executive branch of the government.
   (D) They were afraid that the electoral college system was too democratic.
   (E) They pointed out that the Constitution did not specify the individual rights and freedoms of the citizens.

The United States to 1816

241. Congress passed the Alien and Sedition Acts in 1798 with the goal of
   (A) protecting national security
   (B) preserving individual liberties
   (C) establishing one-party rule
   (D) strengthening federal power over the states
   (E) creating a national standing army

242. Which important legal principle did Chief Justice John Marshall establish in *Marbury v. Madison*?
   (A) the balance of power
   (B) judicial review
   (C) the right to legal representation
   (D) the presumption of innocence
   (E) the right to remain silent

243. The purchase of the Louisiana Territory was inconsistent with Thomas Jefferson's professed political belief that
     (A) the United States should not take any more land from the Indians
     (B) the United States should not expand any farther to the west
     (C) the Constitution should be strictly observed according to its literal wording
     (D) France would attack the United States after the sale of the land
     (E) it was not his duty as president to take advantage of the chance to buy the land

244. The term *impressment* refers to
     (A) making boys and men within a specified age range sign up for a national military draft
     (B) kidnapping men and forcing them into service in the navy or merchant marine
     (C) calling all the boys and men of a town together for military training at specified times
     (D) forcing Indians who were settled on desirable farmland to move elsewhere
     (E) forcing Indians to live only on land set aside for them by the U.S. government

245. Whose ideas had the greatest influence on Alexander Hamilton's economic theories?
     (A) Samuel Adams's ideas
     (B) Benjamin Franklin's ideas
     (C) Thomas Jefferson's ideas
     (D) John Locke's ideas
     (E) Adam Smith's ideas

246. The Democratic-Republican Party was characterized by all the following positions EXCEPT
     (A) support for agriculture as the mainstay of the U.S. economy
     (B) belief that the states should have more power than the central government
     (C) support for an alliance with Britain
     (D) support for an alliance with France
     (E) belief that the government had only those powers specifically described in the Constitution

247. Which statement best describes American foreign policy under the Washington administration?
    (A) The United States allied with France against Britain.
    (B) The United States allied with Britain against France.
    (C) The United States allied with Spain against rebellious Latin American colonies.
    (D) The United States concentrated on taking over more territory.
    (E) The United States remained officially neutral toward all other nations.

248. The War of 1812 had all the following results EXCEPT
    (A) forging a permanent alliance between Britain and the United States
    (B) strengthening U.S. control over the Northwest Territory
    (C) enlarging the United States with the acquisition of the Florida Territory
    (D) substantially weakening the Federalist Party
    (E) leaving the Indian population without the support of a foreign power

249. Secretary of the Treasury Alexander Hamilton took or vigorously supported all the following steps to place the United States on a sound financial footing EXCEPT
    (A) raising the national debt ceiling
    (B) establishing a national bank
    (C) establishing a national currency
    (D) selling government bonds
    (E) raising taxes and establishing new taxes

250. Thomas Jefferson signed the Embargo Act into law in order to
    (A) improve the U.S. international trade balance
    (B) put a stop to the practice of impressment
    (C) cut off trade relations with Britain and France
    (D) establish trade relations with Britain and France
    (E) make the United States economically self-sufficient

251. In response to the passage of the Alien and Sedition Acts, Democratic-Republicans
    (A) argued for the passage of stronger and more punitive measures against disloyal citizens
    (B) suggested a constitutional amendment to protect the rights of foreign visitors
    (C) threatened to impeach the president unless the acts were repealed
    (D) supported state laws declaring that the acts were unconstitutional and therefore nonbinding on the states
    (E) advocated a formal alliance with Britain against France

252. What was the cause of Pennsylvania's Whiskey Rebellion of 1794?
(A) determination that Philadelphia should continue to be the capital city
(B) opposition to the state constitution
(C) antislavery sentiments
(D) new federal taxes
(E) the temperance movement

253. The first U.S. political parties, the Democratic-Republicans and the Federalists, organized themselves, respectively, around
(A) Alexander Hamilton and John Adams
(B) John Adams and Aaron Burr
(C) Aaron Burr and James Madison
(D) James Madison and Thomas Jefferson
(E) Thomas Jefferson and Alexander Hamilton

254. The Twelfth Amendment, ratified in 1804, changed the
(A) electoral college system by which the president was chosen
(B) voting procedures of the Senate
(C) voting procedures of the House
(D) process by which Supreme Court justices were approved
(E) Supreme Court's jurisdiction over international lawsuits involving the United States

255. George Washington is unique among U.S. presidents because he
(A) had served as a general in the armed forces
(B) did not belong to or represent any political party
(C) supported American neutrality in foreign affairs
(D) had never before been elected to national office
(E) was appointed, not elected, to the presidency

256. The goal of the War Hawks of the 1812 Congress was to
(A) see George Clinton elected president
(B) stop trading with both Britain and France
(C) drive the British from Canada and the Spanish from Florida
(D) come to an agreement with Britain over the Northwest Territory
(E) forge a lasting alliance with France

257. The political leaders of the United States during the presidencies of Washington, Adams, Jefferson, and Madison generally had all these characteristics in common EXCEPT
(A) they were from old established colonial families
(B) they were well educated and highly literate
(C) they had played crucial roles in winning U.S. independence
(D) they were from New England or the Northeast
(E) they believed in the ideals of the Enlightenment

258. Aaron Burr is a notable figure in U.S. history for all of the following EXCEPT
(A) fatally wounding Alexander Hamilton in a duel
(B) leading a mutiny of his troops during the Revolutionary War
(C) presiding over the impeachment trial of Justice Samuel Chase
(D) being indicted and tried for treason against the United States
(E) participating in the hotly contested presidential election of 1800

259. Why was Washington, D.C., chosen as the national capital?
(A) It had a central location in the United States.
(B) It was named in honor of the first president.
(C) It was on a major river.
(D) It was in the South.
(E) It was the location of important political meetings in colonial days.

260. Why did the southern colonies accept the total ban placed on the importation of kidnapped Africans and their sale into slavery after 1808?
(A) Slavery was proving economically costly.
(B) The slave population would sustain itself through live births.
(C) Newly arrived Africans were harder to train than American-born slaves.
(D) Southerners thought that northerners profited too much from the slave trade.
(E) Southerners were beginning to consider a plan of gradual abolition.

261. Which of the following did NOT serve in the first presidential cabinet?
(A) Benjamin Franklin
(B) Alexander Hamilton
(C) Thomas Jefferson
(D) Henry Knox
(E) Edmund Randolph

262. The principle of judicial review, established during the Jefferson administration, gives the Supreme Court the power to
(A) propose amendments to the Constitution
(B) refuse to hear any case the justices feel does not merit their attention
(C) review the decisions of justices serving on lower courts
(D) determine the constitutionality of any federal or state law
(E) veto a bill proposed by both houses of Congress

263. What effect did the Napoleonic Wars have on the American economy?
(A) They caused a boom because of large purchases of American-made arms and ammunition.
(B) They caused a boom because of the rise in manufacturing jobs in the North.
(C) They caused a boom because European nations began trading with the United States instead of trading with one another.
(D) They created a depression because Americans left their jobs to sail to Europe and fight.
(E) They created a depression because Europe stopped buying American cotton and other products.

264. What happened at the Hartford Convention of 1814?
(A) Federalists drew up a list of suggested amendments to the Constitution.
(B) New England states voted to secede from the United States.
(C) Massachusetts sent a commission to Great Britain to negotiate its own peace treaty.
(D) Opposition party members discussed a plan to assassinate President Madison.
(E) The Federalist Party agreed to disband.

265. Zebulon Pike is a significant figure in U.S. history for
(A) discovering the source of the Mississippi River
(B) helping to establish the borders of the future Great Plains states
(C) leading expeditions through the Louisiana Territory
(D) conspiring with Spain against the U.S. government
(E) climbing the highest mountain in North America

266. What was the XYZ Affair of 1797?
  (A) an attempt by French government agents to bribe U.S. diplomats
  (B) an attempt by British government agents to bribe U.S. diplomats
  (C) a public scandal resulting from corruption within the John Adams administration
  (D) a series of last-minute judicial appointments on John Adams's last night as president
  (E) a secret agreement between Britain and France to declare war on the United States

267. Which was NOT one result of the Battle of the Fallen Timbers (1795)?
  (A) Friendship was declared between the United States and various Indian tribes of the Northwest Territory.
  (B) The Miami, Kaskaskia, and other tribes sold their ancestral lands to the U.S. government.
  (C) The United States and the tribes agreed on a permanent border between U.S. and Indian territory in the northwest.
  (D) The Miami and other tribes retained absolute rights over their new territory.
  (E) The U.S. government and the Indians agreed to exchange prisoners of war.

268. The Lewis and Clark expedition brought back detailed information on the people, animals, plants, and natural features of all the following present-day states EXCEPT
  (A) Colorado
  (B) Idaho
  (C) Montana
  (D) North Dakota
  (E) South Dakota

269. The Treaty of Ghent established all of the following EXCEPT
  (A) peace between Great Britain and the United States
  (B) an exchange of prisoners of war
  (C) the creation of a commission to determine control over certain disputed territories and boundaries
  (D) peace between the United States and the Indians, and between Great Britain and the Indians
  (E) the resumption of trade between Britain and the United States

270. Which of the following created a division within the Federalist Party?
  (A) George Washington's election for a second term
  (B) George Washington's insistence on maintaining U.S. neutrality in foreign affairs
  (C) John Adams's insistence on maintaining peace with France
  (D) Thomas Jefferson's decision to purchase the Louisiana Territory
  (E) Alexander Hamilton's support for a national bank

271. Which was NOT one factor in the massive slowdown in westward migration during the decade before 1815?
  (A) the War of 1812
  (B) a severe economic depression
  (C) the lack of efficient transportation and good roads
  (D) continual armed conflict with the Indians on the frontier
  (E) congressional refusal to consider establishing slavery in the West

272. As of the end of 1816, which of the following had NOT been awarded statehood?
  (A) Florida
  (B) Kentucky
  (C) Louisiana
  (D) Ohio
  (E) Tennessee

273. Which is NOT one reason why the United States declared war on Great Britain in 1812?
  (A) The United States wanted to expand into Canada and Florida.
  (B) The United States had recently purchased the Louisiana Territory.
  (C) British ships were forcing Americans into service in the Royal Navy.
  (D) Britain had provided arms to some of the Indian tribes in the Northwest Territory.
  (E) The United States blamed Britain for the economic depression in the inland frontier region.

274. Which was NOT one goal of the Lewis and Clark expedition?
  (A) to make accurate maps of the Louisiana Territory
  (B) to search for a water route across North America from the Atlantic to the Pacific
  (C) to register all the Indian tribes living in the Louisiana Territory
  (D) to study the various types of plants and animals in the Louisiana Territory
  (E) to establish friendly relations with Indian tribes in the region

275. What role did Alexander Hamilton play in the presidential election of 1800?
   (A) He urged Congress to break the deadlock by voting for Thomas Jefferson.
   (B) He urged Congress to break the deadlock by voting for Aaron Burr.
   (C) He ran the first "negative campaign" against his opponents.
   (D) He ran as the first third-party candidate.
   (E) He urged the passage of a constitutional amendment to change the electoral process.

CHAPTER 4

The 19th Century: Politics, Economics, and Culture to 1865

National Politics and Foreign Affairs to 1860

276. One purpose of issuing the Monroe Doctrine was to
(A) declare absolute neutrality in foreign affairs outside U.S. borders
(B) declare support for any western colony in rebellion against a European nation
(C) urge Latin American colonies to rebel against European nations
(D) ban European colonization in the Western Hemisphere
(E) forge an alliance between the United States and the colonies of Latin America

277. The Five Civilized Tribes of the Southeast include all of the following EXCEPT
(A) the Cherokee
(B) the Choctaw
(C) the Creek
(D) the Sac and Fox
(E) the Seminole

278. Which is NOT one change that occurred in U.S. politics during the first four decades of the 19th century?
(A) Some states revoked the voting rights of free African-American men.
(B) States dropped the property-ownership requirement for voters.
(C) Civil servants were rotated out of office after fixed short terms.
(D) National party conventions selected the candidates for president and vice president.
(E) Senators were popularly elected rather than chosen by state legislatures.

279. Congress accepted the Missouri Compromise because it
   (A)   swung the balance of power in Congress toward the free states
   (B)   swung the balance of power in Congress toward the slaveholding states
   (C)   maintained the balance of power in Congress where it was
   (D)   convinced the South that slavery would soon spread throughout the United States
   (E)   convinced the North that slavery would soon be abolished

280. The term *filibusters* refers to Americans who
   (A)   illegally seized control of Latin American territory
   (B)   agitated for all-out war against Spain
   (C)   urged the repeal of the Monroe Doctrine
   (D)   supported spending limits on campaigns for high office
   (E)   advocated full citizenship for the Indians

281. The Whig Party was founded by men who objected to significant gains in power by the
   (A)   presidency
   (B)   Senate
   (C)   House of Representatives
   (D)   Supreme Court
   (E)   states

282. The Know-Nothing Party was founded in the 1840s by those who opposed
   (A)   abolition
   (B)   slavery
   (C)   immigration
   (D)   western expansion
   (E)   imperialism

283. Which was NOT one plank of the Republican Party platform in the campaign of 1856?
   (A)   to admit Kansas into the United States as a free state
   (B)   to abolish slavery throughout the United States
   (C)   to ban the spread of slavery into U.S. territories
   (D)   to prevent the U.S. annexation of Cuba
   (E)   to finance the construction of the transcontinental railroad

284. Which was NOT one position taken by the Republican Party during the election of 1860?
(A) opposition to any expansion of slavery in the territories
(B) denunciation of the raid on Harpers Ferry
(C) support for preservation of the Union
(D) opposition to land grants for western settlers
(E) support for protective tariffs and the transcontinental railroad

285. According to the Indian Removal Act of 1830, the United States would
(A) buy all Indian lands in the organized states or territories from the Indians at fair market value and resettle the Indians in the unorganized territories
(B) accept lands of consenting Indian tribes in the organized state or territories in exchange for equivalent land in the unorganized territories
(C) force all Indians to move from the United States to the U.S. territories
(D) force all Indians to leave the United States and its territories
(E) resettle all Indians in specific territory west of the Mississippi River, organize the territory into two states, and eventually admit those states to the Union

286. Which was NOT one reason why South Carolina passed the Ordinance of Nullification of 1832?
(A) The Tariff Acts were passed from unconstitutional and corrupt motives.
(B) The Tariff Acts did not operate equally on all the states.
(C) The taxes specified in the Tariff Acts were unreasonably high.
(D) The revenue raised by the Tariff Acts would be used for an unconstitutional purpose.
(E) The Tariff Acts were unconstitutional because they were passed without the consent of the people being taxed.

287. In 1854, the United States used "gunboat diplomacy" to force a favorable trade relationship on
(A) Canada
(B) Great Britain
(C) Japan
(D) Mexico
(E) Panama

288. Which does NOT describe one aspect of the presidential campaign of 1840?
(A) Harrison won the election because his campaign successfully presented him as a "log-cabin" candidate.
(B) Both Van Buren's and Harrison's supporters attacked the opposing candidate with highly exaggerated personal slurs.
(C) For the first time in presidential politics, the candidates made speeches directly to the crowds.
(D) With restrictions on voting dropped throughout the states, voter participation reached a new high.
(E) Van Buren refused to speak on the issues of the day in order to avoid alienating any potential voters.

289. The United States annexed the Oregon Country in 1846 by signing an agreement with
(A) Canada
(B) France
(C) Great Britain
(D) the Nez Perce, Kiowa, and Chinook nations
(E) Russia

290. Which of the following made it possible for the United States to enforce the Monroe Doctrine in the decades before the Civil War?
(A) full military support from Great Britain
(B) full military support from Spain
(C) Mexico's declaration of independence from Spain
(D) the growing size and strength of the U.S. Army and Navy
(E) the abrupt withdrawal of Russian claims to territory in the Pacific Northwest

291. Which was NOT one provision of the Missouri Compromise of 1820?
(A) Missouri would enter the United States as a slaveholding state.
(B) Maine would enter the United States as a free state.
(C) Slavery would be banned in all U.S. territory north of Missouri's southern border, except Missouri itself.
(D) The Northwest Ordinance of 1787 would be repealed.
(E) The Missouri legislature would create a plan to phase slavery out gradually.

292. The Free-Soil Party, founded in 1848, comprised all of the following EXCEPT
(A) northern Democrats
(B) southern Democrats
(C) antislavery Whigs
(D) abolitionists
(E) westerners

293. Which historical event is referred to as the Trail of Tears?
(A) the secession of Texas from Mexico
(B) the migration of the pioneers from Missouri to the West
(C) the forced relocation of the Five Civilized Tribes to Indian Territory
(D) the state funeral of William Henry Harrison
(E) the state funeral of John Quincy Adams

294. In the Adams-Onís Treaty of 1819, the United States gained territory in the
(A) Northeast
(B) South
(C) Great Lakes region
(D) Great Plains region
(E) Southwest

295. Why did Andrew Jackson lose the presidential election of 1824?
(A) He did not receive a clear majority of votes in the electoral college.
(B) He did not come in first in the electoral college vote.
(C) He did not win the national popular vote.
(D) He was not listed on the ballot in all the states.
(E) He was not the choice of his party's national caucus.

296. The doctrine of nullification supports which of the following political positions?
(A) that each state should divide its electoral votes among the presidential candidates according to their percentage of the popular vote
(B) that the presidential candidate who wins the national popular vote must succeed to the presidency
(C) that only taxpayers and property owners should have the right to vote
(D) that the federal government has the right to overturn unconstitutional state laws
(E) that a state cannot be forced to obey a federal law it regards as unconstitutional

297. What was the main issue in the presidential election of 1844?
    (A) the abolition of slavery
    (B) popular sovereignty
    (C) westward expansion
    (D) the domestic economy
    (E) European immigration

298. John Quincy Adams is a notable figure in history for all of the following EXCEPT
    (A) becoming a forceful advocate for the abolition of slavery
    (B) establishing the terms of the Monroe Doctrine
    (C) leading U.S. troops to victory in the War of 1812
    (D) serving in Congress for 18 years
    (E) serving as secretary of state under President James Monroe

299. Which is NOT one way in which the Cherokee nation had, by 1830, adapted itself to the customs and culture of the United States?
    (A) converting to Christianity and building churches
    (B) creating a writing system and publishing a newspaper
    (C) establishing farms and plantations
    (D) declaring themselves a sovereign nation
    (E) invoking the Constitution in their own defense against the state of Georgia

300. The Convention of 1818 established all of the following EXCEPT
    (A) a permanent border between the Louisiana Territory and Canada
    (B) a permanent border between the Louisiana Territory and Spanish territory
    (C) U.S. fishing rights off the coast of Newfoundland
    (D) joint occupation of Oregon Country by Britain and the United States
    (E) 10-year rights of free settlement for both British and Americans in Oregon Country

301. In his Proclamation on the Nullification Issue (1832), President Andrew Jackson used all the following arguments EXCEPT
  (A) that no law or tariff could possibly apply with perfect equality to all subjects
  (B) that each state had a clear constitutional obligation to obey federal laws
  (C) that no state legislature had the right, without proof, to impute corrupt motives to members of Congress
  (D) that even in the case of oppressive and unendurable federal laws, the states had no right to resist compliance
  (E) that Congress had the constitutional right to raise revenue in whatever manner and amount it deemed appropriate and necessary

302. The Rush-Bagot Agreement of 1817 governed which of the following issues?
  (A) the maintenance of warships on the Great Lakes
  (B) the permanent boundary between Indian territory and the United States
  (C) international shipping rights on the Mississippi River
  (D) territorial claims to the Oregon Country
  (E) the northern border of the Louisiana Territory

303. President Millard Fillmore invoked the Monroe Doctrine to oppose an attempted French annexation of
  (A) the Bahamas
  (B) Cuba
  (C) Haiti
  (D) Hawaii
  (E) Martinique

304. What was the major issue in the national election of 1832?
  (A) the establishment of a permanent Indian frontier
  (B) a proposed constitutional amendment to phase out slavery
  (C) whether or not to send military aid to France
  (D) the admission of Pacific coastal territories as new states
  (E) the future of the Second Bank of the United States

305. Which was NOT one provision of the Kanagawa Treaty of 1854?
   (A) that Japanese and U.S. officials would negotiate any issues or business not covered by the treaty, as needed
   (B) that U.S. ships would only be permitted to enter and trade in certain specified Japanese ports
   (C) that U.S. citizens staying temporarily in Japanese ports would be subject to the same restrictions as Chinese and Dutch traders at Nagasaki
   (D) that the United States and Japan would commit to a permanent alliance
   (E) that any privileges Japan granted to any other nation would also be extended to the United States

Culture, Society, and Reform to 1865

306. Which was the first U.S. college or university to offer four-year college degrees to women and Africans on equal terms with white male students?
   (A) Bryn Mawr College, Bryn Mawr, Pennsylvania
   (B) Oberlin College, Oberlin, Ohio
   (C) Radcliffe College, Cambridge, Massachusetts
   (D) University of Pennsylvania, Philadelphia, Pennsylvania
   (E) Yale University, New Haven, Connecticut

307. During the mid-1800s, the majority of European immigrants came to the United States from
   (A) Ireland
   (B) the Mediterranean
   (C) Poland and Russia
   (D) Scandinavia
   (E) southeastern Europe

308. Which is NOT one reason why the early Mormons aroused so much antagonism among non-Mormons?
   (A) In Mormon-dominated communities, only Mormons had the right to bear arms.
   (B) Mormon business practices discriminated against non-Mormons.
   (C) Mormons did not tolerate criticism of their doctrines or practices.
   (D) Mormons openly supported abolition in the slaveholding state of Missouri.
   (E) Mormon doctrines and practices, particularly polygamy, were considered blasphemous by non-Mormons.

309. The temperance movement advocated
    (A) reform of the U.S. penal codes and prison system
    (B) a more liberal immigration policy
    (C) citizenship for the Indians
    (D) equal rights for women
    (E) abstention from drinking alcoholic beverages

310. Which of the following did NOT play a major role in organizing the Seneca Falls Convention of 1848?
    (A) Aimee Semple Macpherson
    (B) Mary Ann McClintock
    (C) Lucretia Mott
    (D) Elizabeth Cady Stanton
    (E) Martha Wright

311. What was the primary goal of the American Colonization Society?
    (A) to end slavery by expelling African-Americans from the United States
    (B) to establish Indian reservations on valuable arable land
    (C) to encourage settlement of the Great Plains and the West
    (D) to enable and encourage free Africans to resettle in northwestern Africa
    (E) to annex all the unsettled territory between the United States and the Pacific Ocean

312. David Walker is historically significant for all of the following EXCEPT
    (A) publishing the first national newspaper for African readers
    (B) writing an African-American version of the Declaration of Independence
    (C) founding the Massachusetts General Colored Association
    (D) writing and distributing the *Appeal to the Colored Citizens of the World*
    (E) serving as an outspoken advocate of abolition

313. The Seneca Falls Convention of 1848 was called primarily in order to
    (A) declare that women should have the same civil and legal rights as men
    (B) integrate American society along race, gender, and class lines
    (C) revise the Declaration of Independence
    (D) force Congress to grant women the right to vote
    (E) do away with the capitalist economic system

314. Which was NOT one result of the slave rebellion led by Nat Turner in Virginia?
   (A) Southern legislatures sharply curtailed slaves' few rights and freedoms.
   (B) Southerners blamed the abolitionist newspaper *The Liberator* for the rebellion.
   (C) A series of slave uprisings took place throughout the South.
   (D) Turner and several of his followers were tried and executed.
   (E) Fifty or sixty white people were killed.

315. Which is NOT one reason why Horace Mann of Massachusetts was an important figure in educational reform?
   (A) He raised teachers' salaries and founded teacher training programs.
   (B) He advocated the elimination of corporal punishment from the classroom.
   (C) He suggested that compulsory schooling was only necessary for students entering one of the professions.
   (D) He excluded all sectarian influence from the public school system.
   (E) He broadened the curriculum and brought it up to date.

316. On what grounds did the states justify denying women the right to vote?
   (A) on the grounds that women had the same legal status as slaves
   (B) on the grounds of centuries of tradition of male authority
   (C) on the grounds of strict construction of the Constitution
   (D) on the grounds that government must be by the consent of the governed
   (E) on the grounds that women were illiterate and uneducated

317. Which European did NOT write a classic work of nonfiction based on his or her travels through and observations of the United States before the Civil War?
   (A) Charles Dickens
   (B) Frances "Fanny" Kemble
   (C) Alexis de Tocqueville
   (D) Frances Trollope
   (E) Oscar Wilde

318. In the decades before the Civil War, the South comprised all these social classes EXCEPT
(A) wealthy planters
(B) wealthy financiers and businessmen
(C) independent small farmers
(D) the rural poor, or "poor whites"
(E) slaves

319. All of the following were significant American authors of the early to mid-19th century EXCEPT
(A) Frederick Douglass
(B) Ralph Waldo Emerson
(C) Henry James
(D) Henry David Thoreau
(E) Walt Whitman

320. Sojourner Truth is a notable figure in U.S. history as all of the following EXCEPT
(A) a forceful public speaker on abolition
(B) an advocate of women's rights
(C) the author of a notable slave narrative
(D) an active recruiter of black troops for the Union Army
(E) a conductor on the Underground Railroad

321. Which notable American writer of the antebellum era is NOT correctly matched with his or her best-known literary work?
(A) James Fenimore Cooper, *The Last of the Mohicans*
(B) Emily Dickinson, *Leaves of Grass*
(C) Nathaniel Hawthorne, *The Scarlet Letter*
(D) Herman Melville, *Moby-Dick*
(E) Harriet Beecher Stowe, *Uncle Tom's Cabin*

322. The popular patriotic song and future U.S. national anthem "The Star-Spangled Banner" was written to commemorate the defense of
(A) Fort Duquesne, Pennsylvania
(B) Fort McHenry, Maryland
(C) Fort Sumter, South Carolina
(D) Fort Ticonderoga, New York
(E) Fort Vincennes, Ohio

323. During the antebellum era, American women gained all of the following rights EXCEPT
 (A) the right to vote if free and age 21 or older
 (B) the right to keep and use their maiden names after marriage
 (C) the right to earn a college or university degree
 (D) the sole ownership of any wages they earned, if married
 (E) the right to acquire and control property, if married

324. The purpose of the Morrill Act of 1862 was to support
 (A) the assimilation of Indian tribes into the U.S. economy and society
 (B) the organization of the unsettled western and Great Plains territories
 (C) the sale of public lands in the West to individual farmers and their families
 (D) college training in practical sciences such as engineering and agriculture
 (E) the U.S. annexation of certain strategically important offshore islands

325. Alexis de Tocqueville's *Democracy in America* is best described as
 (A) a comparison of the American and French forms of government
 (B) an analysis of the people of the United States and their national character
 (C) an essay explaining why the American form of government was bound to fail in the long run
 (D) a travelogue describing the landscapes, large cities, factories, and small towns throughout the settled areas of the United States
 (E) a lengthy description and analysis of the history, formation, and viability of the republican form of government in the United States

Economic and Industrial Development to 1865

326. The perfection of the mechanical reaper had all these important effects EXCEPT
 (A) crop yield rose to previously unimaginable levels, making farmers' profits soar
 (B) food prices dropped drastically, making it possible for workers to live on wages without subsistence farming
 (C) farmers were encouraged to move west, where they could buy good farmland cheaply
 (D) the Great Plains and the West became profitable farming economies without relying on slave labor
 (E) small family farms became a thing of the past because they were no longer profitable

327. Which is NOT one reason why industrialization developed slowly in the South?
(A) The agricultural economy was so profitable that wealthy southerners had no incentive to build factories.
(B) The majority of the southern population was too poor to provide a market for manufactured goods.
(C) The system of slave labor discouraged immigrants from settling in the South.
(D) Technological advances such as the steamboat were of no relevance or benefit to the southern economy.
(E) Wealthy planters considered themselves socially superior to men engaged in manufacturing, business, and trade.

328. The "mill girls" of the Lowell textile mills and similar New England companies were attracted to this type of work for all the following reasons EXCEPT
(A) clean and comfortable boardinghouses
(B) substantially higher wages than they could earn elsewhere
(C) the protection of a labor union
(D) time to pursue cultural and intellectual interests
(E) three meals a day at no cost to themselves

329. Which was NOT one effect of the canal boom in Illinois, Indiana, Ohio, and Pennsylvania?
(A) It gave rise to tremendous growth of interstate trade in the region.
(B) It brought about the transfer of unclaimed lands into state and private ownership.
(C) It connected the region economically to the old Northeast.
(D) It helped to cause the Panic of 1837.
(E) It contributed to a shift in the region's economy from primarily agricultural to primarily industrial.

330. Henry Clay's American System called for all of the following EXCEPT
(A) a national bank
(B) protective tariffs
(C) a national transportation system
(D) a sound national currency
(E) a free-trade agreement with Great Britain

331. Which of the following was the primary cause of the explosion of internal trade that took place in the early 1800s?
(A) the creation of a national bank
(B) the development of refrigeration
(C) the abandonment of the gold standard
(D) the improvements in long-distance transportation
(E) the signing of international trade agreements

332. Which best describes the effect of the cotton gin on the southern economy?
(A) It caused a major economic boom.
(B) It caused a temporary financial panic.
(C) It did not affect the southern economy.
(D) It made the South much more prosperous than the North.
(E) It eased the shipment of southern cotton to the northern textile mills.

333. The Erie Canal provided an efficient, direct trade route between Lake Erie and the
(A) Allegheny River
(B) Delaware River
(C) Hudson River
(D) Monongahela River
(E) Ohio River

334. Why was beaver fur so highly prized by consumers in the 1820s and 1830s?
(A) It was thick and warm.
(B) It was waterproof.
(C) It was beautifully marked.
(D) It was inexpensive.
(E) It was scarce.

335. The six-shot revolver rose to national prominence when
(A) the Texas Rangers introduced it into battle during the Mexican War
(B) the Mormons traveled westward to establish a community in the West
(C) the American settlers of Texas rebelled against the Mexican government
(D) the Mexican Army led a successful rebellion against Spain
(E) Andrew Jackson led U.S. troops in the First and Second Seminole Wars

336. The economy of the antebellum South was primarily dependent on
(A) large-scale agriculture
(B) manufacturing and industry
(C) employment in the civil service
(D) international trade
(E) banking and finance

337. What caused the Panic of 1837?
(A) the election of Martin Van Buren as president
(B) the issuance of the Monroe Doctrine
(C) the completion of the Erie Canal
(D) the expiration of the charter of the Second Bank
(E) the outcome of the Nullification Crisis

338. Major new technologies or inventions of the antebellum Industrial Revolution included all of the following EXCEPT
(A) the cotton gin
(B) the light bulb
(C) the spinning jenny
(D) the steam-powered engine
(E) the telegraph

339. Which was NOT one effect of the creation of a national system of roads, canals, and a railroad?
(A) It hastened the full settlement of the western territories.
(B) It increased the social and political divide between North and South.
(C) It bolstered the economy by creating new markets for goods.
(D) It strengthened economic connections between distant regions of the country.
(E) It gave rise to more clashes between the settlers and the Indian population.

340. The cotton gin's purpose was to speed up the process of
(A) planting cotton
(B) picking cotton
(C) separating cotton seeds from cotton fibers
(D) spinning raw cotton into thread and yarn
(E) weaving cotton thread or yarn into fabric

341. Which does NOT describe one standard aspect of work in the mills and factories of the North in the decades before the Civil War?
  (A) Children under 15 were forbidden by law to work except on Saturdays.
  (B) Owners could pay whatever wages they chose.
  (C) There were no laws to regulate safe working conditions.
  (D) Compensation for injury or serious illness depended on the owner's generosity.
  (E) The workweek was 60 or more hours over six days.

342. What was the purpose of the Land Law of 1820?
  (A) to encourage easterners to help settle the West
  (B) to reserve specific western lands for settlement by the Indians
  (C) to sell government-owned land to individual settlers at a profit
  (D) to set aside government-owned western lands for a transcontinental railroad
  (E) to provide economic relief for the West after the Panic of 1819

343. What effect did the Mexican Revolution of 1821 have on the U.S. economy?
  (A) It temporarily halted Mexican exports to the United States.
  (B) It temporarily halted U.S exports to Mexico.
  (C) It established new and irksome barriers to free travel between U.S. territory and Mexico.
  (D) It eliminated high protective tariffs on U.S. exports to Mexico.
  (E) It drove up the price of Mexican exports to the United States.

344. What was the outcome of the Nullification Crisis of 1832–1833?
  (A) President Andrew Jackson repealed the Tariff Act of 1828.
  (B) South Carolina temporarily seceded from the United States.
  (C) Congress agreed to lower the tariff rate gradually over 10 years.
  (D) Congress persuaded the tariff opponents that the Tariff Act benefited them economically.
  (E) Each state held a referendum on the Tariff Act of 1828.

345. The Clayton-Bulwer Treaty of 1850 dealt with the issue of
  (A) construction of the transcontinental railroad
  (B) boundaries of the Indian territory
  (C) mining regulations in the West
  (D) ownership and use of the Bessemer process
  (E) rights over a potential canal between the Atlantic and Pacific Oceans

346. Which was NOT one important effect of the opening of the Erie Canal?
  (A) Several important manufacturing cities sprang up along the canal route.
  (B) Road-building projects throughout the region were abandoned.
  (C) Settlers began migrating westward into the Great Lakes region in large numbers.
  (D) Shipping costs for loads of goods dropped dramatically from the overland prices.
  (E) New York became the busiest and wealthiest of the Atlantic port cities.

347. Which of the following inventions achieved major success as a direct result of the growth of the railroads?
  (A) the automobile
  (B) the cotton gin
  (C) the elevator
  (D) the telegraph
  (E) the telephone

348. Which figure is NOT correctly matched with his major contribution to the Industrial Revolution in the United States?
  (A) Samuel Colt—the six-shot revolver
  (B) Robert Fulton—the first practical steamboat
  (C) Paul Moody and Francis Cabot Lowell—the power loom
  (D) Elisha Otis—the mechanical reaper
  (E) Eli Whitney—the cotton gin

349. What is one important reason for the decline of the fur-trading industry in the late 1830s?
  (A) the beginning of massive westward migration
  (B) the decimation of the Rocky Mountain beaver population
  (C) the continual improvements in transportation
  (D) a sharp rise in long-distance shipping costs
  (E) continual resistance by Indian tribes in the region

350. Which best explains why southerners opposed the Tariff Acts of 1816 and 1828?
- (A) They were afraid these acts would provoke other countries to tax American cotton.
- (B) They believed these acts were part of a scheme to abolish slavery.
- (C) They did not support the settlement of the western territories.
- (D) They automatically rejected all legislation proposed by northern legislators.
- (E) They felt that the American System was not a sensible economic plan.

351. Which is NOT one reason why the steamboat was a significant improvement over the keelboat?
- (A) It greatly lessened the human effort required to navigate upstream (i.e., against the current).
- (B) It could carry larger loads of goods than the keelboat.
- (C) It took much less time than the keelboat to travel the same route.
- (D) It improved and increased connections among the towns along its route.
- (E) It was more durable than the keelboat.

352. Which was NOT a contributing cause of the Panic of 1819?
- (A) The nations of Europe had recovered economically from the Napoleonic Wars.
- (B) The Second Bank declared that individual loans must be repaid in "hard money."
- (C) The Second Bank of the United States called in all state loans.
- (D) Several consecutive poor harvests led to famine and high prices.
- (E) The European demand for American imports dropped.

353. Which best describes the shift in the economy of the Midwest after the opening of the Erie Canal?
- (A) from farming to ranching
- (B) from manufacturing to agriculture
- (C) from dairy farming to planting and harvesting
- (D) from mining to manufacturing
- (E) from agriculture to manufacturing

354. What was the purpose of the protective tariffs Congress passed in 1816 and 1828?
(A) to equalize the northern and southern economies
(B) to encourage international trade
(C) to support the purchase of American-made goods
(D) to encourage people to settle the western territories
(E) to support southern agriculture

355. How did the Panic of 1837 affect the settlement of the West?
(A) It stimulated westward migration.
(B) It slowed westward migration to a trickle.
(C) It had no effect on westward migration.
(D) It spurred Congress to pass laws restricting westward migration.
(E) It encouraged European immigrants to remain in the Northeast.

356. The federal government organized the Nevada Territory in response to the
(A) boom created by the discovery of the Comstock Lode
(B) migration of the Mormons from western to eastern Utah Territory
(C) Gold Rush shift from individual prospecting to organized large-scale mining
(D) serious threat of a large-scale Indian rebellion against the government
(E) need of a buffer state between the Mormon community and California

CHAPTER 5

The 19th Century: Westward Expansion to 1865

Westward Expansion to 1835

357. All of the following were significant figures in the early exploration of the West EXCEPT
(A) William Ashley
(B) Robert Fulton
(C) Manuel Lisa
(D) Stephen Long
(E) Jedediah Smith

358. Which is NOT one reason why the Mexican government encouraged U.S. citizens to settle Texas during the 1820s?
(A) Texas was sparsely populated.
(B) Mexico was vulnerable to invasion through Texas.
(C) The Comanche, Kiowa, and other tribes frequently raided settlements in the region.
(D) American settlers would establish an organized government and bring control to the region.
(E) Mexico hoped eventually to sell Texas to the United States for a high price.

359. Which factor was the main obstacle to the settlement of Spanish California before about 1800?
(A) the California climate
(B) geographical factors
(C) frequent Indian raids
(D) the failure of the fur-trading industry
(E) Mexico's declaration of independence from Spain

360. In the 1820s, which was NOT one advantage Texas had over the western U.S. territories as a place for a pioneer family to settle?
(A) Texas was a largely self-governing state that held regular free elections.
(B) Land in Texas was being sold much more cheaply than in the West.
(C) American settlers in Texas were exempt from paying taxes and tariffs.
(D) A pioneer could claim a much greater amount of land in Texas than in the West.
(E) The Mexican government granted special privileges to Texans that the U.S. government did not grant to settlers in the West.

361. The Great Migration of 1815–1819 was fueled by all of the following EXCEPT
(A) western land grants made to veterans of the War of 1812
(B) the displacement of Indian peoples north of the Ohio River
(C) improved transportation, such as steamboats and paved roads
(D) the annexation of new territory from Britain and Spain
(E) the new economic prosperity of the Midwest

362. The common factor among all the Indian tribes of the Great Plains was
(A) they all spoke the same language
(B) they were all ethnically related to one another
(C) they constantly warred with one another
(D) their culture was based on riding horses
(E) their culture was based on subsistence farming

363. Which best describes the first group of U.S. citizens to visit Spanish California?
(A) surveyors laying plans for a transcontinental railroad
(B) trailblazers and surveyors from the fur-trading industry
(C) Christian missionaries sent west to convert Indians
(D) officers and troops sent west to build forts
(E) sailors from whaling and trading ships

364. Which was NOT one result of the Black Hawk War of 1832?
(A) The United States purchased a large tract of land on the western bank of the Mississippi from the Sac and Fox tribe.
(B) The U.S. government formally apologized to the Sac and Fox for repeated violations of the terms of war.
(C) More than 80 percent of the rebelling Sac and Fox Indians were killed
(D) The northern section of the Permanent Indian Frontier was moved 50 miles westward.
(E) Black Hawk was regarded throughout the United States as a hero.

365. Which does NOT describe the first battle (August 1823) between the United States and the Indians in the Northwest?

(A) The Sioux and the Missouri Legion fought against the Arikara tribes.

(B) The Arikara and the Missouri Legion signed a peace treaty at the end of the battle.

(C) British troops and volunteers took part in the battle in support of the Arikara.

(D) The Arikara were hostile because they saw the approach of the Americans as a threat to their economic interests.

(E) Two members of the Missouri Legion who disagreed with the treaty burned the Arikara village, causing the tribe to migrate northward.

366. It was possible for settlers and traders to travel along the Santa Fe Trail all the way from

(A) San Diego, California, to St. Louis, Missouri

(B) San Diego, California, to Santa Fe, New Mexico

(C) St. Louis, Missouri, to Santa Fe, New Mexico

(D) Independence, Missouri, to Santa Fe, New Mexico

(E) Independence, Missouri, to San Diego, California

367. Which best accounts for President Andrew Jackson's Indian policy?

(A) He was determined to protect southern frontier interests.

(B) He opposed chattel slavery in the South and throughout the territories.

(C) He wanted to protect the Cherokee, Seminole, and other nations from the threat of U.S. settlement and expansion.

(D) He believed in strict construction of the U.S. Constitution.

(E) He supported full U.S. citizenship for the Indian nations of the Southeast.

368. How did Illinois deal with the question of slavery when it became a state in 1818?

(A) All slaves resident in Illinois were emancipated in 1818.

(B) All slaves resident in Illinois would continue to be enslaved; as of 1818, slavery was outlawed in the state under all other circumstances.

(C) All slaves resident in Illinois were given the opportunity to earn their freedom after 1818.

(D) All slavery in Illinois would be permanently outlawed as of its 10th anniversary as a state.

(E) All Illinois slaveholders would be required to move out of the state in 1818 or free their slaves.

369. What was the primary reason American settlers flocked to Texas during the 1820s?
(A) Texas would become an independent republic in 1836.
(B) The Mexican government was developing a plan to phase out chattel slavery.
(C) Land prices in Texas were much lower than in the western U.S. territories.
(D) The region was culturally and linguistically part of Latin America.
(E) Both the U.S. and Mexican governments encouraged settlement of Texas.

370. What was the central issue discussed at the Prairie du Chien Conference of 1825?
(A) organizing the western U.S. territories into states
(B) establishing a line of forts along the U.S.-Mexican border
(C) determining whether the Rio Grande or the Red River was to be the border between Mexico and the United States
(D) establishing a Permanent Indian Frontier by mutual agreement between the U.S. government and the Indian nations
(E) routing of the transcontinental railroad, which was then in the planning stages

371. Why did the British support Shawnee chief Tecumseh in his stand against U.S. settlement of lands south and west of Lake Michigan?
(A) They believed that the land belonged by rights to the Shawnee and other tribes.
(B) They supported the creation of an Indian state as a buffer between the United States and Canada.
(C) They hoped to annex the Great Lakes region themselves.
(D) They wanted revenge against the United States for winning the Revolutionary War.
(E) They resented the alliance between the United States and France.

372. Which region of the future United States was known as the "Great American Desert" between about 1820 and 1860?
(A) Southwest
(B) Pacific Northwest
(C) Rocky Mountains
(D) Canadian border area
(E) central Great Plains

373. As of its completion in 1850, which was NOT a major stop along the Cumberland, or National, Road to the Midwest?
(A) Baltimore, Maryland
(B) Columbus, Ohio
(C) Indianapolis, Indiana
(D) Pittsburgh, Pennsylvania
(E) Wheeling, Virginia (later West Virginia)

374. The United States acquired land in which present-day state(s) in the Black Hawk Purchase (1832)?
(A) Alaska
(B) Arizona and New Mexico
(C) Georgia
(D) Iowa
(E) Wisconsin

375. Secretary of War John C. Calhoun drew up a plan for a line of U.S. forts along the western frontier for all the following reasons EXCEPT
(A) to protect the United States against attacks and raids by the Indians
(B) to make it more difficult for foreign fur-trading companies to encroach on the U.S. market
(C) to establish customs houses to regulate trade along the frontier
(D) to gather scientific information about parts of the West that only the Indians had so far explored and settled
(E) to put a stop to further westward expansion by the United States

376. Sac and Fox chief Black Hawk is a significant figure in U.S. history because he
(A) led a heroic rebellion of the Sac and Fox against U.S. troops
(B) successfully assimilated the Sac and Fox into American society and culture
(C) appealed to the Supreme Court to allow the Sac and Fox to remain on their ancestral lands
(D) wrote the only detailed autobiography by an Indian chief of the mid-19th century
(E) negotiated an exemption for the Sac and Fox to continue living east of the Permanent Indian Frontier

377. On what grounds did Texas justify its 1835 rebellion against Mexican rule?
  (A) Texas did not want to be part of a Spanish-speaking Catholic culture.
  (B) Texas did not support the Mexican rebellion against Spanish rule.
  (C) Texas wanted to establish a slaveholding society, which was illegal under Mexican rule.
  (D) Texas considered the Mexican government illegitimate.
  (E) Texas wanted to become part of the United States.

Westward Expansion, 1836–1865

378. What happened at the Alamo in 1836?
  (A) Texas declared independence from Mexico and became a republic.
  (B) Mexico laid siege to the Alamo and won control of it in a battle with Texas.
  (C) Sam Houston and the Texans defeated Santa Anna and the Mexicans in battle.
  (D) Mexico declared its independence from Spain and established a republic.
  (E) Santa Anna overthrew the Mexican government and declared himself a military dictator.

379. Which does NOT describe one effect of the Pike's Peak Gold Rush of 1859?
  (A) a surge in the population of western Kansas Territory
  (B) the creation of new markets for farm and ranch produce
  (C) a movement for statehood organized by the "fifty-niners"
  (D) the development of new towns and cities in the territory
  (E) a move to declare an independent republic

380. What did the United States most want to achieve at the Fort Laramie conference with the Plains tribes?
  (A) free access across the Great Plains for westbound pioneers
  (B) the purchase of lands on which the government wanted to built a railroad
  (C) preservation of the buffalo population for the future
  (D) full U.S. citizenship and assimilation of the Plains tribes
  (E) peace among the various Plains Indians tribes

381. All of the following were significant figures in the Mexican War EXCEPT
(A) Antonio López de Santa Anna
(B) John O'Sullivan
(C) James K. Polk
(D) Winfield Scott
(E) Zachary Taylor

382. When did the United States acquire the last of the territory that would make up the 48 contiguous states?
(A) during the Revolutionary War
(B) during the Mexican War
(C) during the 1850s
(D) during the Civil War
(E) after the Civil War

383. According to the Homestead Act of 1862, which was NOT one qualification a person had to meet in order to acquire a homestead of 80 to 160 acres?
(A) to be male
(B) to be at least 21 years old, or the head of a family, or a veteran
(C) never to have taken up arms against the United States or aided its enemies
(D) not to rent or resell the homestead during the first five years after filing the claim
(E) to live on and cultivate the land personally for five years

384. The Oregon Trail was established as a result of
(A) a U.S. government scheme to seize Mexican territory in the Southwest
(B) the construction of the transcontinental railroad
(C) the attempt to establish a westward route that avoided contact with Indian settlements
(D) improvements in the design of wheeled vehicles such as wagons
(E) the Rocky Mountain fur trade

385. Which of the following eventually became a major element of U.S. culture as a result of the Gold Rush?
(A) cigarettes
(B) chewing gum
(C) orange juice
(D) blue jeans
(E) soda

386. By 1860, almost all of the Indian tribes had succumbed to relocation to all these present-day states EXCEPT
(A) the Dakotas
(B) Montana
(C) Nebraska
(D) Oklahoma
(E) Wyoming

387. The Mormons settled in the unorganized territory near the Great Salt Lake in the 1840s because
(A) they were no longer willing to live in a country that practiced chattel slavery
(B) they hoped to profit by trading with the westbound forty-niners
(C) they wanted to settle as far as possible from the Indians
(D) their wagons could not take them any farther across the terrain
(E) they did not want to obey the laws of the United States

388. Which of the following was NOT a significant figure in the settlement of the Oregon Country (later called Oregon Territory)?
(A) John Floyd
(B) Stephen Watts Kearney
(C) Hall Jackson Kelley
(D) John McLoughlin
(E) Narcissa Whitman

389. At the Laramie Conference of 1851, the Plains tribes agreed to all of the following EXCEPT
(A) an end to intertribal warfare and raids
(B) defined boundaries to each tribe's territory
(C) full U.S. citizenship for all Indians by 1881
(D) safe passage for westbound pioneers passing through Indian territory
(E) the construction of roads and U.S. military forts in Indian territory

390. Which was NOT one of the terms President James K. Polk offered to Mexico in 1845 in an attempt to avoid an all-out war?
(A) to purchase the province of New Mexico outright for cash
(B) to purchase California outright for cash
(C) to forgive Mexican debt owed to the United States
(D) to agree on the Rio Grande as the U.S.-Mexican border
(E) to eliminate protective tariffs on Mexican imports

391. In which transaction or agreement did the U.S. government acquire the last of the territory that would eventually become the 48 contiguous states?
(A) the Gadsden Purchase
(B) the Mexican Cession
(C) the Louisiana Purchase
(D) the annexation of Texas
(E) the Adams-Onís Treaty

392. Which was NOT one effect of the Gold Rush on the society and/or economy of California?
(A) a surge in population
(B) an increase in crime and violence
(C) the rapid acquisition of wealth by the skillful or lucky
(D) the establishment of slavery
(E) an increase in ethnic diversity

393. What was the cause of the Mexican War?
(A) the admission of Texas into the United States
(B) the declaration that Texas was an independent republic
(C) the election of James K. Polk as president of the United States
(D) the election of Mariano Paredes as president of Mexico
(E) the dispute over the border between Mexico and Texas

394. The Pike's Peak Gold Rush of 1859 caused a surge in the population of which future state?
(A) California
(B) Colorado
(C) Nevada
(D) New Mexico
(E) Utah

395. Which was NOT one factor in the conflict that developed between the Plains tribes and the United States during the 1840s?
(A) The westbound pioneers hunted the buffalo to near-extinction.
(B) The Gold Rush dramatically increased the flow of westbound traffic along the Oregon Trail.
(C) When the buffalo herds moved, the Plains hunters followed, thus encroaching on the territory of other tribes.
(D) Severe droughts and dust storms caused famine and starvation throughout the Great Plains.
(E) The westbound pioneers' livestock competed with the buffalo for grazing lands.

396. The Mexican Cession included territory that would later become all of these states, in whole or in part, EXCEPT
(A) Arizona
(B) California
(C) Oklahoma
(D) Utah
(E) Wyoming

397. Nebraska Territory included all or parts of the following present-day states EXCEPT
(A) Iowa
(B) Montana
(C) Nebraska
(D) North Dakota
(E) South Dakota

398. The term *manifest destiny* is related to which of the following?
(A) the abolition of slavery
(B) voting rights for women
(C) placing limits on immigration
(D) territorial expansion to the Pacific
(E) the balance of federal powers

399. John C. Frémont is a notable figure in U.S. history for his achievements in all these areas EXCEPT
(A) exploration of the West
(B) invention and technology
(C) land surveying
(D) national and California politics
(E) the military

400. Which was NOT one provision of the Treaty of Guadalupe-Hidalgo?
(A) The Rio Grande would be the border between Mexico and the United States.
(B) The United States would pay Mexico $15 million.
(C) Slavery would not be permitted in the territory the United States gained as a result of the war.
(D) Mexico would pay any financial claims made by U.S. citizens against its government.
(E) Mexico would give a vast amount of territory, called the Mexican Cession, to the United States.

401. The location of which of the following accounts for the geographical oddity of the Oklahoma panhandle?
(A) the Missouri Compromise line
(B) the Mason-Dixon Line
(C) the Continental Divide
(D) the Mississippi River
(E) the transcontinental railroad

402. Wagon trains took the Oregon Trail westward through all the following present-day states EXCEPT
(A) Idaho
(B) Kansas
(C) Montana
(D) Nebraska
(E) Wyoming

403. What caused the Mormon War of 1856–1857?
(A) Mormons claimed that the U.S. government had violated their First Amendment rights.
(B) Mormons flouted the authority of federal judges in Utah Territory.
(C) Shoshone and Paiute tribes took up arms against the Mormons to defend their ancestral territory.
(D) Non-Mormon settlers disputed Mormons' rights to settle in certain territory in the West.
(E) The U.S. government ordered the Mormons to move west after the discovery of the Comstock Lode.

404. Which was NOT one effect of the Laramie treaty of 1851?
(A) The Plains tribes were deprived of their right to roam freely over the Great Plains.
(B) The Indian population was shifted from the Great Plains to the Dakotas and the Rockies.
(C) The hunting culture of the Plains tribes was lost.
(D) The U.S. government worked with the Plains tribes to ease their assimilation into mainstream American society.
(E) The Plains tribes became dependent on the charity of the U.S. government.

405. Which was NOT one reason why California was a rough, dangerous place to live during the Gold Rush?
  (A) Most of the thousands of new immigrants were young single men.
  (B) The transcontinental railroad was already under construction.
  (C) The population was ethnically and linguistically diverse.
  (D) There was no organized law enforcement.
  (E) The gold was a constant temptation to theft and even murder.

406. Which was NOT one provision of the Pacific Railway Act of 1862?
  (A) A railroad would be constructed on public land.
  (B) A telegraph line would be built, running alongside the railroad.
  (C) The U.S. government would provide land grants to companies willing to build the railroad.
  (D) Compensation for railroad construction would vary according to the difficulty of the terrain.
  (E) All railroad workers would be paid for their labor; the use of slave labor was expressly banned.

407. The Pony Express closed down shortly after, and as a result of, the
  (A) completion of the telegraph lines
  (B) establishment of passenger stagecoach service
  (C) completion of the transcontinental railroad
  (D) outbreak of the Civil War
  (E) discovery of the Comstock Lode

408. Which was NOT one step in the process of the U.S. annexation of California?
  (A) The governor of Monterey granted 50,000 acres of land to Johannes Sutter in 1839.
  (B) U.S. settlers at Sonoma declared an independent "Bear Flag Republic" in July 1846.
  (C) After the Mexican War broke out, the U.S. Navy occupied the port of Monterey in June 1846.
  (D) John C. Frémont led the California Battalion to victory at Los Angeles in August 1846.
  (E) Mexico formally ceded California to the United States in January 1847.

409. Which was NOT among the serious risks or hardships faced when
traveling west on the Oregon Trail?
(A) lack of trained medical assistance for women giving birth
(B) threats of flash floods, severe storms, and serious heat waves
(C) the spread of serious illness through a wagon train
(D) the risk of supplies running out
(E) constant and often fatal attacks by Apaches and Plains Indians

410. Before 1858, how was the U.S. mail carried between the West coast
and the East?
(A) overland by railroad
(B) overland by special couriers
(C) overland by stagecoach
(D) by ship via Panama
(E) by riverboat

411. During the 1840s, which did NOT help to make the former
Great American Desert a desirable place for pioneers to settle?
(A) the development of the steel-bladed plow and the mechanical reaper
(B) the cessation of conflict between settlers and Indians
(C) successful experiments with cultivating wheat
(D) the ability to ship large loads of crops by railroad
(E) the abundance of natural grass for livestock

CHAPTER 6

The War Between the States

The Division Between North and South, 1830–1850

412. All of these people played significant roles in the abolitionist movement EXCEPT
- (A) Susan B. Anthony
- (B) John Brown
- (C) Frederick Douglass
- (D) William Lloyd Garrison
- (E) Harriet Tubman

413. In what way did the Second Great Awakening reinforce the abolitionist movement?
- (A) by preaching that slaveholding was a matter of individual conscience
- (B) by arguing that the federal government should emancipate the slaves
- (C) by teaching slaves to read the Bible and attend church services
- (D) by insisting that it was sinful to hold another human being in slavery
- (E) by declaring that slaves were property, not people

414. What was the purpose of the Underground Railroad?
- (A) to take revenge against free or enslaved Africans who had crossed the wills of white people in the South
- (B) to spearhead a campaign for a national antilynching law
- (C) to relieve traffic congestion on the streets in the largest cities
- (D) to link the Atlantic and Pacific coastal populations
- (E) to help escaping slaves gain their freedom

415. The Compromise of 1850 included all of the following provisions EXCEPT
    (A) California would be admitted to the United States as a free state
    (B) slavery would remain legal in Washington, D.C.
    (C) the state of Texas would pay all debts incurred by the Republic of Texas
    (D) the Fugitive Slave Act of 1850 would become law
    (E) unorganized Mexican Cession territory would be divided into two sections, New Mexico and Utah

416. Which of the following did NOT publish an important, bestselling slave narrative during the antebellum era?
    (A) William Wells Brown
    (B) William Craft
    (C) Harriet Jacobs
    (D) Sojourner Truth
    (E) Booker T. Washington

417. The territories acquired in the Mexican War remained without governments until 1850 because
    (A) Mexico was mounting a determined attack to retake some of the territories
    (B) Congress could not agree on whether slaveholding would be permitted in the territories
    (C) the U.S. government had not yet paid Mexico the agreed price for the territories
    (D) Congress had not arrived at an acceptable policy for American Indians living in the territories
    (E) the people of the territories had not yet been given a chance to vote for their own leaders

418. Which was NOT one provision of the Fugitive Slave Act of 1850?
    (A) Slavery was permanently banned in the nation's capital as of the passage of the act, excluding people who were already slaves.
    (B) A slaveowner could reclaim a runaway slave at any time, no matter how long ago he or she had escaped.
    (C) Special courts would hear cases in which a recaptured person claimed that he or she was legally free.
    (D) No one claimed as a runaway slave could testify in his or her own defense.
    (E) Aiding an escaped slave was a crime subject to heavy fines and imprisonment, even in free states and territories.

419. What was the uniting factor of the various groups who came together to form the Free-Soil Party in 1848?
(A) support for the gold standard
(B) support for strict constructionism
(C) support for protective tariffs
(D) support for abolition
(E) support for manifest destiny

420. How did the election of 1848 change the shape of national politics?
(A) The supporters of abolition now had greater say in Congress.
(B) The opponents of abolition now had greater say in Congress.
(C) The new president was determined to settle the question of slavery.
(D) The new president represented a major new political party.
(E) The new president was committed to preserving the union of North and South.

421. When Congress annexed Texas as a slaveholding state, it maintained the balance of sectional power by
(A) granting Texas the power to divide itself into two to five states, all slaveholding
(B) extending the Missouri Compromise boundary westward
(C) admitting California to the United States as a free state
(D) agreeing to ban slavery in western territory then under consideration for purchase
(E) forming the Free-Soil Party and supporting Martin Van Buren for president

422. Which does NOT describe a compromise proposed and debated in Congress on the slaveholding or free status of the Mexican Cession?
(A) to extend the Missouri Compromise line westward to the Pacific, banning slavery north of the line
(B) to shelve the issue, leaving it to be decided by the Supreme Court
(C) to grant the settlers of the individual territories the right to vote on the issue for themselves
(D) to ban slavery outright throughout the territories
(E) to ask the president to decide the issue and agree to abide by his ruling

423. Which was NOT one important effect of the Underground Railroad?
- (A) It gave white abolitionists a chance to be of real use in the fight for emancipation.
- (B) It hastened the end of the Civil War.
- (C) It disproved southern claims that black people could not fend for or take care of themselves.
- (D) It helped to fight racism by uniting black and white Americans in a common cause.
- (E) It helped thousands of enslaved Africans gain their freedom.

424. Which was NOT one of the nation's important abolitionist newspapers?
- (A) *Frederick Douglass' Paper*
- (B) *Freedom's Journal*
- (C) *The Liberator*
- (D) *My Bondage and My Freedom*
- (E) *The North Star*

425. The term *Mason-Dixon Line* refers to the border between
- (A) Pennsylvania-Maryland and Delaware-Maryland
- (B) Texas and Mexico
- (C) Nebraska Territory and Kansas Territory
- (D) slaveholding territory and free territory
- (E) the Confederacy and the Union

From Disagreement to the Outbreak of War, 1850–1860

426. Which region of the country did NOT vote heavily for Abraham Lincoln in the election of 1860?
- (A) the Southeast
- (B) the Great Lakes
- (C) the Northeast
- (D) the Pacific coastal states
- (E) the Mid-Atlantic

427. Which does NOT help explain why southerners who were too poor
to own slaves still supported the institution of slavery?
(A) Wealthy planters hired men from the small-farmer class as overseers.
(B) Planters as a class could bring considerable pressure to bear on anyone
who opposed them.
(C) Ordinary working people in the South did not believe that
African-Americans were good workers.
(D) The existence of slavery meant economic opportunities for white
people as bounty hunters, informers, and so on.
(E) Independent small farmers and even "poor whites" considered
themselves racially and socially superior to slaves.

428. Southerners banned the sale of the bestselling novel *Uncle Tom's Cabin*
and dismissed its author as a madwoman because it
(A) justified their view that slavery was morally permissible
(B) depicted slavery as morally wrong and slavers as corrupt
(C) depicted romantic relationships between African-Americans
and whites
(D) predicted that the South would lose the Civil War
(E) portrayed African-Americans as equal to whites

429. The Crittenden Compromise of 1860 suggested all of the following
EXCEPT
(A) that slavery be permanently banned north of the Missouri
Compromise line and permanently guaranteed south of it
(B) that Congress could not abolish slavery in states where it already
existed
(C) that Congress must compensate slaveowners financially if it abolished
slavery in Washington, D.C.
(D) that the federal ban on the slave trade be strictly enforced
(E) that each state should develop its own plan for the gradual abolition
of slavery

430. Which was NOT one important effect of the passage of the
Kansas-Nebraska Act?
(A) Abraham Lincoln decided to run for national office.
(B) Several southern states threatened to secede from the United States.
(C) Missouri residents illegally voted a pro-slavery legislature into office
in Kansas.
(D) John Brown and his supporters began planning an armed slave
uprising.
(E) Several minor political parties came together to form the Republican
Party.

431. The Republican Party was a first in U.S. history because it embodied the political principle of
(A) sectionalism
(B) popular democracy
(C) popular sovereignty
(D) anarchy
(E) states' rights

432. Which incident was NOT a direct result of the political conflict that raged in Kansas during the late 1850s?
(A) Congressman Preston Brooks's criminal assault on Senator Charles Sumner
(B) John Brown's massacre of five proslavers at Potawatomie Creek
(C) Henry Ward Beecher's campaign to send rifles for the defense of the Kansas Free-Soilers
(D) James Buchanan's election to the presidency of the United States
(E) Senator David Atchison's mustering of a mob of proslavers in Missouri

433. Which is NOT one reason why the West supported the Republican candidates in the elections of 1856 and 1860?
(A) Westerners wanted to enter the United States as free states.
(B) Western farmers did not want to compete economically with slaveholding farmers.
(C) The West and the North shared economic and business ties.
(D) The West did not want the South gaining more political power in Washington, D.C.
(E) The West was the home of the strongest wing of the abolitionist movement.

434. What was the final result of the conflict between proslavery and antislavery forces in Kansas Territory?
(A) Kansas was admitted to the United States as a slaveholding state.
(B) Kansas was admitted to the United States as a free state.
(C) Kansas joined the Confederacy as a slaveholding territory.
(D) Kansas was reorganized as two territories, one slaveholding and one free.
(E) Kansas was reorganized as part of the Nebraska Territory.

435. Which is NOT one argument Chief Justice Roger Taney used in his opinion for the defense in *Dred Scott v. Sanford*?
(A) The United States must reestablish the transatlantic African slave trade.
(B) The framers of the Constitution had never intended it to apply to Africans.
(C) The Fifth Amendment made antislavery laws illegal.
(D) The Missouri Compromise had been illegal because it affected property rights.
(E) Slave status was permanent and applied everywhere, including free states or territories.

436. Which is NOT one reason why the Republicans chose Abraham Lincoln instead of William Seward as their presidential candidate in 1860?
(A) Lincoln had made fewer enemies than Seward in national politics.
(B) Lincoln was clearly committed to the abolition of slavery.
(C) Lincoln was considered more moderate than Seward on the issue of slavery.
(D) Lincoln's home state of Illinois was considered crucial to a Republican victory in November.
(E) Lincoln appealed to many voters because he was both a self-made man and an articulate speaker.

437. The term *popular sovereignty* is best defined as
(A) the legal right of every adult resident of a locality to vote in elections
(B) direct election of representatives by their constituents
(C) the right of citizens to determine laws by direct vote
(D) the constitutional right of U.S. citizens to participate in their own government
(E) the right of citizens to overturn legislation by direct popular vote

438. All of the following played significant roles in the political conflict in "Bleeding Kansas" EXCEPT
(A) David Atchison
(B) John Brown
(C) Millard Fillmore
(D) James Lane
(E) Wilson Shannon

439. Which does NOT help explain why Stephen Douglas was an unpopular candidate throughout the South in the 1860 election?
(A) He opposed secession.
(B) He represented the Democratic Party.
(C) He urged the people to accept the results of the 1860 election.
(D) He supported the Kansas-Nebraska Act.
(E) He supported popular sovereignty in the territories.

440. All of the following contributed to the formation of the Republican Party EXCEPT
(A) the Compromise of 1850
(B) the passage of the Kansas-Nebraska Act
(C) the repeal of the Missouri Compromise
(D) the struggle for political supremacy in Kansas Territory
(E) the raid on Harpers Ferry

441. Which does NOT help describe the role played by slave narratives in the nation's deepening sectional division?
(A) They converted thousands of readers into active supporters of abolition.
(B) They infuriated southerners with their depiction of slaves' everyday lives.
(C) They gave rise to at least one armed slave rebellion.
(D) They provided the enslaved people with a powerful voice of their own.
(E) They brought African-Americans into positions of social and political prominence.

442. The Illinois Senate campaign that pitted Democrat Stephen Douglas against Republican Abraham Lincoln was important because the
(A) voters had their first opportunity to support or oppose a Republican candidate for Congress
(B) debates between the candidates clearly articulated the political issues of the day for the ordinary voters
(C) results of the election confirmed that Douglas would never be president of the United States
(D) candidates' positions demonstrated that there could be no compromise on the issue of slavery
(E) results of the election confirmed that Illinois had no sympathy with the slaveholding South

443. What compromise did Henry Clay offer southern congressmen
in exchange for their agreement to accept California as a free state?
(A) the admission of Texas as a slaveholding state
(B) the admission of Nevada as a slaveholding state
(C) the repeal of the Missouri Compromise
(D) the repeal of the Wilmot Proviso
(E) the passage of a new Fugitive Slave Act

444. How did President James Buchanan respond to the secession
of the southern states and the creation of the Confederacy?
(A) He took no official action to reunite the nation.
(B) He asked Congress to declare war on the Confederacy.
(C) He sent federal troops into the South to maintain order.
(D) He held a series of meetings with Confederate President Jefferson
Davis.
(E) He resigned from the presidency.

445. What role did the federal government play in the political turmoil
in Kansas Territory during the 1850s?
(A) It deliberately kept the conflict alive for as long as possible.
(B) It refused to consider the territory's application for statehood.
(C) It refused to take any action.
(D) It supported the proslavery legislature.
(E) It supported the antislavery legislature.

446. In *Dred Scott v. Sanford*, the Supreme Court ruled that
(A) slavery could not be banned in any state except by the voters
of that state
(B) the federal, state, and territorial legislatures had no power to ban
slavery
(C) slavery could never be legalized north of the Missouri Compromise
line
(D) slaveholding states would have five years to develop plans to phase
slavery out
(E) slavery could not be abolished where it already existed, but it could
not be allowed to spread any farther

447. According to the Kansas-Nebraska Act, the slaveholding or free status of each territory should be decided by
- (A) the rules set forth in the U.S. Constitution
- (B) the principles expressed in the Declaration of Independence
- (C) an official statement issued by the president
- (D) a two-thirds majority vote in Congress
- (E) free elections by the residents of the territories

448. What happened at Harpers Ferry, Virginia (later West Virginia), in 1859?
- (A) Federal troops put down a secessionist uprising against the United States.
- (B) Federal troops put down an abolitionist uprising against the United States.
- (C) Virginia issued a statement that it was seceding from the United States.
- (D) Southern and northern troops fired on one another for the first time.
- (E) The western counties of Virginia began making plans to apply for independent statehood.

449. Which does NOT describe one aspect of the May 1856 confrontation between Senator Charles Sumner and Congressman Preston Brooks?
- (A) Brooks accosted Sumner in the Senate chamber and beat him nearly to death with a cane.
- (B) The House of Representatives voted to expel Brooks but not by the required two-thirds majority.
- (C) Sumner leveled a gun at Brooks from across the Senate chamber during debate.
- (D) Brooks was condemned as a criminal in the North and praised as a hero in the South.
- (E) Sumner gave a passionate antislavery speech that included direct criticism of Senator Andrew Butler, Brooks's cousin.

450. People throughout the North were alarmed by the *Dred Scott v. Sanford* decision because it
- (A) meant the discontinuation of the Underground Railroad
- (B) indicated that the nation would have to resort to a civil war to settle the question of slavery
- (C) called for "separate but equal" facilities for African-American business customers
- (D) implied that slavery might legally spread back into the North
- (E) explicitly denied the right of any black person to full U.S. citizenship and civil rights

451. All these groups combined to form the Republican Party EXCEPT
   (A)   antislavery Democrats
   (B)   the Federalist Party
   (C)   the Free-Soil Party
   (D)   antislavery Know-Nothings
   (E)   the Whig Party

452. Which was NOT among the seven states that seceded from the Union
   and formed the Confederate States of America before the Civil War
   broke out?
   (A)   Georgia
   (B)   Mississippi
   (C)   South Carolina
   (D)   Texas
   (E)   Virginia

453. Who were the Border Ruffians and how did they get their nickname?
   (A)   They were Illinois frontiersmen who habitually crossed the border
         into neighboring Indian territory to hunt or plunder.
   (B)   They were Creek and Cherokee who fought a border war to overturn
         the forced relocation of their people.
   (C)   They were Texans who fought to extend their northern border above
         the Missouri Compromise line.
   (D)   They were Missourians who crossed the border into Kansas Territory
         and used terrorist tactics to fix the election results.
   (E)   They were Mexicans who continually raided Texas border towns with
         the intention of reclaiming the territory south of the Red River.

454. Which was NOT one important effect of the passage of the Fugitive Slave
   Act of 1850?
   (A)   The Underground Railroad became more active.
   (B)   Slavery became economically more profitable than before.
   (C)   Thousands who had passively opposed slavery became active
         abolitionists.
   (D)   Thousands of free Africans living in the North emigrated to Canada.
   (E)   The Supreme Court ruled that slave status was permanent and
         irrevocable.

455. Why did proslavers oppose the passage of a homestead bill?
(A) They did not want the United States to expand to the Pacific.
(B) They believed that the western territories belonged by rights to the Indians.
(C) They were afraid of losing their power base in national politics.
(D) They opposed the sale of public lands on constitutional grounds.
(E) They insisted on higher land prices than those supported by the bill's advocates.

456. Which was NOT part of the Democratic Party platform on which James Buchanan ran for president in 1856?
(A) support for maintaining U.S. neutrality in foreign affairs
(B) support for the Kansas-Nebraska Act
(C) support for the principle of popular sovereignty
(D) opposition to the Know-Nothing Party and movement
(E) opposition to any discussion of the slavery issue

457. What was the most crucial political difference between North and South during this period?
(A) The people of the South were polarized on the issue of slavery while the people of the North were largely in agreement.
(B) The North was becoming a society of one-party rule while the South still had two functioning parties.
(C) The North began preparing for war much earlier than the South.
(D) Dissenting voices were still strongly heard in the North but not the South.
(E) The South hoped to avoid war if at all possible while the North embraced the idea of war.

458. South Carolina seceded from the United States because
(A) John Brown led an armed rebellion in Virginia
(B) Abraham Lincoln was elected president
(C) the Missouri Compromise was repealed
(D) the Kansas legislature drafted a free-state constitution
(E) the Wilmot Proviso was introduced in Congress

459. Northern and western opponents of the Kansas-Nebraska Act objected
to it because they believed it would
(A) expand slavery into the West, thus robbing workers of wage-earning
jobs
(B) take away people's right to vote in the territories
(C) reinforce the provisions of the Missouri Compromise
(D) expand federal powers over the individual states
(E) curtail the power base of the southern sympathizers in Congress

460. Between 1828 and 1860, congressional debate over applications
for statehood focused primarily on the issue of
(A) land grants
(B) temperance
(C) women's suffrage
(D) slavery
(E) free public education

The Civil War, 1861–1865

461. Which best explains why the Confederate troops lost the Battle
of Gettysburg?
(A) They did not have enough reinforcements.
(B) They were outnumbered by the Union troops.
(C) They did not have command of the high ground.
(D) They were fighting in Union territory for the first time.
(E) Their commanders were good at discipline but poor at strategy.

462. When Abraham Lincoln began the Gettysburg Address by saying that
the United States was founded on the proposition that "all men are created
equal," he was quoting the
(A) Bill of Rights
(B) Civil Rights Act
(C) Constitution
(D) Declaration of Independence
(E) Fugitive Slave Act

463. Which advantage did the Union NOT enjoy over the Confederacy
at the beginning of the Civil War?
(A) control over the majority of American industry and material resources
(B) location of major national railroads in Union states
(C) the loyalty and support of the U.S. Navy
(D) a larger population from which to draw troops
(E) superior and more experienced military leaders

464. Northerners who opposed the Civil War showed their opposition by
  (A) joining the Confederate Army or moving to the South
  (B) leaving the United States for Canada or Great Britain
  (C) flying the Confederate flag
  (D) openly expressing their opinions in speeches and newspaper articles, and voting for candidates who shared their opinions
  (E) trying to nullify the election of Abraham Lincoln as president of the United States

465. What was the main purpose of the naval blockade of the South during the Civil War?
  (A) to capture the capital city of the Confederacy
  (B) to force Jefferson Davis to emancipate all southern slaves
  (C) to take control of the railroad system
  (D) to block Confederate access to the Mississippi River
  (E) to prevent goods and supplies from reaching the Confederacy

466. Which was NOT one element of the Union strategy to win the war?
  (A) establishing a military alliance with Britain and France
  (B) capturing the Confederate capital city of Richmond, Virginia
  (C) blocking Confederate access to the Mississippi River
  (D) taking control of the southern railroads
  (E) using the Mississippi River to cut off the western half of the Confederacy

467. Which was NOT a key Union victory in the Civil War?
  (A) Battle of Antietam
  (B) Battle of Gettysburg
  (C) Battle of Manassas (Bull Run)
  (D) Battle of Shiloh
  (E) Battle of Vicksburg

468. The Civil War was fought on the battlefields of all the following states EXCEPT
  (A) Georgia
  (B) New York
  (C) Pennsylvania
  (D) South Carolina
  (E) Virginia

469. Which of the following events began the Civil War?
  (A) John Brown's raid on Harpers Ferry, Virginia
  (B) South Carolina's secession from the United States
  (C) the Confederate attack on Fort Sumter, South Carolina
  (D) the issuance of the Emancipation Proclamation
  (E) the siege of Richmond, Virginia

470. Confederate commanders Robert E. Lee and Joseph E. Johnston fought an almost entirely defensive war because
  (A) they were geographically hemmed in and their troops were usually outnumbered
  (B) they did not have the military experience and expertise of the Union commanders
  (C) their goal was to protect the South from invasion, not to invade and conquer the North
  (D) they lacked any foreign military allies
  (E) they knew from the beginning that it would not be possible to win the war

471. The Union victory at New Orleans was of great strategic importance for all these reasons EXCEPT
  (A) it gave the Union control of the Mississippi River from the south
  (B) it reduced the Confederate Navy by several ships and ironclads
  (C) it enabled the Union to attack the Confederacy from a new direction, inside Confederate territory
  (D) it made possible the naval blockade of the port of New Orleans
  (E) it was the first step in the Union plan to cut off the western half of the Confederacy

472. What effect did the First Battle of Manassas (Bull Run) have on the Confederate troops?
  (A) It made them aware they were facing a formidable opponent in what would probably be a long war.
  (B) It made them realize they did not have sufficient resources to win a war against the Union without foreign allies.
  (C) It convinced them that the Confederacy would win an easy victory and thus encouraged many soldiers to leave the army.
  (D) It showed them that the naval blockade of New Orleans would be a decisive factor in the war.
  (E) It gave them a new confidence in their own fighting ability and encouraged most troops to reenlist for another year.

473. Which was NOT one reason for the Confederacy's attempt to carry the war into the West?
(A) to force the Union to divide its troops between two fronts
(B) to abandon the South because it could not be militarily defended
(C) to seize the gold, silver, and other mineral wealth of the West
(D) to circumvent the naval blockade of the South by establishing an east-west communication and trade route
(E) to influence the territorial governments to pass laws allowing the spread of slavery

474. Which of the following was NOT an important African-American spy for the Union during the war?
(A) Allan Pinkerton
(B) John Scobell
(C) George Scott
(D) Mary Touvestre
(E) Harriet Tubman

475. What was the result of the Second Battle of Manassas (Bull Run)?
(A) The Confederates permanently gained control of the Potomac River.
(B) President Lincoln dismissed General George McClellan from command of the Army of the Potomac.
(C) Lines of communication between the Union commanders and the White House were temporarily severed.
(D) The Confederates began a march on Washington, D.C.
(E) The Confederates planned an invasion of the North as their next step.

476. Which was NOT among the extraordinary powers President Lincoln assumed with the outbreak of the Civil War?
(A) He suspended the writ of habeas corpus.
(B) He called for military volunteers for a three-year term of service.
(C) He expanded the size of the regular army and navy.
(D) He dismissed Congress for the duration of the war.
(E) He called for a naval blockade of the Confederacy.

477. Vicksburg, Mississippi, was of great strategic importance to both sides because it
(A) was the capital city and seat of the Confederate government
(B) was the junction of several southern railway lines
(C) commanded the Mississippi River from high cliffs
(D) was the only site in the South with a substantial number of factories
(E) was the largest and most cosmopolitan city in the Confederacy

478. The Emancipation Proclamation had all the following effects EXCEPT
- (A) to increase the African-American commitment to the Union cause
- (B) to bring about a speedy conclusion to the war
- (C) to bring tens of thousands of former slaves into the Union Army
- (D) to signal the end of the era of compromise over slavery
- (E) to rob the Confederacy of thousands of viable soldiers

479. Which was the primary cause of Robert E. Lee's decision to invade Union territory in the spring of 1863?
- (A) the siege of Vicksburg
- (B) the loss of the Potomac River
- (C) the capture of Richmond
- (D) the death of General Jackson at Chancellorsville
- (E) the victory at Fredericksburg

480. The Confederate victory at Chickamauga, Tennessee, prolonged the war because it
- (A) distracted Union forces from the main theater of war in Virginia
- (B) inspired Confederate troops in the Southwest to victory over Union forces
- (C) reopened the lines of communication between the eastern and western halves of the Confederacy
- (D) prevented Union troops from invading the South from the northwest
- (E) made Great Britain reconsider an earlier refusal to send military aid to the South

481. Which of the following does NOT accurately describe African-American participation in the Civil War?
- (A) About 180,000 men enlisted and fought in the Union Army.
- (B) Boys too young to enlist ran errands and carried messages for the soldiers.
- (C) Black regiments from all the states fought with distinction.
- (D) Most black soldiers who fought for the Union came from the Confederacy.
- (E) The Confederate side refused to trust any slaves or former slaves by allowing them to enlist or participate in the war.

482. Horace Greeley's 1862 editorial "The Prayer of the Twenty Millions" urged President Lincoln to
   (A) be merciful to men holding high political or military office in the Confederacy after the war
   (B) immediately order full emancipation throughout the Confederacy
   (C) hold a peace conference with the Confederate president Jefferson Davis
   (D) allow the Confederacy to secede on peaceful terms
   (E) move the Union capital to a safer location farther north

483. Which is NOT one reason why the capture of Atlanta, Georgia, was a major objective for the Union Army?
   (A) It boasted most of the South's few munitions factories.
   (B) It was an important symbol of Confederate wealth and power.
   (C) It would provide a dramatic boost to Union morale during a difficult period of the war.
   (D) Its capture would enable the Union to retake control of the Mississippi River.
   (E) It was a major source of supply for the Confederate Army.

484. Which new state was formed during the Civil War?
   (A) Arkansas
   (B) Kansas
   (C) Maryland
   (D) Nebraska
   (E) West Virginia

485. Which is NOT one reason why the Sioux west of the Missouri River rose up in armed rebellion in 1862?
   (A) They could not provide for themselves on the reservation lands they had been awarded.
   (B) They supported the Confederacy in exchange for greater civil rights.
   (C) A poor harvest caused famine and starvation.
   (D) They were frequently defrauded by white traders.
   (E) The U.S. government did not make its promised payments on time.

486. Which of the following did NOT play a significant role in the Union military forces?
   (A) David G. Farragut
   (B) Ulysses S. Grant
   (C) Thomas "Stonewall" Jackson
   (D) William T. Sherman
   (E) Philip Sheridan

487. Once the Union troops captured Atlanta, Georgia, in 1864, they took all the following steps EXCEPT
    (A) ordered the evacuation of all civilians from the city
    (B) destroyed all public buildings
    (C) wrecked the railroads and railroad stations
    (D) cut the telegraph lines
    (E) destroyed all private property

488. Why were southerners confident, early in the war, that Britain and France might aid the Confederacy?
    (A) British and French leaders disapproved of slavery.
    (B) Britain and France wanted to protect their interest in the American cotton crop.
    (C) Britain and France were still actively engaged in the transatlantic slave trade.
    (D) British and French military experience would help the South win the war.
    (E) Britain and France did not support the Republican victory in the 1860 election.

489. What did the Union Army accomplish at the Battle of Shiloh?
    (A) It pushed the Confederate Army out of western Tennessee.
    (B) It surrounded and laid siege to the Confederate capital city.
    (C) It took back control of the Mississippi River from the Confederates.
    (D) It cut off the lines of communication between the eastern and western halves of the Confederacy.
    (E) It forced the Confederate troops to retreat south of Pennsylvania for the rest of the war.

490. Mathew Brady is important to the history of the Civil War because he
    (A) was one of the most successful of the Confederate spies
    (B) led the Union Navy in the Battle of New Orleans
    (C) served as an aide-de-camp in the Army of the Potomac
    (D) documented the war in thousands of photographs
    (E) designed the ironclad warships used throughout the war

491. Black regiments played major roles in all the following military actions EXCEPT
    (A) Fort Henry, Tennessee
    (B) Fort Wagner, South Carolina
    (C) Honey Springs, Indian Territory (Oklahoma)
    (D) Island Mound, Missouri
    (E) Port Hudson, Louisiana

492. The Gettysburg Address expresses all the following principles EXCEPT
- (A) government by the consent of the governed
- (B) the equality of all the people of the nation
- (C) the greatness of the sacrifice made by the soldiers on both sides
- (D) the need for all Americans to dedicate themselves to the cause of freedom
- (E) the need for foreign allies to join the fight for freedom

493. Historians believe that the Confederacy might have won the war in 1861 if the army had followed up its victory at the First Battle of Manassas (Bull Run) by
- (A) assassinating President Lincoln
- (B) defeating the Army of the Potomac
- (C) capturing Richmond, Virginia
- (D) marching on Washington, D.C.
- (E) calling for a peace conference with the Union commanders

494. Which was made legal by the terms of the Confiscation Act of 1862?
- (A) the Emancipation Proclamation
- (B) the secession of the southern states
- (C) the suspension of the writ of habeas corpus
- (D) the extension of the military volunteer term from 90 days to three years
- (E) the creation of the Freedmen's Bureau

495. Which is NOT one reason for the importance of the Union victory at Antietam in the fall of 1862?
- (A) It halted the momentum the Confederate Army had gained from its victory at the Second Battle of Manassas (Bull Run).
- (B) It resulted in the capture of General Robert E. Lee.
- (C) It gave the North new confidence in an eventual Union victory.
- (D) It allowed President Lincoln to issue the preliminary to the Emancipation Proclamation.
- (E) It blocked the planned Confederate invasion into Union territory and carried the fighting back into Virginia.

496. Which does NOT describe one important result of the Union victory at Fort Donelson?
- (A) General Ulysses S. Grant achieved his first widespread recognition.
- (B) The Union regained its hopes of ultimate victory over the Confederacy.
- (C) The Union Army established its control over the Mississippi River.
- (D) The Confederate Army lost a sizeable and irreplaceable store of ammunition.
- (E) The Union Army established a power base from which to invade the South.

497. The Battle of Gettysburg was an important turning point in the war primarily because it
- (A) proved that the Confederates could never win a victory in the North
- (B) showed that the Union generals were superior strategists and tacticians
- (C) gave the Union control over all southern railroads
- (D) eliminated the possibility of the Confederates capturing Washington, D.C.
- (E) persuaded President Lincoln to name General Ulysses S. Grant as general in chief of the entire Union Army

498. Which is NOT one reason why Abraham Lincoln was reelected in 1864?
- (A) The tide of the war had turned decisively in favor of the Union.
- (B) The voters hesitated to change to a new leader during a war.
- (C) There was widespread support for Lincoln's determination to restore the Union without slavery.
- (D) Emancipated African-Americans voted for Lincoln in huge numbers.
- (E) The Confederate states did not vote in the election.

499. The Emancipation Proclamation of January 1, 1863
- (A) freed all slaves in the Union
- (B) freed all slaves in the Confederacy
- (C) freed all slaves in both the Confederacy and the Union
- (D) required all slaves to register with the U.S. government
- (E) gave all adult male slaves the right to vote

500. Why did Lincoln use the army to prevent Maryland from seceding from the Union?
   (A) to warn the rest of the South that he would not tolerate further secession
   (B) to prevent the Union's capital from being surrounded by Confederate states
   (C) to keep the support and loyalty of the Maryland voters
   (D) to maintain Union access to the Atlantic coast
   (E) to prove to the Confederacy that the Union Army was too strong to lose the war

ANSWERS

Chapter 1: Beginnings

1. (E) Throughout all the centuries of European imperialism, the conquerors very rarely made any effort to accommodate themselves to the cultures of the lands they invaded. Instead, they imposed their own cultures on the peoples they conquered.

2. (B) According to current archaeological knowledge, human beings are not native to the Americas. They came to the Americas thousands of years ago by walking across the Bering or Beringia land bridge that connected Alaska and Siberia. This bridge has been covered by water since perhaps 11,000 BC, giving an approximate end date to the time when the Asian nomads might have crossed it in search of food or a warmer climate. The term *Native Americans* is therefore a misnomer, as is the term *Indians*. (See the Author's Note at the front of this book and answer 7 below.)

3. (E) The first transatlantic voyage among the five choices was that of Christopher Columbus, a Genoese Italian who sailed west in 1492 under the sponsorship of Queen Isabella of Spain.

4. (A) It is a historical axiom that the side with the more powerful weapons always wins the war. The Europeans had guns; the Indians had bows and arrows. The conquest was bound to end in victory for the men with the guns. The Europeans had one other highly effective weapon, although they were unaware of it and made no deliberate use of it—germs. Indians had never been exposed to smallpox and other diseases the Europeans carried with them; therefore, they had built up no natural immunities and they died by the tens of thousands.

5. (D) The French motive for exploring the Americas was purely financial. They did build permanent settlements in eastern Canada, but this was largely an outgrowth and consequence of establishing the fur trade.

6. (B) As a general rule, Native American tribes did not interfere with one another at all. Some were hostile, but most either maintained peaceful trade relations or ignored one another's existence. When conflicts broke out among northeastern tribes, the leaders developed the Iroquois Confederacy—centuries before the Europeans and their American descendants would create the United Nations.

7. (D) Columbus never learned that he had not reached Asia; he thought the islands of the Caribbean were "the Indies," as Europeans at that time referred to India. This is the source of the term *West Indies*, which is still used as a name for the Caribbean islands, and of the misnomer *Indians*, which has stuck to the first peoples of the Americas ever since. Not until Magellan's voyage of 1519 did Europeans prove it was possible to reach Asia and return to Europe by sailing west.

8. (C) The French did not come to North America in order to establish a new civilization on the order of Europe; they were interested in economic profit from the fur trade. They confined themselves to establishing major settlements in eastern Canada—with the sole exception of New Orleans. New Orleans was the major shipping port for exporting French furs and other goods, and importing goods from Europe. It was strategically located at the mouth of the Mississippi River, North America's major north-south trade highway.

9. (D) Until Cabot returned from his first voyage, Europeans generally believed that Columbus in his first voyage to the Caribbean had actually reached "the Indies," as they called India. It is not certain exactly where Cabot landed, but it was in the area of northern Maine or Canada; the descriptions he and his crew brought back to Europe clearly showed that they had not found Asia, but that there was a previously unknown landmass in between.

10. (A) The Iroquois Confederacy was one of the world's first attempts to resolve conflicts peacefully, through discussion, rather than always settling them on the battlefield. Popularly elected elders and chiefs of the Seneca, Onondaga, Oneida, Cayuga, Mohawk, and later Tuscarora tribes met to discuss and resolve conflicts among their people.

11. (E) Pizarro is best known for his conquest of the Incan Empire in 1532; he did not explore any part of the future United States. In 1565, Menendez de Áviles founded the first permanent European settlement in the future United States—St. Augustine, on the peninsula the Spaniards had named *Pascua Florida*. In 1540, Coronado and his party became the first Europeans known to have seen the Grand Canyon; they traveled as far north as the Colorado River. In 1528, Cabeza de Vaca and several other Spaniards were separated from their party; they threw in their lot with the local Indians and became the first Europeans to explore Texas and the Southwest. In 1542, de Soto and his party became the first Europeans to cross the Mississippi River, having explored most of the future southeastern United States.

12. (C) Virginia, the first colony claimed in the name of Queen Elizabeth I, was much larger than the present-day state of Virginia; it reached north to New York City and south to Florida.

13. (D) The early French settlers achieved a measure of friendly cooperation with the Algonquin and other tribes in eastern Canada and the Great Lakes region. The early English settlers accepted help and hospitality from the Delaware, Iroquois, and other tribes along the Atlantic coast, in Jamestown and in New England. Relations between Spaniards and Indians, however, were for the most part violent and hostile. The Spaniards were zealous Catholics, thus they considered the Indians heathens; they meted out violent and brutal treatment of any Indians they encountered.

14. (A) Byrd (1674–1744) was born in the colony of Virginia, well after the age of discovery and exploration of the New World; he was a wealthy planter and a diarist whose records are of great interest to historians. Raleigh first claimed the Virginia territory in the name of Elizabeth I; he and John White founded the colony of Roanoke in the 1580s. John Smith was among the founders of the Jamestown colony in 1607; he thoroughly explored the entire Chesapeake region during his first year in North America. In 1609, Hudson and his crew explored the Chesapeake and Delaware Bays and sailed upriver as far as Albany in search of the elusive Northwest Passage.

15. (B) The Spanish architectural styles, Catholic churches and missions, and Spanish place-names are clear indications of their early settlements in the South and the Southwest. The Spaniards also established the first permanent European settlement in the future United States—St. Augustine, Florida. Hernando de Soto and his party of conquistadors roamed the Southeast in search of gold; they were the first Europeans to explore this region and to see the Mississippi River. The Spaniards originally claimed more than two-thirds of what would later become the United States; the one region they did not explore was the Northeast.

16. (E) The physical environment was the determining factor in early North American cultures. Each group adapted itself to the climate and resources of the place it chose to settle in. Thus, the Plains tribes roamed with the herds on which they depended for food, the Zuni and Anasazi built thick-walled adobe structures that stayed cool in the extreme southwestern heat, and so on.

17. (A) Bolivar was a leading figure in the Latin American revolutions of the 1830s. Cabrillo and Ferrelo were among the first Europeans to explore the coast of California by boat; Cabrillo was the leader of the expedition and Ferrelo piloted the ship and published an account of the voyage. Serra was a Catholic missionary who founded the first European settlements in California. Vizcaíno followed along the route established by Cabrillo. He named the port of San Diego and drew maps of the California coast that were so detailed and accurate they remained in use for nearly 200 years.

18. (B) Georgia was settled in the early 1700s, much later than the other British colonies. Anyone who owed vast debts in England could settle in Georgia and start out with a clean slate.

19. (E) The Fundamental Orders describe the structure of the government for the settlements of Wethersfield, Windsor, and Hartford, which had agreed to unite as the colony of Connecticut. The orders establish the procedures for choosing a governor, magistrates, and other officials.

20. (A) Outrage over the legal proceedings at Salem eventually halted the trials—but not before 19 people were hanged, despite no crimes having been proved. No evidence was ever presented apart from the bare accusations of witchcraft. All sides belatedly acknowledged that Puritan zeal had gone too far. The overall effect was greatly to weaken Puritan authority in New England.

21. (D) The colonies of New Haven (later Connecticut) and Rhode Island were founded by people who believed in freedom of religious worship and at least some separation of church and state. Yale College was founded at New Haven as a liberal alternative to Harvard. Puritan society was religiously exclusive, and many viewed it as harsh, joyless, and unreasonably demanding, particularly in its attempts to dictate private behavior.

22. (C) At this time, only the Quakers practiced full gender equality in their religious services. Hutchinson was a Congregationalist and therefore not an official minister of her church. However, there were no rules to prevent her from leading private discussions of the Bible and the sermons of the city's leading ministers. Hutchinson aroused the wrath of the town fathers not only because her sessions were so popular, but because she was openly critical of their leadership. Put on trial and found guilty as a threat to their authority, she moved to the more liberal colony of Rhode Island.

23. (B) Choice (A) is wrong because the outcome was the opposite—the Virginia House of Burgesses decreed that the colonists would settle where they liked. Choice (C) is wrong because slavery was already legal in some areas. Choice (D) is wrong because Bacon's Rebellion had nothing to do with the division of Carolina into North and South. Choice (E) is wrong because the rebellion had the opposite effect; it made southern planters decide that they needed an unpaid labor force that was under their total and permanent control. The men of Bacon's Rebellion had once been indentured servants; once they worked off their debts to the large planters, they established their own small farms and thus became the planters' economic rivals. Thus, Bacon's Rebellion had the ultimate effect of stimulating the rise and spread of slavery throughout the colonies, especially on the tobacco and cotton plantations of the South.

24. (E) Slavery was never widespread in Pennsylvania, but it was legal for a time. The colony was, however, the home of the first antislavery society in North America, and home to a sizeable population of free Africans.

25. (B) Bradford was governor of Plymouth Colony and the author of *Of Plymouth Plantation*, an eyewitness account of the colony's history from its founding until 1646. Choice (A) describes John Smith, choice (C) William Penn, choice (D) Walter Raleigh, and choice (E) Richard Nicolls.

26. (A) Once the era of Puritan theocracy came to an end in the late 17th century, the self-governing towns of New England became the closest thing the United States has ever known to true popular democracy. As a general rule, all male church members were eligible for office, and all had a say in any laws made in the town. Although 17th- and early 18th-century New England was overwhelmingly white, free African men had the same rights as those of European descent. Women could not vote in a town meeting, but they certainly had the chance to discuss the issues with their husbands or brothers at home; this was a reasonable approximation of meaningful input.

27. (B) In the 1650s, Maine became a province of the Massachusetts Bay Colony and was considered a part of the state of Massachusetts until 1820, when it was admitted to the United States under the Missouri Compromise as an independent free state. The extremely cold winters prohibited rapid settlement and fast population growth, which is why Maine did not establish itself as an independent colony.

28. (C) For the Puritans, church and state were the same thing. One building did duty as the town hall during the week and the meetinghouse on Sundays. Only church members were permitted to have a say in the local government. Williams argued for freedom of religious worship, taking the position that a person's civil rights should not be affected by his or her membership in a particular church.

29. (E) The rise of manufacturing would not begin until the 19th century. The other four choices describe conditions in the colonies north of Maryland. New York, Boston, and Philadelphia all had their wealthy neighborhoods, cultural advantages, booksellers, and print shops. Even people who were not primarily farmers grew or raised their own food as a way of life; almost everyone had, at the very least, a vegetable plot, a few fruit trees, a flock of chickens, and a pig.

30. (E) Doctor Rush (1746–1813) was a Philadelphia native whose eventful life and career are notable for many more reasons than those described in choices (A) through (D). He represented Pennsylvania during the Second Continental Congress, and he was a member of the state's ratifying convention for the Constitution. He served as treasurer of the U.S. Mint for a number of years. He founded or helped to found at least three Pennsylvania colleges. He was highly influential in improving the medical process of diagnosing illnesses. Rush even reunited John Adams and Thomas Jefferson in friendship, 12 years after these two longtime colleagues had parted in enmity.

31. (B) An overseer's job means just what the word says—to oversee, or supervise, the slaves working in the plantation fields, much as a factory foreman would supervise his workers in the North. Wealthy planters hired overseers from among the small-farmer class. The overseer exercised absolute authority and generally maintained iron disciplinary rules.

32. (A) Maryland was founded as a safe haven for Catholic immigrants fleeing persecution in Britain, which had alternated between Anglican and Catholic monarchs since first creating the Anglican Church in 1534. Treatment of subjects who did not embrace the monarch's faith depended entirely on the monarch's whim; some were tolerant, others much less so. Charles I granted the charter of Maryland (named for Queen Henrietta Maria) in 1632.

33. (D) The English Bill of Rights was passed in the wake of the Glorious Revolution, a peaceful regime change brought about by Parliament. The Bill of Rights was important for the future United States because it was an assertion of legislative supremacy in government. It created a constitutional monarchy in which the monarch was the head of state but had almost no governing powers. Thus the English Bill of Rights served as a model for the colonists, who would develop a government in which the legislature was the strongest branch.

34. (A) A theocracy is a government in which a religious organization makes all the civil laws. At this time in history, the Quakers were the only group that treated men and women as equals in the worship service, permitting women as well as men to preach. Massachusetts Bay was a low-church Anglican community in which women might lead informal religious meetings in their own homes, but they were not eligible to enter the ministry.

35. (E) The land that became Vermont was within the borders of the 13 colonies, but this territory was a bone of contention among Massachusetts, New Hampshire, and New York. Leader Ethan Allen declared Vermont's independence in 1777 (at which time it was known as "New Connecticut"). Vermont joined the United States in 1791, after New York finally consented to give up its claims to the territory.

36. (E) King Philip's War was a series of late 17th-century raids, kidnappings, and armed attacks between the New Englanders and the Wampanoag and Narragansett tribes. The New Englanders accurately considered it the greatest calamity to befall their society in its brief history. Although the armed conflicts eventually died down and a treaty was signed, it did nothing to resolve the bitter cultural differences and territorial conflicts between colonists and Indians.

37. (A) A mercantile economy is a society based on thriving trade—buying and selling. This type of society did not develop in the South because each plantation was a self-contained world that made or grew almost everything it needed. The small farmers also saw to their own families' needs, on a much more modest scale. The economy was based on subsistence farming and also on large-scale farming, largely for export. Wealthy planters certainly could and did purchase luxury items, but the bulk of their trading or shopping was done outside the local area.

38. (D) The Mayflower Compact was an agreement among the company of Pilgrims who founded the colony of Plymouth. It described the agreed-on system of government for the colony, which would be democratically ruled by majority vote among adult male church members. A constitution is defined as a founding document that describes the structure of a government; therefore, this is the best answer choice.

39. (B) Roanoke was the first British settlement to be founded; leader John White left Roanoke for England, to bring back a shipload of supplies. When he returned, the colony and its people had vanished without a trace. Jamestown was founded 13 years before Plymouth; Boston and Richmond would be founded much later.

40. (B) The colonists reasoned that British authorities were too far away to enforce the Navigation Acts and paid very little attention to them. Obeying the letter of the Navigation Acts would have cut deeply into their profits and harmed the local economy. The courts, merchants, and shipowners agreed to turn a blind eye to any violations of the Navigation Acts.

41. (E) According to the custom of the times a statement such as "She muttered something when she passed my daughter on the street, and my daughter became seriously ill that night" was enough evidence for a court to convict the accused of witchcraft. Obviously, there could be no defense against such a claim except a protestation of innocence. A rash of these types of accusations led to the execution of a number of people in Salem in the infamous 1690s witch trials before public outcry against the proceedings became strong enough to halt them.

42. (C) In early colonial times, the colonists and the Indians recognized deep, impassable divisions in culture, religion, and overall worldview that still exist to this day. The Native American culture is much less materialistic than mainstream American culture. Native Americans believe in respecting the natural environment and caring for it, while the conquering Americans continue their history of dominating and using the environment and its resources for profit. The "green revolution" that mainstream U.S. culture began to embrace in the early 21st century is the closest it has ever come to adopting any aspect of the Native American way of life.

43. (E) The *middle passage* was the nightmare journey of the slave ships from Africa to either the Americas or the Caribbean islands. Abolitionist and former slave Olaudah Equiano, who survived the middle passage, described it in harrowing detail in his famous autobiography *The Interesting Narrative of the Life of Olaudah Equiano*. The Africans were packed below decks in chains, with barely room to turn around, let alone any light, sanitary facilities, or fresh air. Many died of the dreadful conditions. Others threw themselves overboard in terror on the rare occasions when they were allowed on deck for air and exercise.

44. (B) The Dutch purchased Manhattan Island from the Lenape and Delaware tribes for trade goods and 60 guilders (the equivalent of about $1,000 today). They established a thriving mercantile city called New Amsterdam on Manhattan's southern tip; the larger surrounding colony was known as New Netherland. In 1664, the British invaded New Netherland; Governor Peter Stuyvesant surrendered without a fight, and the British divided the colony into two sections, naming one New York and the other New Jersey.

45. (D) The overall effect of the Navigation Acts was to control and restrict colonial trade for the financial advantage of the mother country. The acts stated that all European goods exported to the colonies must be routed through Great Britain, that all trade with the colonies must be carried out on British ships with crews that were at least three-fourths British, and that the colonies could only export goods within the British empire.

46. (A) The documentation of Pocahontas's life is sketchy; she was the daughter of Wahunsonacock (Powhatan), the chief of the nation of Algonquin tribes living near the Jamestown colony. Credible eyewitness accounts describe her frequent visits to the Jamestown colony. Her friendly behavior to the colonists, and theirs to her, helped to cement good relations between the two peoples. The legend that she threw herself across John Smith's body to save him from death is a popular fixture of American mythology; it almost certainly never happened.

47. (A) Although slavery was legalized in all the British colonies between 1694 and 1750, it was much more common in the South because of economics. Cotton, rice, and tobacco were labor-intensive crops, and plantation farming would not have been profitable in pre-industrial times with a paid labor force. Therefore, white southerners insisted on maintaining a system of slavery. The trade in African slaves was not outlawed until after the American Revolution, and racial prejudice certainly existed in the North as well as the South.

48. (E) The Shoshone people were not northeastern, but western—their lands were in the region of present-day Montana and the Rocky Mountains. Lewis, Clark, and their party of explorers first met the Shoshone people on their 1803 expedition westward.

49. (B) Metacomet, called King Philip in English, was a Wampanoag chief. King Philip's War broke out because the various local tribes, mainly the Wampanoag and Narragansett, felt that the colonists in Massachusetts Bay and Plymouth were encroaching on their land. The war lasted for about a year, during which hundreds of colonists were killed or kidnapped, and many towns burned.

50. (C) The Maryland Toleration Act, also called "An Act Concerning Religion," established that all Marylanders who believed in the Christian Holy Trinity were free to worship as their individual conscience dictated, without molestation or persecution. The document even went so far as to protect Trinitarian Christians from casual insults (what we would today call "hate speech"); such insults were punishable by fines, with repeat offenders risking whippings and prison sentences. Despite its name, the Toleration Act was not tolerant toward atheists or nonbelievers who spoke out; anyone who denied the existence of God, the divinity of Jesus, or the doctrine of the Holy Trinity could be put to death.

51. (D) The Great Awakening began around 1740. It was a major revival of religious fervor, involving melodramatic sermons, revival meetings, open confessions, and the widespread rejection of the doctrine of predestination. Men preached instead that a person could be saved by his or her own intense, sincere faith in God. It resulted in the founding of many new Baptist and Methodist congregations throughout the colonies.

52. (C) Captive narratives were the popular bestsellers of the day because of their subject matter. A captive narrative was a nonfiction work describing the author's experiences of being kidnapped by Indians. This was a relatively frequent occurrence during the late 17th and early 18th centuries, particularly in New England. It generally happened during an Indian raid on a settlement. Prisoners would be forced to go with the Indians and would live with them, often for many weeks or months; the Indians usually asked for a ransom. Most often, the captives were eventually released; during their captivity they were normally treated very well.

53. (A) Smallpox was one of the greatest killers in colonial North America; it decimated the Indian population and was almost as dangerous for the Europeans and their descendants. In 1721, Dr. Zabdiel Boylston of Boston (a great-uncle of President John Adams) devised a method of preventive care called variolus inoculation. This meant infecting a healthy person with a very mild case of smallpox, on the theory that he or she had enough strength to combat the germs, and on recovery would be forever immune to the disease. Boylston's method was highly effective; a death rate of more than 1 in 6 smallpox victims dropped to a death rate of fewer than 1 in every 100 inoculated patients. Note: The method described in choice (B) was developed in the following century and replaced variolus inoculation because it was less risky.

54. (D) Choice (A) is wrong because, obviously, no human being in history has ever been content to live as a slave. Choice (B) is wrong because it does not follow from the question; the Quakers' speaking out would help the movement to grow. Choice (C) is wrong because it was not especially easy to escape, and it grew more difficult as time went on. Choice (E) is wrong because Parliament never outlawed a colonial abolitionist movement. The abolitionist movement depended for its success on the sympathy and participation of white people (mostly northerners) with political power. Since the everyday realities of plantation slavery happened far away, the North as a whole remained unaware for decades of how serious the situation was.

55. (C) The early New England colleges were founded specifically to educate young men for the ministry. By the time of the French and Indian War, the curriculum embraced other areas besides theology; a college education was usual for young men entering a variety of professions, such as medicine, business, or law. An education was a desirable (although not mandatory) stepping-stone to political leadership; in the pre-Revolutionary era, most of the prominent political leaders came from the educated class.

56. (E) The churches of colonial New England preached the doctrine of predestination: that God predetermined a soul's fate before birth. Neither sincere faith nor good deeds could save a person who was not predestined for salvation; however, everyone still had to profess faith and behave well because these were two sure signs that a person was saved. Jonathan Edwards was considered a dangerous radical because he openly disagreed with the doctrine of predestination. Instead, he preached the doctrine of redemption by sincere repentance for one's sins; he argued that a penitent could be reborn in God's love. He suggested, in other words, that a person could play a role in his or her own salvation.

57. (C) By the 17th century, two schools of thought had developed in the Church of England. High-church Anglicans preferred a ceremonial style of worship similar to the Catholic mass. Low-church Anglicans preferred and imitated the much more spartan style of the Calvinist service. The low-Anglican Puritans got their name because they wanted to purify a church that they felt had strayed from its Protestant beliefs; unable to purify it to their satisfaction, they broke away from it. These Puritans, or Separatists, would eventually become known as Congregationalists.

58. (B) The jury acquitted journalist John Peter Zenger of libel because his facts were accurate and his statements were not seditious—that is, the jury believed they were unlikely to stir up the public to rebellion against the government. This established the important principle of freedom of the press—if writers can demonstrate that their facts are accurate, they cannot be censored or punished. The court declared that Zenger was free to criticize the government in print, as long as he could prove his statements were true. Ever since this time, freedom of the press in the colonies and later the United States has been limited to opinions and true facts.

59. (B) West (1738–1820) revolutionized the genre of history painting by portraying French and Indian War heroes in accurate, modern-day uniforms, rather than in the ancient classical garb dictated by tradition. Copley (1738–1815) broke new ground with his portrait of Paul Revere, showing the silversmith on the job in his shirtsleeves rather than clad in his Sunday best. He painted many famous figures of the colonial era, including John and Samuel Adams. Peale (1741–1847) is best known for a full-length portrait of two of his sons on a staircase, so lifelike that it reportedly fooled George Washington into greeting the boys one day as he hurried by. Stuart (1755–1828), like Copley, is best known as a portraitist; the likeness of Washington on the dollar bill is copied from a Stuart portrait. Thomas Eakins (1844–1916) was a great American painter and teacher of the late 19th century.

60. (D) The colonists were, as a group, lively writers and voracious readers, but not of prose fiction. There were two main reasons for this. First, religiously conservative colonists considered novels a dangerous amusement, likely to lead to licentious behavior—this affected both readers and writers. Colonial America did not produce even one novel. Second, the great tradition of the English novel was in its infancy in the 1700s, so there were very few prose fiction works to choose from. However, the British colonies were a literate society and Benjamin Franklin was only one of many busy publishers and printers. Poetry (particularly religious poetry), sermons and theological works, ancient and modern history, current political essays, biography, and autobiography—particularly action-packed "captive narratives" like Mary Rowlandson's—all sold well.

61. (E) In the southern colonies, it was illegal for slaves to learn to read or write. Although enslaved women were required to take care of white children from babyhood, they were never asked to teach them schoolbook lessons. Many slaves did somehow manage to acquire literacy—sometimes with the help and encouragement of liberal or kind white people—but this was never openly acknowledged by society.

62. (D) Franklin was what is often described as a "Renaissance man"—a figure who showed creative ability in many fields. He founded Philadelphia's first fire insurance company, hospital, library, and intellectual society. He was a moving spirit behind the redesign of the streetlights and the paving of the streets. He printed and wrote many articles for both *Poor Richard's Almanack* and the *Philadelphia Gazette*, which was the most successful newspaper in the colonies. He invented not only the lightning rod but bifocal glasses and the enclosed stove (the latter was perfected by others later).

63. (B) Bradstreet (1612–1672) was an acclaimed colonial-era poet. Mather (1639–1723) was a famous Boston minister who wrote widely on theology and history. Rowlandson (c. 1635–1678) published a bestselling account of her experience of being kidnapped by Wampanoags during King Philip's War. Sewall (1652–1730) published works on a number of topics ranging from biblical prophecies to the abolition of slavery. His diary documents New England's transition from a theocracy to a more secular, business-minded society. Emerson (1803–1882) was a major essayist and poet of the mid- to late 19th century.

64. (A) Puritanism was very slow to give up its cultural stranglehold over New England. In Great Britain, Puritan leader Oliver Cromwell—the only commoner ever to rule England—closed all the London theaters because he believed that actors were immoral people, that the drama portrayed a false picture of real life, and that playgoing encouraged audience members to behave riotously. Cromwell's spiritual descendants in New England shared these beliefs. There was no live theatrical entertainment in the colonies north of New York. Traveling theatrical troupes were very popular in the South, however.

65. (B) Phillis Wheatley came to the colonies on a slave ship as a small child. She was fortunate enough to be purchased by wealthy people who raised her almost as their own daughter, encouraging her to read, write, and study, and only requiring a few light household chores from her. Wheatley's *Poems on Various Subjects, Religious and Moral*, the first book written and published by an African-American, was printed in Great Britain in 1772 and in Philadelphia in 1786.

66. (C) The moment they reached their teens, sometimes earlier, colonial children were considered old enough to start learning a trade. Girls stayed home (or occasionally went to live with other families) and learned to run a household by helping their mothers with the weaving, spinning, cooking, cleaning, and so on; boys were usually bound out to masters (such as wheelwrights or blacksmiths), exchanging their labor for room, board, and learning on the job. Children did not usually earn any significant wages. There was certainly time for play, but work was the main focus for both adults and older children. Schooling was limited to the essentials; young children learned to read, write, and do simple math. Higher education was considered necessary only for young men who intended to enter the ministry or one of the professions (such as medicine or law).

67. (A) The reverse of choice (A) is true; it was quite common for a man to marry and remarry and remarry because his life expectancy was much longer than his wife's. The procedures for delivering babies were so primitive that the death rate was very high for mothers; burning to death was another common fate for women because their long skirts easily caught fire at the open hearth where they cooked the meals (enclosed stoves were not developed in the colonies until the late 1700s). Widowers usually lost no time in remarrying, especially if they were left with children.

68. (D) Although playing and singing was an everyday activity for a great many colonists, and many enjoyed attending musical performances by professionals, American cities lagged behind their European counterparts in accepting music as a viable full-time profession. The first U.S. opera companies and symphony orchestras would not be established until the 19th century. Before that time, a professional musician in the colonies could pick up a living the same way many freelance musicians do today. He or she (usually he) could teach individual pupils in their homes, play in the band in various theaters, perform solo or with a pickup group in concerts in large cities, provide dance music at formal balls and more casual community festivities, and play during religious services and weddings.

69. (E) Edwards and Whitefield were both highly influential revival preachers. Whitefield was so famous that he was given newspaper coverage in the colonies in a way no preacher had ever enjoyed; it is fair to say that he was a celebrity before the concept of celebrity existed. Edwards was well known for his terrifying, dramatic sermons, such as the famous "Sinners in the Hands of an Angry God."

70. (B) Phillis Wheatley is one example of a female author; she was in fact the first African-American to publish a book. (See answer 65.) Midwives, of course, were all women; male doctors did not usually deliver babies in this time and place. Quakers allowed women to preach on an equal footing with men. Women taught their own children, and they often ran the small village schools in which the youngest children were taught to read and write.

Chapter 2: The War for Independence

71. (B) The Proclamation of 1763 was issued after the Treaty of Paris, described in choice (A). It set aside all the land between the 13 colonies and the Mississippi for the Indians and made it illegal for the British colonists to buy any of that land for themselves. In other words, it drew a boundary line and decreed that British colonists must live east of the border and Indians must live west of it.

72. (C) Franklin found the Iroquois Confederacy an impressive example of a working union among tribes with common interests and concerns. He made this the basis for the Albany Plan of Union, which, like the Iroquois Confederacy, left each colony self-governing and independent, but united them for their mutual protection against outside threats.

73. (E) The first four choices all describe important effects of the French and Indian War. Choice (E) is the opposite of what happened; fighting on the same side in a war against an enemy nation created a bond and a sense of national identity among the British colonists.

74. (A) France gave up all the land east of the Mississippi River, except the city of New Orleans, to Britain. It gave the rest of its colonial holdings to Spain in order to prevent a British takeover of the entire continent. During Napoleon's military campaigns, France would take back the territory it had ceded to Spain—and Napoleon would then sell the vast Louisiana Territory to the United States in an event known as the Louisiana Purchase.

75. (C) The French and Indian War broke out because both France and Britain claimed the right to settle the Ohio Valley.

76. (D) The Albany Plan of Union was loosely modeled on the Iroquois Confederacy. It was intended as an association of sovereign states that would remain separate for their individual pursuits but united for their mutual security and protection.

77. (A) As a result of the French and Indian War, Canada became a British colony. Its association with Britain lasted well into the 19th century.

78. (C) The original French settlers had treated the Indians very well; therefore, the Indians began the war on the French side. However, Indians felt only minimal trust in any Europeans, and they fought in their own best interests. In 1758, when the tide of war turned against France, the Indians went over to the British side.

79. (B) The war had been fought to secure the British colonial borders in North America, and it ended on terms that were highly favorable to Britain and to the colonies. The colonies had gained a great deal of new territory. Because the colonies were the primary beneficiaries of the war, Britain thought it was only fair they should share in the burden of the war debt.

80. (E) The British had cannons and the French had none. This was the main reason for the British victory.

81. (A) Colonial disunion before the French and Indian War is illustrated by the fact that only 7 of the 13 colonies sent representatives to the 1751 meeting at which Benjamin Franklin proposed the Albany Plan of Union. The war would prove a powerful unifying force in the colonies, as would the acts of Parliament that followed the war.

82. (B) The Delaware, Huron, Iroquois, and Shawnee tribes made an agreement with the British agents because, although French-Indian relations had been friendly and mutually profitable up to that time, the British were now offering the Indians better trade goods at a better exchange rate.

83. (B) Choice (A) is wrong because the French were not disputing British ownership of the Atlantic coast colonies. Choice (C) is wrong because this describes the entire present-day United States, a great deal of which was claimed by Spain in 1753. Choice (D) is wrong because this describes the Louisiana Territory that the United States would later purchase from France. Choice (E) is wrong because the disputed territory touched only the two easternmost Great Lakes and extended south to the Gulf of Mexico. The French and British were fighting over the land between the Mississippi River and the settled British colonies.

84. (D) The French viewed the obvious British ambition to expand westward with concern. This was not due to any worries about the British takeover of French settlements because there were no such settlements, except for forts and trading posts. Rather, the French did not want to lose control of their easy access to the Ohio and Mississippi Rivers because continued success in the fur trade depended on this access.

85. (C) Barely out of his teens at the time, Washington was given a major's commission in the British Army and handed a letter to deliver to the French military authorities. Written by Governor Dinwiddie of Virginia, the letter reminded the French that Virginia had a longstanding claim to the Ohio Country and warned the French to withdraw their forces from the area.

86. (A) The French and Indian War was over on the battlefield around 1760; France signed over the considerable Louisiana Territory (covering almost all the central portion of the future United States except Texas) to Spain to ensure that Britain could expand no farther west than the Mississippi River. The balance of power was a very important principle among European nations; if any one became too strong, the others would generally unite against that one.

87. (A) The Albany Plan of Union describes two branches of a general government for all the colonies: an executive called the President-General, and a legislature called the Grand Council. The document describes different duties and responsibilities for each of the two branches. Similarly, the U.S. Constitution describes a three-branch government, in which the executive, legislative, and judicial branches have distinct powers.

88. (C) In the Treaty of Paris, France ceded the disputed territory between the Mississippi and the British colonies to Britain. The only exception was the port of New Orleans, which France had ceded to Spain in 1762. France also ceded its Canadian territory to Britain. As part of the same treaty, Britain took over Florida from Spain; Spain would temporarily recover Florida after the American Revolution.

89. (E) The British Army was a regular army—in other words, a professional military organization of full-time, career officers and men. There was no such professional army in the colonies; they did not even have organized militias at this time. Perhaps not surprisingly, the British regulars showed nothing but contempt for the volunteer colonial soldiers—a contempt that extended itself even to the appointed American officers like George Washington. The cold shoulder the British gave the Americans, and the American resentment at the snub, created a mutual hostility that carried over into the Revolutionary era that lay just ahead.

90. (E) The French were well established in the area of Fort Duquesne (on the border of present-day Pennsylvania and Ohio). Washington had only a few hundred men to support him, including Indian allies and members of the Virginia militia. Unable to storm Fort Duquesne, Washington and his men withdrew and built their own fort, called Fort Necessity. Vastly outnumbering the Virginia troops, the French laid siege to the fort and soon forced a surrender. Washington agreed to retreat to Virginia with his troops.

91. (B) The point of the general government as described in the Albany Plan of Union was to eliminate parliamentary authority over the colonies. The Albany Plan of Union describes a colonial parliament—a unicameral legislature with a royally appointed executive, to govern the colonies instead of the British Parliament.

92. (D) By this date, the colonists had not yet gone so far as to say the king had no authority over them. They were British subjects, and the king had the right to do what he liked with his own territory. However, the colonists also believed in the British principle of government by the consent of the governed, and of their right to protest royal policies with which they disagreed. As a result of their objections, the terms of the Proclamation of 1763 were relaxed and western settlement continued.

93. (C) The colonial assemblies called upon the able-bodied men for defense in emergency situations such as Indian raids. The situation was the same in all the colonies; there was no regular drill or practice, only citizen soldiers who served when called on. There was no standing army in the colonies; there was no equivalent of the National Guard. In case of war, it was the duty of the British Army to defend Britain's colonies. The French and Indian War marked the first time most of the colonists had seen any military action, and they were very ill-prepared for it.

94. (D) The colony of South Carolina had the same borders in 1763 that the state of South Carolina has today. South Carolina did claim a narrow slice of western territory after the French and Indian War but would before long give up its claim in favor of Tennessee.

95. (D) The Indians would never deliberately ally themselves with the losing side in a battle; they had no reason to feel any personal loyalty to either the French or the British and supported whichever side appeared more likely to further their own territorial and economic interests. Note on choice (B): General Edward Braddock ordered the construction of a wagon road from Baltimore to Fort Cumberland, so that his troops could be supplied more easily. This road would eventually be extended as far as Illinois, greatly facilitating the early settlement of the Midwest. Today it is U.S. Route 40.

96. (B) Because rioting and violence in the streets of Boston became so common in the period immediately following the Townshend Acts, British officials in Boston asked for troops to be sent to the city to maintain order. The Bostonians deeply resented the presence of an army of occupation in peacetime.

97. (E) When the Massachusetts Government Act disbanded the Massachusetts legislature, its leaders met privately and agreed to urge their counterparts in the other colonies to meet in some central location and organize a united colonial response to the Intolerable Acts. This meeting is known to history as the First Continental Congress.

98. (A) The committees of correspondence were generally made up of members of the elected colonial assemblies. The leaders made a point of establishing these committees because at this time in history, news was slow to travel over a long distance. By making it an official responsibility, the leaders ensured that important breaking news of acts of Parliament would spread throughout the colonies as quickly as possible. The First Continental Congress was convened as a result of communication among these committees.

99. (E) The Stamp Act long predated the Intolerable Acts. As a result of the other four acts, Parliament closed the port of Boston, revoked the Massachusetts Charter, protected royal officials from being tried for crimes in Massachusetts, and stated that the army could force citizens to provide food and housing for soldiers.

100. (D) The Massachusetts legislature remained in session until after the Boston Tea Party, when it was disbanded by act of Parliament. Note on choice (C): The John Singleton Copley portrait of Samuel Adams shows him holding the Massachusetts royal charter and pointing to the provision that banned the deployment of troops in peacetime. It is historically important because it was the first painting in the future United States to capture a leader at a dramatic moment in history, in the same way that a newspaper photograph or a video clip would do today.

101. (C) The celebrated Boston Tea Party of December 16, 1773, was a protest against a British attempt to manipulate the colonists into paying a tax that they opposed on principle. Perhaps because the Boston Tea Party involved the deliberate destruction of valuable property, Parliament cracked down very hard on Bostonian defiance, making Massachusetts an example to any other colony tempted to defy parliamentary authority. The Intolerable Acts became law in 1774.

102. (A) The Boston Massacre hardly deserves its melodramatic name. It arose from the Bostonians' objections to the occupation of the city by troops in peacetime. One evening, a small mob of colonists gathered in a public area to jeer at the recoats on duty. When the colonists began throwing stones at the soldiers, the soldiers fired a few shots in self-defense; in the ensuing brawl, five people were killed.

103. (E) Britain had full authority to make its colonies obey its trade rules. Colonies were never allowed to establish their own international trade relationships; they could trade only with the parent country and only on its financial terms. The colonial objection to the Sugar Act was that it violated two important civil rights—the right not to be taxed without consent and the right to be tried by a jury if accused of a crime. In addition, the colonists were alarmed at the prospect of economic ruin by the sudden enforcement of a rule that had been allowed to slide for many decades.

104. (A) Delegates to the First Continental Congress agreed on a document called the Declaration and Resolves, which included the provisions described in choices (B) through (D). The delegates discussed a complete break with Britain but could not agree on the issue. It was the Second Continental Congress that would declare American independence.

105. (B) All the colonists were British citizens, entitled to the same rights and privileges as those who lived in England. The Magna Carta, signed by King John in 1215, first granted the principle of government by the consent of the governed, stating that the English barons (the earliest form of Parliament) had the authority to take action against the monarch if he or she broke the law. This was confirmed even more strongly in the English Bill of Rights of 1689, which stated that the monarch had no authority to enact laws without parliamentary consent and that members of the House of Commons must be freely elected. Since the French and Indian War, every act of Parliament—whether it involved new taxes, the presence of a standing army in peacetime, or the denial of the right to trial by jury—had denied the colonists their right to a voice in their own government.

106. (D) With the passage of the Intolerable Acts, Samuel Adams and the leaders of the disbanded Massachusetts Assembly urged a meeting of the leaders from all the colonies to discuss a united colonial response to Britain.

107. (C) Parliament did not have to pass a new law to send troops to maintain order in Boston; it had already done so once before. The troops were only removed as a safety measure after the Boston Massacre.

108. (E) Despite the fact that they had fired on unarmed civilians, the redcoats who took part in the Boston Massacre received the full benefits of the judicial system. They were arrested and tried for murder; like all defendants, they were presumed innocent, with the burden on the prosecution to prove their guilt. John Adams, one of Boston's ablest lawyers, defended them. Though his decision to do so was politically unpopular, he insisted that if the colonists wanted justice for themselves, they must extend it to the redcoats. The jury acquitted the redcoats because they were the victims of an unprovoked attack.

109. (C) Connecticut schoolmaster Hale (1755–1776) was not a writer of political pamphlets, but a volunteer spy for the Continental Army. He was captured on his first mission and executed for treason. Pennsylvania lawyer Dickinson (1732–1808) wrote *Letters from a Farmer in Pennsylvania*, a famous attack on the legitimacy of the Townshend Acts. Maryland lawyer Dulaney (1722–1797) wrote *Considerations on the Propriety of Imposing Taxes . . .* , the best-known and most cogent argument against the concept of "virtual representation." Jefferson's *Summary View of the Rights of British America* was a reasoned protest against the Intolerable Acts. Otis (1725–1783) was the author of *The Rights of the British Colonies Asserted and Proved*, which appeared after the passage of the Sugar Act.

110. (A) The colonists never disputed the fact that they were British subjects—this was the whole reason they were so upset about the Stamp Act and the other parliamentary attempts to tax them. As British citizens, they had certain rights, among which was representation in their own government. Parliament could not offer them fair representation for the reasons described in choices (B) through (E).

111. (B) The time for armed resistance had not yet arrived; the colonies did not begin organizing militias until the early 1770s. The other four choices all describe various means of colonial resistance to the Stamp Act.

112. (A) The English word *quarter* has a number of correct definitions; the Quartering Act gets its name from the definition of *quarters* as "a place to live." Just as a military quartermaster is responsible for providing food and shelter for the troops, the Quartering Act required the civilians to provide room and board for them at any time when the army requested it.

113. (D) Choices (A) and (B) are wrong because although they did happen, they were still a little way in the future. The direct result of the Intolerable Acts was to bring the leaders of all the colonies together in support of Massachusetts, which was the main target of the acts. This proved that the colonies had set aside any internal suspicion and distrust to come together in a true union because Britain had proved itself to be the common enemy of all of them. All of them felt threatened by the Intolerable Acts because if such acts could be enforced against one colony, they might later be enforced against any or all of the others.

114. (E) The first shots of the Revolution were fired on Lexington Green in April 1775, while the colonial leaders were still awaiting the parliamentary response to the Declaration and Resolves. The Second Continental Congress, which had already planned to meet in May if no parliamentary response was received, ended up having to confront an outbreak of war. The Battles of Breed's Hill and Bunker Hill took place on June 16, about a month after Congress convened.

115. (B) The colonists petitioned Parliament in writing and boycotted imported British goods. Brawling between colonists and sailors of the Royal Navy also became common. Parliament responded by lowering the tax; on their side, the colonists agreed to accept the reduced tax as a legitimate trade regulation.

116. (D) The Boston Tea Party is the first documented instance of colonists throwing a cargo overboard into the sea. In Rhode Island in 1765, resistance to the enforcement of the Sugar Act took somewhat less radical forms: deliberate refusal to cooperate, secretly bringing disputed cargo ashore and hiding it from the inspectors, and failing to show up at a shipowner's trial so that the case was bound to be dismissed. When the courts did have to convict a shipowner of smuggling and seize his ship, they often sold it back to him at an absurdly low price.

117. (C) The Stamp Act was passed in the spring of 1765; the Virginia resolutions described in choices (A), (B), (D), and (E) were passed in May 1765 in response. The purpose of the resolutions was to set down the burgesses' reaction to the Stamp Act in the written record. Choice (C) describes the Virginia resolution of June 1776; the Second Continental Congress voted unanimously (with one abstention) in favor of this resolution in July.

118. (A) Dickinson was among the most prominent of the many patriots who hesitated to take the step of dissolving the colonies' connection to Great Britain. He argued for prudence, for waiting until word of support might come from France, for waiting to see how the Continental Army succeeded against the redcoats. He believed that the time for a declaration of independence had not yet arrived. Some of his reasons are summarized in choices (B) through (D).

119. (B) British officials knew perfectly well that no real Indians participated in the Boston Tea Party; the Indians were not involved in the colonists' quarrel with Britain. The colonists knew that Parliament would accurately pinpoint the source of the damage. The disguise was essential not to blame the Indians, but to protect the individuals, because destroying the cargo was certainly a crime and might possibly be construed as treason against the Crown. People who witnessed the event could truthfully say they recognized no one they knew under the war paint, blankets, and feathers; even the participants, if questioned, could deny recognizing one another. The disguises were highly effective; to this day, historians are not certain who boarded the *Dartmouth* that night.

120. (C) The *Gaspée* was a British ship whose commission was to enforce regulations against smuggling. The colonists found this irksome and infuriating, as regular inspections and seizure of goods ate into their profits and wasted their time and effort. Smuggling was such a matter of course in Rhode Island that most colonists did not consider it illegal—or believe that it should be illegal. Of course, the British customs crews took the opposite view. Therefore, conflict between the two was inevitable and frequent. The *Gaspée* incident is famous for its extreme violence; the captain was seriously wounded and the ship destroyed.

121. (A) Joseph Galloway of Pennsylvania proposed a middle course between declaring independence and maintaining the status quo. According to his plan, the colonies should continue to be self-governing but should also establish a national assembly that would function as an American branch of Parliament. This national assembly would be made up of elected representatives from all the colonies, headed by a royally appointed president-general. The Galloway Plan of Union was narrowly defeated by majority vote.

122. (D) Throughout the controversy between the colonies and Britain, Pitt supported the colonists' view that Britain could regulate their trade but not tax them without their consent. Grenville and Townshend argued the opposite side. Grenville had first proposed the Stamp Act; Townshend gave his name to the Townshend Acts of 1767. Blackstone wrote an influential pamphlet supporting the doctrine of virtual representation. Hutchinson, the royal governor of Massachusetts, supported the parliamentary majority.

123. (E) Parliamentary leaders were astonished at the outrage with which the colonists greeted the passage of the Stamp Act. The response from all the colonies was the same: violence against the persons and property of the stamp inspectors, articulate protests in print, and an absolute refusal to obey the new law. With the stamp inspectors reporting their utter inability to carry out their duties, Parliament had little choice but to withdraw the act.

124. (D) Thomas Whately, a member of the House of Commons and the principal author of the Stamp Act, was the first person to advance the argument of "virtual representation" in print. He argued that Parliament represented the interests of all citizens throughout the British Empire, regardless of whether the geographically distant districts (such as those in India or North America) had actual representatives seated in the House of Commons.

125. (A) The Boston Massacre and the Boston Tea Party made Parliament single out Massachusetts as the target of parliamentary wrath, as embodied in the Intolerable Acts. The Revolutionary War began in Massachusetts because the redcoats were stationed in Boston; this meant that Boston was threatened more directly than any other colony.

126. (A) Jefferson's argument that King George III was directly responsible for many colonial grievances went far beyond any other argument in print at that time. Jefferson's *Summary View* prefigures the Declaration of Independence, with its long list of specific charges against the king, its reminder that the king is subject to the nation's laws, and its insistence that the people need not obey the king when he breaks the laws. Choices (B) through (D) describe arguments previously made by many writers. Choice (E) is wrong because the colonists never disputed Britain's right to regulate trade.

127. (C) In October 1765, the Stamp Act Congress passed a list of resolutions that spelled out colonial objections to the Stamp Act. The colonists were all British subjects; therefore they had all the same rights as their fellow citizens who lived in the British Isles. Among those rights were the right to trial by jury, the right (of the qualified voters) to vote for representatives in the government, and the right not to be taxed without the consent of those representatives. The Stamp Act violated all three of these rights. The colonists also opposed it and other recent acts of Parliament on the grounds that they would impoverish a prosperous society.

128. (B) Adams agreed to defend the redcoats as a matter of principle. He argued that if the colonists demanded for themselves the right to trial by jury, they could not fairly deny that right to anyone else. Public feeling was very strong against the redcoats, and many looked askance at Adams; however, he refused to back down. He did not support the British side—he was an ardent patriot and among the most vocal supporters of American independence in the spring of 1776—but he insisted on the principle of equal justice for all. He won his case on the grounds that the colonists had been the aggressors in the incident.

129. (E) The Tea Act was passed largely as a favor to British merchants in India, who had millions of pounds of tea in their warehouses and no buyers for it. The colonial boycott on British imports continued, and the colonists drank smuggled Dutch tea instead. Parliament agreed to allow the East India tea to be shipped directly to the colonies, where it would be sold at a special low price that made it even cheaper than the Dutch tea. However, the low price included the tax that the colonists objected to on principle—again, the issue was taxation without the consent of the people taxed. In addition, colonial merchants were alarmed about the overall economic implications of the Tea Act.

130. (B) The Stamp Act itself sets out the fees for each type of document, in great detail. Stamped paper would be required for a host of professional licenses, legal documents, newspapers, pamphlets, deeds, bonds, mortgages—even playing cards. The act's references to the admiralty and ecclesiastical courts alarmed the colonists because they strongly believed in the colonial system of common-law courts with juries. Admiralty courts had no juries, and their traditional purpose was only to deal with cases involving ships and shipping, not with tax disputes. Ecclesiastical courts were church courts presided over by bishops; they assumed broad authority to try any case involving moral failings. The colonies had no bishops or ecclesiastical courts; the Stamp Act's hint that Britain might attempt to establish them in the colonies alarmed everyone.

131. (D) The Sons of Liberty and the Daughters of Liberty were what we would today call political activists. They stirred up public sentiment against taxation without representation. Since the Boston Tea Party was an illegal act involving the destruction of valuable property, the Massachusetts Assembly would not have openly or officially planned or approved it. However, many of the assemblymen were patriots and Sons of Liberty, and several may very well have taken part in the Tea Party.

132. (A) The Declaratory Act was passed in response to colonial opposition to the Stamp Act. Parliament recognized that the Stamp Act could not be enforced and, therefore, repealed it. At the same time, Parliament issued the Declaratory Act, stating that Parliament had total authority to make laws for the colonies and that the colonies must obey parliamentary laws.

133. (C) Colonists grudgingly accepted the amended Sugar Act as a legitimate attempt to regulate trade, which they freely acknowledged that Britain had every right to do. Trade regulations were one thing; direct taxes or other punitive measures on which the colonists had had no opportunity to vote were another thing altogether.

134. (D) Each colony was administered by a freely elected legislature. Voting rights were limited to free adult men who met the requirements of age and property ownership (these varied among the colonies). However, government by an elected lawmaking body of representatives was the form of government that prevailed in the individual colonies. Britain, of course, was a constitutional monarchy, and the colonists were British citizens, but actual day-to-day government was local.

135. (C) Planning for the invasion of Canada began in the spring of 1775, immediately after the Battle of Bunker Hill. There were relatively few British troops garrisoned in Canada, so it might be an easy victory; the largely French population in Canada resented the British presence and thus were likely allies for the Americans; Canada would be a welcome addition to the group of American colonies; and the loss of Canada would eliminate any chance of a British invasion from the north. Neither Congress nor the American military commanders expected Britain to abandon Boston to defend Canada; victory in Massachusetts was far more important to Britain, both strategically and psychologically.

136. (C) Choice (C) is much too sweeping. Britain agreed that the United States had the exclusive right to expand eastward as far as the Mississippi, but Britain still maintained its ties to Canada, including what was then called Oregon Country in the West (parts of which were also claimed by Russia, France, and Spain). In 1846, Britain and the United States would divide Oregon Country along the present U.S.-Canadian border.

137. (A) The reason George Washington chose to attack on Christmas night was to surprise the Hessians, who had been celebrating the holiday and were totally unprepared for the ambush. The Americans left their campfires burning on the Delaware's western banks, crossing the river quietly during Christmas night. The attack was successful because it caught the enemy unprepared.

138. (E) Even the most conservative colonists opposed the Stamp Act, the Townshend Acts, and the other assorted acts of Parliament that infringed on their rights as British citizens. However, the loyalists, or Tories, believed that it was possible to work out their differences with Britain by some means that stopped short of actual armed rebellion, which many of them believed to be treason against their king. The patriots, or Whigs, took the opposite view—that the monarch forfeited his subjects' loyalty when he took away their rights.

139. (B) The idiom "offering an olive branch" means "making a peace offering." Conservative leaders in the Second Continental Congress, led by John Dickinson of Pennsylvania, urged passage of the Olive Branch Petition as a last resort before formally severing ties with Britain. Choice (C) describes the Declaration of Independence, choice (D) describes *Common Sense*, and choice (E) describes the Declaration of the Causes and Necessity for Taking Up Arms.

140. (B) The British planned to take over New York, thus separating New England from the rest of the colonies. They planned to take over the two sections in turn. Philadelphia was the capital city, but its capture would offer the British only prestige, not any real strategic advantage. The royal governor of Virginia did offer emancipation to any slaves who joined the British Army, but this was not part of an overall military strategy. The British did hire Hessian (German) mercenaries to fight on their side, but France and Britain were traditional enemies. France came into the war on the American side after the Battle of Saratoga in 1777.

141. (D) The actual reference in the Declaration is one of many grievances the colonies had against the British king; it blames him for continuing the transatlantic slave trade and describes it as "violating [the] most sacred rights of life and liberty." Jefferson did not state or suggest that the United States of America would emancipate its slaves. However, the southern delegates insisted that the reference be removed. Since the delegates had agreed that any vote in favor of independence must be unanimous, the southerners gained their point.

142. (A) Englishman Thomas Paine emigrated to the colonies shortly before the tension between them and Parliament turned into an all-out war. He published *Common Sense* in 1776. His arguments against hereditary monarchy as a viable form of government, and against reconciliation with England, persuaded many Americans to support independence. Paine was not quite an anarchist, but he did believe that government was inherently evil because it tended to oppose and suppress individual liberty. He urged Americans to declare independence and to create a national legislature with a mix of elected and appointed officials from all the colonies.

143. (B) General Arnold helped to bring the guns from Fort Ticonderoga to the defense of Boston and later was largely responsible for the victory at Saratoga. Colonel Hamilton began the war as a captain of artillery and was soon promoted to aide-de-camp to General Washington. General Putnam led the troops to victory at Bunker Hill in the first months of the Revolution. Washington's command of the Continental Army is, of course, common knowledge. Franklin was too old to take part in combat; he served his country during the revolution as a statesman.

144. (C) The redcoats had marched from Boston to Concord to find a hidden stash of weapons. After the skirmish at Lexington, they continued to Concord, took what weapons they found, exchanged more fire with the minutemen, and began the march back to Boston. The minutemen followed them and laid siege to the city; this would soon lead to the Battles of Breed's Hill and Bunker Hill.

145. (E) Because they had never developed technologically powerful weapons, Indians had always fought like guerrillas. They crept along in hiding and caught the enemy by surprise. The Continental Army profited by its own experience of fighting Indians, attacking the redcoats by stealth whenever possible during the war. Europeans believed in fighting across open fields, but the Americans knew that they could gain nothing by fighting that type of battle. They were often outnumbered, they were poorly equipped, and they were up against a disciplined and experienced opponent.

146. (C) Washington's own men never lost confidence in him, but Congress was growing tired of watching him fight a defensive war. More seriously, his troops were barefoot, dressed in rags, and without food or blankets, and Congress had no power to raise money with which to buy these things. In spite of the brutal conditions at Valley Forge during that winter, there were no desertions. This can only be attributed to personal loyalty to the commander.

147. (A) *The American Crisis* is the collective title of a series of essays Paine published during the Revolutionary War. The essays helped to create and maintain enthusiasm for the patriot cause; this was very important, because the Continental Army was made entirely of civilians who had a free choice whether to enlist. Since the soldiers were woefully ill-equipped and poorly paid when paid at all, there was little incentive to enlist apart from their belief in American independence and in the Continental Army's ultimate victory. Paine's essays eloquently fostered faith in the army and the cause.

148. (A) The British surrender at Saratoga in 1777 ended the war in the northern colonies, apart from a battle at Rhode Island in 1778. Saratoga convinced the French that the Americans had a chance to win the war and brought them in against their traditional enemy, Britain. French aid took the form of money, experienced commanding officers, ships, and troops; it was an invaluable element in the eventual American victory.

149. (B) The British knew that the colonists had stashed a large collection of guns and ammunition at Concord, close enough to Boston to be readily available in case of an outbreak of hostility between the redcoats and the citizens. They intended only to collect the weapons and return to Boston, keeping their activity as secret as possible by leaving the city after dark. However, the watchful colonists were aware of their movements, and the minutemen, armed and ready, met them on the village green at Lexington.

150. (E) Jones was made an officer in the fledgling Continental Navy and given command of a frigate. He captured a number of British merchant ships off Nova Scotia and the Bahamas before crossing the Atlantic to take command of a ship he christened the *Bon Homme* (or *Bonhomme*) *Richard* after a fictional character created by Benjamin Franklin. In September 1779, the *Bon Homme Richard* found itself facing the *Serapis*, a modern, 50-gun British ship. Although Jones's ship was smaller and in bad repair, and was severely hampered by an inexplicable attack from a French ship that should have been his ally, Jones led his crew to victory over the *Serapis*. He was hailed as a hero, and the battle proved that the Royal Navy was not invincible in spite of its superior equipment.

151. (D) The patriots rebelling against Britain knew that if the Continental Army lost the war, they all risked severe punishment for committing treason. Because the Tories supported the British Army, they were a genuine and serious threat to the patriots' lives and safety. Therefore, the two sides were bitter enemies. Outspoken Tories were frequently kidnapped, imprisoned, robbed, and humiliated unless or until they agreed to renounce their loyalty to Britain and join the patriot cause. There were a few isolated instances of Tories being hanged—one such Tory was believed guilty of plotting to assassinate George Washington—but for the most part, physical violence was limited to tarring and feathering or similar roughhousing.

152. (A) Arnold knew that he had made valuable and brilliant contributions in command, and resented being passed over for promotion. After a leg wound forced Arnold to withdraw from combat, Washington appointed him military governor of Philadelphia. When Arnold lost that post over questionable financial dealings that led to a court-martial, Washington offered him command of the garrison at West Point. While in Philadelphia, Arnold had met and married loyalist Peggy Shippen. This marriage led to extravagant spending to keep up with his new, largely Tory social circle. When the British offered him a significant sum of money to allow them to take over West Point, he accepted. The conspiracy was uncovered in time, and Arnold ended up accepting a commission in the British Army. He led troops against his own country before the Revolution ended.

153. (C) Throughout his adult life, George Washington had the ability to gain the liking, trust, loyalty, and respect of nearly everyone who knew or worked with him. He was the unanimous choice of the Second Continental Congress to command the troops, just as later he would be the unopposed candidate for president. Washington's troops were paid poorly, when they were paid at all; they were inexperienced and ill-equipped; and Congress had no resources with which to supply them. Troops often deserted, or decided not to reenlist, after a climactic battle was over; but there is a remarkable record of loyalty to Washington among the men who fought under him, particularly when the army was in its most desperate condition in the winter of 1777–1778. Washington was always able to inspire his men with confidence in his ability to lead them.

154. (B) The ships remained in the harbor after the major British victory in Brooklyn because this was as good a strategic position for them as could be found. Washington's troops retreated across the river into Manhattan; General Howe's troops did not immediately pursue them, which historians agree was a serious tactical mistake. Given the huge number of American casualties and the strategic advantage Britain had gained, Howe might well have won the war outright had he remained on the attack. However, he waited several days, which allowed the Continental Army time to regroup.

155. (D) Having been unable to strike a decisive blow in the North, the British switched their attention to the South. General Howe returned to Great Britain in the spring of 1778, leaving Henry Clinton to assume command. Clinton decided to attack the South, which had seen no military action since 1776 and was more or less undefended. Georgia and the Carolinas were taken very quickly, allowing the British to continue north into Virginia.

156. (A) The Declaration of Independence does exactly what its name says—it states that the colonies are now an independent nation, and explains the reasons for taking this step. It is not a formal declaration of war.

157. (A) The British Army was an official organization with a clear chain of command and a high degree of military discipline. Englishmen who enlisted in the British Army received regular wages and served under clearly agreed terms. Deserters were subject to severe punishment. The Continental Army, on the other hand, had no power to prevent its underpaid, undersupplied, and all-volunteer soldiers from deserting whenever they saw fit, which happened all the time, particularly in the first years of the war. Americans were usually very ready to enlist for agreed-upon terms of service, but they saw no reason not to desert if they got bored during a military stalemate, or if their crops needed harvesting, or if they disagreed with their commander's judgment. Pay was irregular, conditions were uncomfortable, and food was often in short supply; few men, once their agreed term of service ended, wanted to reenlist for a second term. Moreover, the Continental Army had no power to punish deserters.

158. (C) The Declaration of Independence was signed in July 1776; the Battle of Saratoga took place in October 1777. Note on choice (A): After the British surrender at Saratoga, the theater of war moved south to Georgia and the Carolinas; there would be no further major battles north of New Jersey.

159. (B) The American Revolution was an era of high ideals; people believed that, in the words of Thomas Paine, the colonists "had it in their power to begin the world over again." In sermons, letters, and published pamphlets and essays, literate Americans argued in favor of many of the major Enlightenment ideals. Gender equality was not among them; the battle for full civil and legal rights for American women would not really begin until the middle of the 19th century. Note on choice (C): Even a few southern planters advocated abolition during the Revolutionary era—some as a matter of conscience, others because slavery was becoming less and less economically viable. During the Revolutionary War, the slave trade was either banned or heavily taxed in all the colonies except Georgia and South Carolina, and would be banned everywhere after 1808. However, when the invention of the cotton gin in 1793 made slavery profitable again, all talk of abolition south of Pennsylvania came to an end.

160. (E) The battle ended with the Americans in retreat, but they had inflicted heavy casualties on the redcoats while losing comparatively few of their own men; in addition, the British did not manage to break the siege. Bunker Hill was an important psychological victory for the Americans, who were now convinced that they could fight the British Army on equal terms. Note on choice (C): Congress appointed George Washington commander in chief of the Continental Army before receiving news of the battle.

161. (A) Indians had always used the Cumberland Gap as the easiest passage through the Appalachians. Colonists had begun to use this natural passage to the West as early as 1750. In 1773, Boone became the first white person to lead a group into Kentucky to settle it. In the spring of 1775, at almost the same time as the Battles of Lexington and Concord, Boone was commissioned to blaze a trail through the Cumberland Gap to the Kentucky River. Choice (B) happened during the Stamp Act crisis, well before the Revolution; *Common Sense* was published about a year after the war began; and choices (C) and (E) took place long after the war ended.

162. (D) There was no Joan of Arc in the Continental Army, leading the troops into battle as a commanding officer. Many women—from Martha Washington down to the humblest private's wife—went to war, facing the same risks and hardships as the men (hunger, fatigue, disease, and the constant danger of being shot). They cooked for their men, washed and mended their clothing, and nursed the sick and wounded. Many women served as spies, especially in cities with substantial Tory populations. There are also documented cases of choices (A) and (B). Deborah Sampson disguised herself as a man and enlisted in the Continental Army under the name "Robert Shurtleff." Mary Ludwig Hayes (or Hays) took over her husband's cannon when he was wounded on the battlefield at Monmouth.

163. (A) The "wilderness campaign" fought between patriotic frontiersmen on one side and Tories, Indians, and redcoats on the other had very little to do with the concurrent Revolutionary War. However, it did affect the location of the western boundary of the United States as specified in the Treaty of Paris.

164. (E) Moultrie commanded the American forces at Fort Sullivan in the 1776 battle for Charleston Harbor. Burgoyne led the British forces at Saratoga in 1777. Carleton and his troops defeated Benedict Arnold and his forces at Lake Champlain in 1776. Cornwallis led troops in the battles around New York City in 1777; he became the leading commander of the southern campaign and surrendered to Washington at the siege of Yorktown in 1781. Howe was the leading British commander of the northern campaign.

165. (D) Jefferson did make the charge paraphrased in choice (D) in the original draft of the Declaration, but it was deleted during the debates in Congress. The other four choices describe the charges the Declaration makes against the king.

166. (E) Both redcoats and minutemen who participated in the fighting at Lexington wrote down their accounts of what happened. These descriptions still exist. Each side claimed that someone on the other side fired first; historians will never know who fired what Ralph Waldo Emerson later described as "the shot heard round the world."

167. (D) Choice (D) goes beyond the language of Article IV, in which each nation agrees to aid the other "as far as circumstances and its own particular situation will permit." Since each nation could determine its own ability to aid the other, Article IV was nonbinding and unenforceable. Choice (A) is implicit in the language of the entire treaty, most especially in Article II. Choice (B) is implicit in Articles I, IV, VIII, and X. Choice (C) appears in Article VI. Choice (E) appears in Article IX.

168. (A) The British sent two 50-gun ships to Charleston Harbor. Meanwhile, the Americans under Colonel William Moultrie occupied and strengthened a fort on Sullivan's Island, strategically positioning its numerous cannons. The British could not land any troops from their ships, nor were their guns able to kill more than a few Americans or to damage the fort. The Americans nearly destroyed both British ships, and there were about 10 times as many British casualties as American. This victory effectively ended the British plan to eliminate the South from the war; they would not invade the region again until 1779.

169. (B) By 1776, so many settlers had poured into Kentucky that the local Shawnee and Cherokee people were being pushed off their land. The Kentucky settlers were in violation of the Proclamation of 1763, which had determined the border between Indian territory and the British colonies. The British and the Indians both gained from their united opposition to the settlers. Settlers fighting on the frontier were distracted from joining the main Revolutionary War battles in the East. At the same time, the conflict between Britain and the colonists gave the Indians the opening to try to drive the settlers out of Kentucky.

170. (A) Washington and the Continental Army lost a series of battles to Howe and the redcoats in the Philadelphia region. The Battles of Paoli, Germantown, and Philadelphia were all British victories.

171. (D) Dawes and Revere were patriots and Sons of Liberty, part of a network of spies who watched the comings and goings of British military officials and American Tories in Boston. The spies learned that the redcoats planned to march on Concord on the night of April 18, seize a cache of arms hidden there, and, with luck, arrest Samuel Adams and John Hancock, who were staying in the area that night. Revere and Dawes rode forth to rouse the militia, warning them to turn out ready for action because the redcoats were marching to Concord. The militia and the redcoats faced one another for the first time on Lexington Green.

172. (E) Pitt was prime minister of Great Britain during the Stamp Act crisis; he advocated repeal of the act. Adams served on a number of important congressional committees, nominated George Washington as commander in chief of the army, and was the most vocal advocate of independence in the Congress. Dickinson spoke for the conservative minority, served as the main author of the Olive Branch Petition, and headed the committee that drafted the Articles of Confederation. Hancock was the president of the Congress. Lee proposed the Virginia resolution that the colonies declare their independence from Great Britain.

173. (A) The Connecticut Assembly sent Ethan Allen and his Green Mountain Boys to Ticonderoga. At the same time, the Massachusetts Committee of Safety sent Benedict Arnold and his troops to the same location. Both parties had the same commission—to take the British forts, manned only by skeleton forces, and transport the cannons to Boston. After initial mutual distrust and resistance, Allen and Arnold worked together to subdue the redcoats and take the cannons, which in the end were held in readiness in northern New York, pending congressional decisions on their deployment. Choice (D) was not the original goal of the mission but was a very important result of it.

174. (E) Retiring to winter quarters, to resume fighting once the weather was sufficiently warm, was standard military practice at the time. The winter truce was necessary because troops could not hunt or gather anything to eat at that season; the risks of death by starvation or freezing were much too high. It was also difficult, if not impossible, for troops to march any distance in conditions of ice and heavy snow. The outcome of the Battle of Trenton had nothing to do with the move to winter quarters, which took place after the Battle of Princeton in January 1777 and ended in March when fighting resumed.

175. (C) Thousands of Africans took part in the war. One of the casualties of the Boston Massacre was the free African merchant sailor Crispus Attucks. African men and boys enlisted in the Continental Army in every colony except Georgia and South Carolina. Hundreds joined an "Ethiopian Regiment" organized by the royal governor of Virginia. Those who fought on the British side did so in exchange for a promise of emancipation, which in many cases they achieved. The one area in which Africans were given no opportunity to contribute was in Congress.

Chapter 3: Founding a New Nation

176. (B) The Northwest Ordinance sets forth the U.S. government plan for the Northwest Territory—the region immediately south and west of the Great Lakes. It consists of rules by which the territory was to be settled and its governments organized and explains the process of applying for statehood.

177. (E) The principle in question is that of total separation of church and state; that no one should have to pay any civil penalty, or forgo any civil right, on account of his or her method of worship. When a colony established an official state church, that church required all residents, whether or not they attended that church, to contribute financially. Many politically prominent Americans believed it was wrong to force citizens to pay money to a church in which they did not want to worship. This accounts for the prominent references to the free exercise of religion in the Bill of Rights, the Northwest Ordinance, and other founding documents.

178. (A) The Articles of Confederation did not permit the federal government to tax the states. This was an impossible way to structure any national government; a national government will have no revenue if it cannot tax the people.

179. (B) Massachusetts farmer Daniel Shays and his followers rebelled when the state legislature began assessing taxes on their land and seizing the land if the taxes were not paid. The rebels argued that the taxes were too hard on the farmers and that the merchant class in eastern Massachusetts must share the burden fairly.

180. (D) Madison was deeply concerned over the weaknesses of the Articles of Confederation, as demonstrated by Shays's Rebellion, by a severe economic depression, by the chronic poverty of the Continental Army, and by conflicts arising between and among the states. His "Vices of the Political Systems of the United States" (1787) did not argue against equal representation of the states in the national Congress. It did make the arguments described in choices (A), (B), (C), and (E).

181. (C) According to Article 8 of the Articles of Confederation, taxation was to be decided by the individual states. Naturally, the states did not want to tax themselves, or to pay more than what their leaders regarded as their fair share of the national revenue. This left Congress without the power to pay national debts, supply the Continental Army, or meet any of its expenses.

182. **(D)** It is a common misconception that voting in the early years of the United States was a whites-only privilege. The early state constitutions use the words *freeman* or *free person* to describe an eligible voter; thus free African men (of whom there were many, especially north of Maryland) could vote if they met the requirements of age and property ownership, which varied slightly from one state to the next. This measure of racial equality was revoked gradually, beginning with Maryland in 1809, as the sectional division between North and South deepened. At this time in history, property owners were considered to have a greater stake in the community, and thus a greater right to a say in the government, than poor people. All states revoked the property-ownership requirement before 1840. Indians were not considered citizens at all; therefore, they were not taxed and they did not have the right to vote. This was not rectified until 1924.

183. **(E)** Loyalists (also called royalists or Tories) were colonists (Americans) who remained loyal to Britain, considered themselves British subjects throughout the war, and either fought on or supported the British Army. During the Revolution, their fortunes and other property, such as real estate, were often seized and turned over to the American cause. The Treaty of Paris urged clemency toward the loyalists, specifying that all was to be forgiven; that they were to have the same rights and privileges as all other American citizens; and that they were to be given every chance to recover their lost property, at their own expense.

184. **(B)** The missing state from the five that comprised the Northwest Territory is Indiana. A glance at a map of the continental United States of the present day shows that these five states were indeed directly northwest of the original 13 states along the Atlantic coast.

185. **(E)** The opposite of choice (E) is true. Britain, France, and the Netherlands encouraged American importers to buy on credit. This flooded the American market with foreign imports at a time when the United States was not exporting much. Because they were buying on credit, the importers spent freely; when the time came to pay the bills, they had to use gold and silver. In this way, most of the hard money in the United States went right back to Europe, leaving Americans with nothing but paper money that was worth much less than its face value because it was not backed by gold and silver reserves.

186. **(C)** The clear, specific, and reasonable set of rules governing the settlement and organization of the Northwest Territory, including the procedure by which each portion of the territory could in future apply for statehood, was a genuine and important achievement. The Articles of Confederation proved an unworkable system of government in just about every other area.

187. **(C)** As soon as the Declaration of Independence was signed and the Virginia resolution was unanimously carried (with one abstention), the colonies were no longer colonies. They were individual states within a new nation, the United States of America. This was when the former colonial assemblies began work on their new state constitutions.

188. (E) Governing the new nation under the Articles of Confederation, Congress established a set of rules for settling the Northwest Territory and eventually accepting its settlers as American citizens. This procedure is called the Land Ordinance of 1787, or the Northwest Ordinance. It banned slavery in the territory but stopped short of emancipating any escaped slaves who found their way there.

189. (C) Under the Articles of Confederation, no individual state had the power to sign a peace treaty without the consent of Congress. Choice (A) appears in Article V, choice (B) appears in Article IV, choice (D) appears in Article VIII, and choice (E) appears in Article VI.

190. (A) *Thoughts on Government* may be considered Adams's response to Thomas Paine's *Common Sense*. Paine argued forcefully that all government was inherently bad because it repressed individual rights and superseded individual judgment. Adams argued that wise government was highly desirable because it was likely to produce a stable, prosperous, and peaceful society.

191. (B) Only in Massachusetts did the people of the state have a chance to read the draft constitution. The first draft approved by the state constitutional convention was read in all the towns. The majority voted against it and offered suggested changes. The final draft (largely written by John Adams) was again sent to the people for approval, along with an essay (generally attributed to Samuel Adams) explaining the convention's reasoning to the people. During the spring of 1780, each clause was ratified by the necessary two-thirds majority vote, and the state constitution became law. This point is important because of the American principle of government by the consent of the governed: the people are sovereign, and it is their representatives' duty to carry out their will. Choices (A), (C), and (D) are wrong because they describe aspects of the process that were common to many of the states besides Massachusetts; Choice (E) is wrong because, while true of other states, it is not true of Massachusetts.

192. (E) The territory that later became the state of Vermont was claimed, in different parts and at different times, by Massachusetts, New Hampshire, and New York. New Hampshire and Massachusetts relinquished their claims to Vermont with little fuss, but New York held out, preventing Vermont from achieving statehood until 1790. The Vermont Constitution is closely modeled on the Declaration of Independence. The Declaration listed the offenses of the king against the colonies; the Vermont Constitution listed the offenses of the New York governors and legislators against Vermont.

193. (B) The Articles of Confederation created no national courts and no chief executive, which eliminates choices (A) and (D). The Articles made no mention of the supreme military commander, which eliminates choice (E). Congress and the individual states had all the power; each had checks over the other, but no one state had power over any of the others, and all states must abide by the final decisions of the Congress. Therefore, the overall governing power was vested in Congress. In practice, of course, Congress was not granted sufficient power to force the states to do much.

194. (B) The purpose of the Annapolis Convention is described in choice (A), but the delegates felt that with only five states present, they could not accomplish this purpose. Instead, they discussed the problems inherent in the Articles of Confederation. This resulted in their official recommendation, made to the individual states and the Congress, that representatives of all the states should gather in Philadelphia in May 1787 to "devise such further provisions as shall seem to them necessary to render the constitution of the federal government adequate to the exigencies of the union." In other words, they called for a Constitutional Convention.

195. (A) The Articles of Confederation are, like the original Constitution, almost silent on the subject of citizens' individual rights. Article IV does specifically grant free interstate travel as the right of "free inhabitants" except for "paupers, vagabonds, and fugitives from justice." Choices (B), (D), and (E) are guaranteed in the Bill of Rights. Choice (C) describes voting rights, which were originally determined by the individual states; later, the Fourteenth, Fifteenth, Nineteenth, and Twenty-Sixth Amendments would address the question of voting rights at the federal level.

196. (D) Articles I and II of the Northwest Ordinance grant all the individual rights described in choices (A), (B), (C), and (E). The ordinance does not mention freedom of speech or freedom of the press.

197. (A) The Articles of Confederation allowed the individual states so much independence that no one state wanted to see any of the others grow too large or powerful. Therefore, territorial expansion was a major concern, and held up the ratification of the Articles until 1781.

198. (D) The Virginia Declaration of Rights would serve as a model for the federal Bill of Rights and for similar measures in other states. It is not a constitution; it does not describe the structure of the Virginia government. It is a declaration of the rights and privileges of the citizens of Virginia, some of which are described in choices (A), (B), (C), and (E). The Virginia Declaration of Rights does not address the question of whether a state has the right to defy a federal law; this question would be taken up in both Virginia and Kentucky during the presidency of John Adams, when Congress passed the Alien and Sedition Acts.

199. (C) Article XIII forbids the states from altering their boundaries without the consent of Congress and the agreement of all the state legislatures.

200. (D) Choice (A) appears in Article V of the Articles of Confederation. Choice (B) appears in Article I, Section 1, of the Constitution. Choice (C) appears in Article II, Section 1 of the Constitution. Choice (E) appears in Article VI of the Constitution. Choice (D) appears in Article VI of the Articles of Confederation and Article I, Section 9, of the Constitution.

201. (B) The colonies established the principle of freedom of the press in the 1730s, when journalist John Peter Zenger criticized the governor of New York in print. With the ratification of the Bill of Rights, the United States became the first nation in the world to pass a law guaranteeing freedom of the press. Choice (A) is wrong because the press does provide an important means for people to discuss their political opinions: journalists write their editorials and articles, and readers respond. Choice (C) is wrong because when a government official has to answer a reporter's question, that reporter represents all of his or her readers who will later have a chance to read or hear the question and the answer. Choice (D) is wrong because the basic job of the press is to inform readers of facts. Choice (E) is wrong because the press plays an important role in reporting any misdeeds committed by government officials. Choice (B) is correct because it does not describe a check on the government's power.

202. (A) If two-thirds of the states request it, or if two-thirds of the senators and members of the House agree to it, Congress must call a national convention for proposing an amendment to the Constitution. The amendment becomes law only if three-fourths of the state legislatures ratify it, or if three-fourths of special conventions called in the states ratify it.

203. (D) The Baron de Montesquieu was the first to describe a three-branch government of checks and balances in *The Spirit of Laws*, his massive work on political theory and history.

204. (D) Article I of the Constitution describes the structure and functions of the legislative branch of the government, including the vice president's role in the Senate. Article II describes the structure and function of the executive branch, including the vice president's responsibility to succeed the president, as described in choice (A).

205. (C) Article II, Section 2, of the Constitution states that the president "shall have the power . . . to make treaties, provided two-thirds of the senators present concur."

206. (B) Federalists were those who supported a federal government—one in which the national and state governments shared the authority to run the country. Therefore, the Federalists supported the Constitution as originally written. The Antifederalists opposed the Constitution because it said nothing about the individual rights and freedoms of the citizens. It was in response to Antifederalist concerns that the Bill of Rights was added to the Constitution.

207. (E) The Preamble declares "We, the People of the United States, . . . do ordain and establish this Constitution for the United States of America." This wording shows the framers' great respect for the principle of what Abraham Lincoln would later describe as "government of the people, by the people, for the people." Almost all of the framers of the Constitution were of British descent, and all believed strongly in this principle, first established as national policy in England in the year 1215.

208. (A) Many people believe the myth that the United States is a democracy; it is not. It is a republic—a form of government in which the citizens elect leaders to represent their wishes, to vote as they would vote, and to give them a voice in their government. No nation in world history is a true popular democracy; it is simply not possible to give all citizens a direct role in their own government in a human society of any size. A *federal* republic is one in which the central government shares power with the individual states or provinces.

209. (E) Under the Articles of Confederation, Congress had been unicameral. Each state had had a number of delegates in proportion to the population, but each state had only one vote. In the Constitutional Convention, there was general agreement on a bicameral legislature. The Great Compromise combined the Virginia Plan's idea for two houses with proportional representation and the New Jersey Plan's idea for two houses with equal representation. Under the Constitution, the states are equally represented in the Senate and proportionally represented in the House.

210. (D) Gouverneur Morris of New York is the author of the Constitution, to the extent that it can be said to have a single author. A committee of five delegates to the convention drafted the document; Morris edited and finalized the draft after open debate. Historians credit Morris as the sole author of the famous Preamble. The other four answer choices all help to explain why Madison is known as "the Father of the Constitution" despite not having actually written its text.

211. (B) All of the framers of the Constitution were regular in their attendance at worship services, whether they were Quakers, Episcopalians, Congregationalists, or Catholics. Religious diversity within the convention itself may have played a role in their decision to include freedom of religious worship as the very first individual right guaranteed to all citizens of the United States.

212. (B) According to Article III, Section 3, treason is defined as either making war against the United States, or giving aid or comfort to enemies of the United States. High government officials can be convicted of crimes, but those crimes only constitute treason if they involve the actions described in choice (B).

213. (D) Choice (D) identifies the first French constitution—which was not written until the Revolution of 1789, some years after the U.S. Constitution. The Declaration of the Rights of Man takes many of its ideas from the Declaration of Independence and the American Bill of Rights, not the other way around. The other four choices were all important influences on the design of the U.S. government.

214. (B) There are really five branches of the U.S. government, each of which can check the powers of the others to a greater or lesser degree: the executive, the judiciary, the legislature, the citizens, and the press. The citizens have the power of their votes; they can send a person to Congress or the White House as their representative, and they can just as easily vote a representative out of office if he or she is dishonest, incompetent, or false. (Of course, in 1789 Senators were chosen by state legislatures, but those state legislatures were elected by the citizens.) Choice (A) is a true statement, but direct communication only gives the citizen the power to make suggestions. Casting a vote is an actual check on a representative's power.

215. (A) According to Article I, Section 3, the Senate has the sole power to try a presidential impeachment. If the Senate votes, by two-thirds majority, that the president is guilty as charged, the Senate can only remove the president from office and ban him or her from holding "any office of honor" in the future. The convicted president is liable for civil and criminal penalties in the courts, but the Senate has no control over this.

216. (C) The Preamble to the Constitution reads as follows: "We the People of the United States, in order to form a more perfect union, establish justice, insure domestic tranquility, provide for the common defense, promote the general welfare, and secure the blessings of liberty to ourselves and our posterity, do ordain and establish this Constitution for the United States of America."

217. (E) In *Common Sense*, Thomas Paine had argued against a hereditary monarchy largely because it elevated people to immense positions of power based solely on the accident of birth. The delegates to the Continental Congress were well-read men who knew their history. They were very well aware of numerous incompetent kings and emperors over the centuries and how disastrous those hereditary rulers had been for their people. The delegates did not believe in letting heredity determine individual rights, legal rights, social privilege, or political power. The new nation they were designing would be a nation wherein, as Thomas Jefferson wrote, all men were created equal, where the laws applied equally to all citizens, and where people rose in society on the basis of merit, not birth. (Sadly, the United States at the time was a two-tier society if not an aristocracy, in which those born Indians or slaves had no rights at all.)

218. (D) It was Alexander Hamilton's idea to use the press to urge New Yorkers to support ratification of the Constitution. Believing that "Publius" should write at least four essays a week, and unable to do so much writing by himself, he pressed his friend and fellow New Yorker John Jay into service. Virginian James Madison was the third and best-prepared author, having taken extensive and detailed notes on the debates during the Constitutional Convention. Hamilton would write 51 of the essays, Madison 29, and Jay, who was badly injured in a street riot early in the process, only 5.

219. (A) As originally written and approved by the members of the Constitutional Convention on September 17, 1787, the Constitution did not have a bill of rights as described in choice (A). The Bill of Rights, consisting of the first 10 amendments, was added to the Constitution on December 15, 1791. Choice (B) appears in Article II, Section 1. Choice (C) appears in Article V. Choice (D) appears in Article III. Choice (E) appears in Article III, Section 2.

220. (B) Indians were not given U.S. citizenship until 1924; they are specifically excluded from the U.S population in Article I, Section 2, of the Constitution. Southern delegates to the Constitutional Convention wanted to count slaves for the purpose of determining population so that their states would have more representatives in Congress. However, they did not want to count them for purposes of taxation, so that their states would be taxed less. Naturally, northern delegates argued that the southerners could not have it both ways; slaves should be counted equally for both population and taxation, or not counted at all. Both sides agreed in the end to count every five slaves as three people, for both taxation and population purposes.

221. (C) The government does have the right to seize private property without consent of the owner when it is in the community's best interest—for example, to lay railroad tracks or build an airport. This is known as the right of eminent domain. The Fifth Amendment only guarantees that the property owner must be fairly compensated.

222. (A) The most famous essay in the *Federalist Papers* is "Federalist 10," which addresses the danger of faction. A faction is, as described in the question, a small group of people who share a common concern or political position—what is today called a lobby or a special-interest group. Madison, who wrote "Federalist 10," pointed out that by their very nature, factions were small; they would never be able to control a government because they would always be outvoted by the majority.

223. (D) Americans who regularly watch crime dramas on television or at the movies are well aware that they have the right to remain silent and to consult an attorney, that the court will appoint them an attorney free of charge if necessary, and that any statements they make can be used against them in court. These are called the Miranda rights because the Supreme Court case *Miranda v. Arizona*, decided in the 1960s, established that the arresting officers must inform all accused persons of their rights. The Constitution guarantees the rights themselves but does not require that accused people be informed of their rights.

224. (A) The states' first attempts at constitutions did not achieve anything like an equal balance of powers within the government; in all cases, the legislature was by far the strongest branch. In those states with bicameral legislatures (which means most of them), the lower house of the legislature was the chief power in the government. The judicial and executive branches had no, or almost no, check on the legislative powers. This caused widespread complaints among the many educated American leaders who believed in the principle of separation of powers in government.

225. (A) The Antifederalists believed that the United States was much too large and diverse a nation to adequately and fairly represent all the far-flung local interests. They were able to bolster this argument with many examples drawn from history. This was not their only objection to the Constitution, but this is the argument they were able to articulate most effectively.

226. (C) The Fourth through Eighth Amendments address the individual citizen's rights under the justice system. The Fourth Amendment protects the citizen from being searched or arrested without a warrant; the Fifth protects him or her from double jeopardy and self-incrimination; the Sixth requires that all trials be speedy, public, and open; the Seventh requires a jury trial in all lawsuits over sums in excess of $20; and the Eighth protects the citizen from excessive fines and cruel or unusual punishments.

227. (B) According to Article II, Section 1, of the Constitution, each elector can vote for two of the presidential candidates. The candidate with the most votes becomes president; the candidate with the next most votes becomes vice president. This is how, in the election of 1796, the United States chose a Federalist president (John Adams) and a Democratic-Republican vice president (Thomas Jefferson). The Twelfth Amendment changed this process to what is described in choice (C): from that time one, the electors have chosen the two executive officers in separate rounds of voting. Very early on, it became customary for the electors to vote along party lines, with the result described in choice (A). However, there is nothing in the law to prevent electors from voting as they choose.

228. (E) *The Life of Equiano* is one of the best-known slave narratives—autobiographies describing the author's experience as a slave and his escape. Ironically, Equiano's autobiography was published in the same year as the U.S. Constitution. Equiano was also known as Gustavus Vassa; he was not only an author, but a notable public speaker on the subject of abolition of slavery and the African slave trade.

229. (A) The Constitution granted each state a number of delegates to the House of Representatives, based on that state's total population—counting every five slaves as three people. Thus, in free states, the Congressmen represented the total population of the state (excluding Indians); but in slaveholding states, they represented only the free (i.e., white) people, since the slaves had no civil rights and no political power and the Indians were not counted. If the number of Congressmen had been based only on the free population, southern states would have had significantly fewer representatives, and, therefore, much less influence over national policy in the decades before the Civil War.

230. (B) Choice (A) is wrong because the *Federalist Papers* defend federalism—a form of government in which the states and the central government share the governing powers. Choice (C) is wrong because "Federalist 10" in particular discusses the dangers of faction (i.e., special-interest groups) at length. Choice (D) is wrong because the *Federalist Papers* defend the division of ruling powers into different branches of the government, as described in the Constitution. Choice (E) is wrong because the U.S. government was a republic—a form of government in which freely elected representatives carry out the will of their constituents.

231. (D) Patrick Henry and George Clinton led the Antifederalist side in a lengthy constitutional debate with the Federalists in the Virginia legislature. The two sides eventually agreed to compromise—Virginia would ratify the Constitution but would propose to add a bill of rights to it. The legislature eventually agreed on a list of 20 suggested amendments. In the end, the Bill of Rights adopted by the federal government reflected most of the Virginia Antifederalists' concerns.

232. (B) Only Congress can declare war, but the president is the commander in chief of the military and has the power to decide how the war will be conducted. In practice, of course, the president does not actually lead troops into battle; he or she communicates constantly with the generals and admirals and takes their experience and advice into consideration in giving orders. As one example of how the system works, Congress formally declared war on Japan in 1941, but President Truman gave the order to drop the atomic bombs on Hiroshima and Nagasaki in 1945.

233. (E) Each state decides how its own governor will be chosen; the Constitution does not determine state laws except to require that they conform to federal laws. Supreme Court justices are nominated by the president and approved by the Senate. The president is chosen by the electors from all the states. In the original Constitution, senators were appointed by the state legislatures; this did not change until the passage of the Seventeenth Amendment in 1913.

234. (C) The first thing on which the delegates agreed was to close the doors and windows of the Pennsylvania State House during the debates. They wanted all representatives present to speak their own minds without fear of any pressures or reprisals coming from outside the building.

235. (D) Choice (A) is a check of the executive branch on the legislative branch. Choices (B), (C), and (E) are false statements. The president nominates justices; the Senate must approve the nominations.

236. (C) The missing freedom is the freedom to petition the government for a redress of grievances.

237. (A) If the president vetoes a bill passed by Congress, Congress can override the veto by a two-thirds majority vote. The bill then becomes law until such time as it is successfully challenged by a case in the Supreme Court.

238. (E) The Eighth Amendment guarantees choice (A). The Ninth and Tenth Amendments guarantee choice (B). The Fourth Amendment guarantees choice (C). The Fifth Amendment guarantees choice (D). The Constitution did not address voting rights at all until after the Civil War, when it guaranteed voting rights to former slaves.

239. (D) The people do not vote directly for the president and vice president; they vote for a slate of electors who have made a (nonbinding, but very rarely flouted) commitment to vote for those candidates. Members of Congress, Supreme Court justices, and governors vote like all other citizens, in their private capacity as individuals.

240. (E) Choice (A) is wrong because all the delegates had agreed to keep their proceedings secret, in order to protect themselves from outside threats or pressure. Choice (B) states the opposite of the reality; the Antifederalists feared a strong central government because it was bound to weaken the states' self-governing powers. Choice (C) is wrong because the president's powers as described in the Constitution are quite limited. Choice (D) is the opposite of the reality; if the president were chosen by direct popular vote, that would be democratic. The Antifederalists' main concern was that the Constitution had no bill of rights.

241. (A) The Alien and Sedition Acts were the first of many such provisions Congress has made in times of war or impending war. At such times, the U.S. government has often curtailed individual liberties because of concern about national security. The Patriot Act, signed in the wake of the 2001 terrorist attack, is among the most recent examples. The Alien and Sedition Acts made it illegal to act or speak against the government, and they allowed the government to deport anyone not a U.S. citizen who seemed to be a threat to national security.

242. (B) *Judicial review* is the power of the Supreme Court to examine the legality of a law passed by Congress. The Supreme Court has the power to repeal any law it deems unconstitutional. This is an important check the judicial branch of the government maintains on the power of the legislative branch.

243. (C) Jefferson's political rival Alexander Hamilton argued that the Constitution had a built-in "elastic clause" that allowed for it to be interpreted in the light of new customs and circumstances as they arose. Jefferson had always argued the opposite: that the Constitution was meant to be strictly obeyed exactly as it was written. Jefferson defied his own position by purchasing the Louisiana Territory; he exercised a power that is not specified anywhere in the Constitution.

244. (B) *Impressment* is an important term for this period of U.S. history because it was a contributing cause to the War of 1812. A ship's crew would literally kidnap men, take them on board, and force or "press" them into service on the ship. Impressment usually happened when two enemy ships met on the high seas, although Britain also pressed its own citizens into service by taking solitary men prisoner in the ports. Both the Royal Navy and the British merchant marine practiced impressment. The U.S. government protested that British ships had no right to press Americans into service, but Britain refused to stop the practice.

245. (E) Scottish economist Adam Smith espoused capitalism, in which business and industries are privately owned and free-market competition determines wages and prices. Hamilton's support for Smith's ideas are largely responsible for the way the U.S. economy took shape.

246. (C) The Democratic-Republicans supported Thomas Jefferson, whose political beliefs are described in choices (A), (B), (D), and (E). The Federalists and their leader, Alexander Hamilton, supported an alliance with Britain. (Britain and France have been allies only since World War I; until that time the two nations were enemies.)

247. (E) Despite having pursued a military career, George Washington did not believe that the United States should get involved in foreign wars. He felt that for one thing, the nation was too young and unformed to be distracted by any political quarrels outside its own borders. Strengthening the U.S. government, putting the nation on a sound financial footing, repaying debts, and other such matters were Washington's priorities. Despite the fact that France had helped the Americans win their revolution against Britain, Washington refused to send U.S. troops to France when the French rebelled against their king.

248. (C) The United States would not acquire Spanish Florida until the Adams-Onís Treaty of 1819.

249. (A) With Hamilton's urging and support, Congress founded the Bank of the United States in 1791 and created the mint that stamped the first U.S. coins in 1792. The soaring national debt led Hamilton to begin selling government bonds to pay it down; he also urged the assessment of new taxes and an increase of those that already existed.

250. (B) The Embargo Act severely curtailed American exports. Jefferson's goal was to stop the practice of impressment by eliminating contact between British and American ships on the high seas. The act backfired because it hurt the American economy by making exports drop to one-fifth of their previous levels. It was repealed after two years.

251. (D) Jefferson and Madison, the most prominent of the Democratic-Republicans, believed that the Alien and Sedition Acts violated First Amendment rights. They urged the passage of the Virginia and Kentucky resolutions, which declared that the states could not be compelled to obey unconstitutional federal laws.

252. (D) Pennsylvania farmers had long turned their surplus grain crops into whiskey, then bartered the whiskey for tools and other supplies they could not make or grow. The new tax on whiskey, created to help pay down the national debt, would eliminate their profits.

253. (E) The Democratic-Republicans supported Jefferson's beliefs: that agriculture was the mainstay of the economy, that the balance of federal power should rest with the states, that the United States should honor its alliance with France, and that federal powers were limited by the exact wording of the Constitution. The Federalists supported Hamilton's beliefs that business, trade, and manufacturing were the cornerstone of the economy; that the balance of federal power should rest with the central government, not the states; that the United States should ally itself with Britain; and that the Constitution was intended to be elastic enough to suit the changing needs of changing times.

254. (A) The Twelfth Amendment is a reworking of the electoral college system outlined in Article II, Section 1, of the Constitution. In 1800, the electoral college resulted in a tie between Jefferson and Aaron Burr. The election then went to the House of Representatives, resulting in a deadlock that the Congressmen were unable to break in 36 attempts. In the end, Jefferson won a majority. The Twelfth Amendment would prevent this situation from occurring again. Note on choice (E): This describes the Eleventh Amendment.

255. (B) Washington did not believe in partisan politics; he neither belonged to nor represented any political party. He is the only U.S. president to claim this distinction. Numerous presidents have maintained isolationism in foreign affairs. A few, such as Jackson, Eisenhower, and Grant, rose from army general to president. Many, such as Reagan and Clinton, had not previously been elected to national office. Choice (E) is simply not true; Washington was twice elected president under the rules of the U.S. Constitution (although he did run unopposed).

256. (C) The War Hawks (a group of Congressmen that included Henry Clay of Kentucky and John Calhoun of South Carolina) enthusiastically supported going to war against Britain. Their chief goal is described in choice (C); they hoped to annex East Florida and perhaps add Canada to the rapidly expanding nation.

257. (D) Of the first four U.S. presidents, Adams was the only representative of New England; the other three were from Virginia. Early U.S. political leaders represented all regions of the country. For example, Alexander Hamilton and Aaron Burr grew up in New Jersey and later represented New York.

258. (B) Burr served with distinction as a high-ranking officer in the Continental Army; he put down a mutiny at Valley Forge in 1778. The notorious duel with Hamilton was the result of years of personal and political enmity. As vice president, Burr presided over the impeachment of Chase, and set several important precedents for future impeachments. Burr was tried for conspiring with Spain but was acquitted due to lack of evidence. In 1800, he and Jefferson received the same number of votes for president in the electoral college, leading to a long-drawn-out deadlock in the House of Representatives.

259. (D) The nation's capital was nothing but a parcel of swampland on the Maryland-Virginia border when it was chosen to be the seat of the U.S. government; it did not even have a name at that time. The location was chosen to pacify southern resentment over the federal assumption of debt owed by northern states. Philadelphia had been the nation's capital for some years; New York served for a short period as a temporary capital city. The District of Columbia was named "Washington" only after it was chosen for the capital.

260. (B) Banning further importation of slaves was, of course, not the same thing as abolishing slavery. Southerners were content to accept the ban for two reasons. The first is given in choice (B): slaves would continue to produce children who would inherit their mothers' slave status in spite of the fact that many of these children had white fathers. The second was fear of future slave uprisings if the African population began to outnumber the white. Importing slaves would make the black population grow faster, since there was very little white immigration into the South from Europe. (In fact, an illegal slave trade would continue for some time.)

261. (A) Benjamin Franklin never served in a presidential administration. His final efforts on behalf of his country were in the Constitutional Convention and on important diplomatic missions in France. Franklin died in 1790, just a few months after George Washington's first election.

262. (D) The principle of judicial review means that the Supreme Court can pass judgment on the legality of any law made by Congress or by one of the individual states. Of course, this can only happen if a citizen decides to bring a case to trial *and* if that case is appealed all the way through the lower court system to the Supreme Court.

263. (E) Most of the American cotton crop was sold to Europe. The Napoleonic Wars involved all the major European powers, as well as some of the minor ones. While the wars went on, international trade slowed to a trickle. With no buyers for their cotton, and with a series of new trade restrictions in place because of the international situation, the South reached the point of economic collapse. American profits would soar after 1815, when the wars ended and the South could once again sell its cotton abroad.

264. (A) The Hartford Convention was a gathering of New England Federalists who opposed both the War of 1812 and the economic and trade policies of the Democratic-Republican administrations. Its members drew up a list of suggested constitutional amendments. These included: requiring a two-thirds majority vote in Congress for admitting new states, declaring war, and halting international trade; limiting the president to one term in office; and banning the possibility of two successive presidents from the same home state. There is evidence that some delegates advocated New England's secession from the United States, but there is no proof that the convention voted on secession or passed any resolutions relating to it.

265. (C) In 1805, Lieutenant Pike accepted a military commission to explore the northern Louisiana Territory. The expedition followed the Mississippi River north to Leach Lake but did not discover the source of the river (Lake Itasca). In 1806, Pike led another expedition, this time heading more or less directly west from St. Louis. At the mountain that now bears Pike's name, the party turned south and penetrated deep into Mexico, where Pike was arrested on suspicion of spying. Unable to prove a case against Pike, the Spanish authorities released him.

266. (A) When U.S. diplomats went to France to negotiate a settlement over the issue of seizure of American ships in the Caribbean, three French agents offered them a substantial bribe and requested approval of a $10 million loan to France. When President John Adams reported the affair to Congress, he referred to the Frenchmen as X, Y, and Z instead of naming them.

267. (D) Fighting broke out between U.S. troops and members of the Miami, Delaware, Shawnee, and other tribes in the Northwest Territory. The Treaty of Greenville settled the terms of the peace in 1795; it includes the provisions described in choices (A), (B), (C), and (E). The treaty generally states that the Indians are to live as they please, unmolested, as long as they maintain peaceful relations with the United States. It specifically forbids the Indians from selling their new territory to any agent except the United States, and it requires them to provide right-of-way and other privileges to Americans on their lands. Therefore the Indians' rights to their own territory were not absolute but limited.

268. (A) Lewis and Clark's route took them through Missouri, along the present Nebraska-Iowa border, and on to Washington and the Pacific coast through the Dakotas, Montana, and Idaho. A glance at a present-day U.S. map shows that the party's route was nearly 200 miles to the north of Colorado.

269. (E) The Treaty of Ghent was signed in that city in December 1814. Apart from a clause stating that the nations would work together to eliminate the slave trade, it does not discuss trade agreements except by implication, with such phrases as "restoring upon principles of perfect reciprocity peace, friendship, and good understanding" between the nations.

270. (C) The Democratic-Republicans supported Adams in his desire to avoid war with France. The Federalists, Adams's own party, were split on the issue. Some Federalists supported Adams, either because he was the president of their own party, or from personal loyalty, or from genuine political conviction. Other Federalists, led by Hamilton, criticized the president and opposed his foreign policy. Adams's hard work to maintain peace with France was successful in the end.

271. (E) War with both British and Indians kept many Americans too busy to think about moving westward. Western traders and farmers were hampered by the lack of any efficient means of transporting their goods east for sale. Meanwhile, in the settled East, the economy had collapsed because the Napoleonic Wars all but halted U.S. exports to Europe. With no spare cash, easterners could not afford to move west.

272. (A) Spain did not formally cede Florida to the United States until 1819; the Florida Territory did not become a state until 1845. Only Indiana and Vermont, plus the four states listed in the other choices, joined the original 13 states before January 1, 1817.

273. (B) The Louisiana Purchase did not affect the decision to go to war except very indirectly. The purchase of the territory had encouraged settlement of the interior, and the interior was suffering an economic depression because the Napoleonic Wars and British naval blockades had temporarily closed the market for American goods. The other four choices all describe the various motives that impelled the United States to declare war on Great Britain.

274. (C) The expedition had several purposes, which are described in choices (A), (B), (D), and (E). The primary purpose was choice (B)—to find the mythical "Northwest Passage." Jefferson's instructions to Lewis and Clark did not include a request to register the Indian tribes they met along the way—merely to establish friendly relations with them and bring back accurate information about their languages, customs, and so on.

275. (A) When Jefferson and Burr both received the same number of votes for president, the election was thrown to the House of Representatives. In 35 additional rounds of voting, the House failed to break the tie. Hamilton disagreed with Jefferson on most major issues, but he actively loathed Burr and considered him unfit for high office. Therefore, Hamilton persuaded the electors to vote for Jefferson. Due to Hamilton's machinations, the tie was finally broken; Jefferson became president, and Burr became vice president. Congress swiftly passed the Twelfth Amendment, which established new electoral procedures in order to prevent a future constitutional crisis like that of 1800.

Chapter 4: The 19th Century:
Politics, Economics, and Culture to 1865

276. (D) Choice (A) is too sweeping because the Monroe Doctrine declared that the United States would regard any European attack on or annexation of territory in the Western Hemisphere as an attack on the United States itself. Choice (B) is wrong because the document declared that the United States would remain neutral between any European colony and its mother country. Choice (C) is wrong because the document declares support not for colonies but for independent republics or nations. Choice (E) is wrong because the document was not a formal alliance with Latin America, merely a gesture of potential support.

277. (D) The missing nation is the Chickasaw; the Sac and Fox nation was a long way to the north, just west of the Great Lakes. The Five Civilized Tribes were the last to leave the Southeast for Indian Territory, having refused to go voluntarily under the terms of the Indian Removal Act of 1830. In 1838 and 1839, they were forced to relocate from central Florida, northern Georgia, eastern Alabama, and northern Mississippi to Indian Territory (eastern Oklahoma). This forced march is called the Trail of Tears because thousands of Indians died en route—probably as many as one-quarter of the total number.

278. (E) Choice (A) is wrong because in 1809, Maryland became the first state to change its constitution so that African men could not vote. Other slaveholding states soon did the same. Choice (B) is wrong because by 1840, all states had dropped the requirement of property ownership, meaning that all free adult men (including Africans in some states) could vote. This had the effect of doubling the number of eligible voters across the nation. Choice (C) is wrong because Andrew Jackson instituted rotations of office in the bureaucracy in order to combat corruption and political patronage. Choice (D) is wrong because the first national nominating conventions were held in 1832 and have been a fixture of U.S politics ever since. Choice (E) is correct because it describes the Seventeenth Amendment, which was not ratified until 1913.

279. (C) The Missouri Compromise maintained the current balance of power in Congress by admitting Missouri to the Union as a slaveholding state and Maine as a free state. It also banned slavery in all territory north of Missouri's southern boundary, excluding Missouri itself. Both sides grudgingly accepted the Missouri Compromise because it maintained the status quo. In addition, southerners accepted it because it did not appear to threaten the system of slavery.

280. (A) During the first half of the 19th century, a *filibuster* was a rogue American adventurer who grabbed Latin American territory, sometimes claiming it for the United States but more often claiming that he and his followers had the right to rule it themselves. Examples include Narciso Lopez's failed attempts to take over Cuba, and William Walker's temporary seizure of Baja California from Mexico. Acting as they did without authority from the U.S. government, filibusters were a national embarrassment and their antics created serious diplomatic problems for the White House. Some Americans, especially southerners, supported the filibusters on the grounds of manifest destiny. The filibuster movement came to an end with the outbreak of the Civil War.

281. (A) The Whigs felt that the presidency had taken too much control from Congress during Andrew Jackson's administration. Some Whig leaders believed that Jackson had abused the power of the presidency; others personally disliked the man for his style and perhaps for his common, log-cabin background.

282. (C) The Know-Nothings were fiercely opposed to immigration, especially Irish immigration. Thousands of Europeans crossed the Atlantic every year, seeking economic opportunity in the United States. Conveniently forgetting that their own parents or grandparents had been immigrants, Know-Nothings embraced the principle of nativism—the belief that people born in the United States deserved greater rights and privileges than immigrants. Their name comes from the response all party members gave when questioned about nativist acts of vandalism, or even about their own party's existence: "I know nothing of that."

283. (B) Choice (B) is too sweeping. The Republican Party of 1856 was certainly an antislavery party, but the candidates did not even suggest emancipating slaves throughout the South. Their goal was to check the spread of slavery in the territories; their motives were a combination of business, political, and humanitarian concerns.

284. (D) The Republicans supported a homestead act—a bill stating that the government would sell a homestead (80 to 160 acres, known as a quarter-section) either free or at a nominal price to anyone who met the requirements (see answer 383). At the end of five years, the farmer would file papers proving that he or she had actually lived and worked on the claim throughout. Once the claim was proved, the farmer owned the land outright. Settlers supported a homestead act because it was a very economical way to start out life; politicians supported it because it sped up the process of settling the West and organizing the territories for admission to the United States.

285. (B) The Indian Removal Act states that any Indian tribe wishing to move west could trade its current territory for equivalent territory west of the Mississippi. If the tribe claimed that it had improved the land, the U.S. government would assess the claim and compensate the tribe financially. The act clearly states that it applies to only "such tribes or nations of Indians as may choose to exchange their lands," and that the new territory into which they moved would be theirs in perpetuity. In actual fact, of course, the act was compulsory, not a matter of choice. It was intended to push the Indians as far as possible to the west of the territory that was continuing to fill up with white settlers (and, in the South, with African slaves as well).

286. (E) South Carolina opposed the Tariff Acts of 1828 and 1832 so strongly that its legislature refused to obey them, declaring them unconstitutional for the reasons described in choices (A) through (D). Choice (E) would not have been a reasonable claim, because the Tariff Acts were proposed in Congress and thus the representatives of the people had every opportunity to debate them and vote on them. (For President Andrew Jackson's response to the specific grievances in the Ordinance, see answer 301.)

287. (C) In the 1640s, the Tokugawa shogunate completed the process of closing Japan off from what it regarded as the corrupting influences of the outside world. Japanese citizens could not leave the islands, and the only contact with foreigners was the closely monitored trading with a small number of Chinese and Dutch merchants. In 1853, the United States sent a small fleet commanded by Matthew Perry to negotiate a trade agreement with Japan. Since Japan had not advanced technologically during its period of isolation, it had no weapons with which to combat the American warships; the Japanese gave in gracefully to the presidential requests (actually more like demands) contained in the papers Perry carried. (For details of the Treaty of Kanagawa, see answer 305.)

288. (E) It was Harrison's campaign advisers, not Van Buren's, who strongly advised their candidate to avoid speaking out on any political issue. Harrison was the Whig's candidate, and the party was made of so many disparate factions that taking a firm position on any issue risked losing votes. The same risk did not apply to Van Buren because, as the incumbent president, his record was already known. In addition, the Democrats were a more united party at that time.

289. (C) By 1825, Spain and Russia had given up their claims to the Oregon Country, leaving the United States, Great Britain, and the Indians in occupation. In 1846, the United States and Britain agreed to extend the U.S.-Canadian border all the way to the westward tip of the mainland, with the United States taking all the land south of the border and Britain taking all the land north of the border plus Vancouver Island. The United States was guaranteed control of Puget Sound as part of the Oregon Treaty.

290. (A) The United States did not have the military might to enforce the Monroe Doctrine. Great Britain, however, did have the necessary military force, and its interests aligned with those of the United States. Britain did not want Spain retaking Mexico or any other Latin American colonies that broke free, because these new republics were profitable markets for British goods. Therefore, Britain placed the full strength of its navy behind the Monroe Doctrine.

291. (E) During the debate over Missouri's application for statehood, Congressman James Tallmadge of New York pointed out that Missouri had violated the Northwest Ordinance, which prohibited slavery in all U.S. territories. Therefore, Tallmadge suggested that Missouri be admitted to the United States on condition that it develop a plan to phase slavery out gradually. This aroused such strong opposition from southern Congressmen that Henry Clay suggested the Missouri Compromise, whose provisions are described in the first four answer choices.

292. (B) The Free-Soil Party was founded on the basis of support for abolition; therefore it was opposed to the interests of the southern Democrats. Settlers of the western territories opposed slavery because they believed it was against their economic interests.

293. (C) The Trail of Tears can refer either to the forced relocation of the southeastern tribes or to the various routes that they used to reach Indian Territory (present-day Oklahoma). The U.S. government escorted tens of thousands of Cherokees, Choctaws, Chickasaws, Creeks, and Seminoles, traveling overland by wagon caravan or upriver by steamboat. Starvation, disease, emotional trauma, steamboat accidents, and exposure to all weather conditions combined to kill off perhaps a quarter of the total number of refugees en route, thus giving the Trail of Tears its name.

294. (B) The United States gained the territories of East and West Florida in this treaty with Spain. The United States actually lost territory in the Southwest, conceding a long-standing Spanish claim that the Red River, not the Rio Grande, was the U.S.-Mexican border.

295. (A) Jackson did win the popular vote in 1824, and he did come in first in the electoral college vote. However, according to the Twelfth Amendment, receiving the largest number of electoral college votes was not enough; the successful candidate must receive a majority of the votes (in other words, 50 percent of the total, plus one). Since no candidate received a majority, the election was thrown to the House, where a clear majority chose John Quincy Adams as president.

296. (E) The doctrine of nullification says that no state can be forced to obey an unconstitutional law. Former cabinet member John C. Calhoun first articulated the doctrine of nullification in an 1828 essay called "The South Carolina Exposition and Protest." He argued that the Tariff Act of 1828, which was opposed throughout the South, was unconstitutional because the tariffs were not being assessed for the purpose of raising revenue but for protecting manufacturing interests over agricultural ones. According to Calhoun's point of view, this was unconstitutional under the Tenth Amendment. (For President Andrew Jackson's response, see answer 301.)

297. (C) The primary issue in 1844 was the potential annexation of Texas and the popular new slogan "manifest destiny"—the belief that the United States had the divine right and duty to take over all the territory between the Atlantic and Pacific Oceans and between Canada and the Rio Grande. James K. Polk, who favored expansion, won the election with a clear electoral majority.

298. (C) Adams served his country in almost every imaginable way except on the battlefield. In addition to the achievements listed in choices (A), (B), (D), and (E), he represented the United States at the Russian court during his youth, served as foreign minister to Holland and Prussia, and served one term as president of the United States. Adams literally served his government throughout his entire adult life; he died on the job, collapsing in the House of Representatives in 1848 at age 80.

299. (D) The Cherokee declared their territory a sovereign nation in 1827—a clear sign of resistance to assimilation within the United States. Since Cherokee territory was officially part of both the state of Georgia and the United States, this created a conflict. When the Cherokee sued Georgia for trying to expel them from their lands, the Supreme Court found that they were not a sovereign nation and, therefore, were not eligible to sue. The other four choices all describe ways that suggest the Cherokee wished to fit into the rest of the nation; Choice **(D)** describes a way in which they clearly preferred to stand apart.

300. (B) The Convention of 1818 addressed minor issues that Britain and the United States had not settled at the end of the War of 1812. Choice (B) does not fit because Britain had no involvement in any border disputes between Spain and the United States. The border described in choice (B) was agreed as part of the Adams-Onís Treaty of 1819.

301. (D) Jackson's proclamation was issued in response to the South Carolina Nullification Ordinance. His own words best sum up his argument: "The ordinance is founded, not on the indefeasible right of resisting acts which are plainly unconstitutional, and too oppressive to be endured, but on the strange position that any one State may not only declare an act of Congress void, but prohibit its execution." Jackson argued that both the Articles of Confederation and the Constitution clearly stated that Congress was the supreme law of the land and that the states must be governed by it. Choices (A), (C), and (E) describe his responses to South Carolina's specific grounds for objecting to the Tariff Acts. The quotation provided here implies that Jackson recognized the right of a state to defy a federal law that was "plainly unconstitutional" or overly harsh.

302. (A) Charles Bagot of Great Britain and Richard Rush of the United States signed this agreement, which limited both nations to a maximum of two warships on each of the five Great Lakes at any one time.

303. (D) During the 1850s, France attempted to force the king of Hawaii to accept annexation more or less at gunpoint. Invoking the principles of the Monroe Doctrine, Fillmore spoke strongly in support of Hawaiian autonomy.

304. (E) In the summer of 1832, Jackson vetoed a bill to extend the charter of the Second Bank for another 20 years. (The bank's charter had four years still to run at this time.) Congress failed to override the presidential veto, and the bank's future became the central issue of the campaign. Jackson believed that the bank catered to foreigners and the wealthy at the expense of the common working people. In his campaign, he successfully portrayed it as the institution of the rich, and he was reelected by a large plurality. Once its charter expired in 1836, the Second Bank continued to operate as an ordinary bank for only five years before it closed.

305. (C) Japan signed the Treaty of Kanagawa more or less at gunpoint. The Japanese had no way to fight off American warships and preferred to concede without losing face, rather than to fight a losing battle and be humiliated. Article V of the treaty specifies that U.S. citizens would not be subject to the same restrictions as the Chinese and Dutch traders, but would be able to move about freely in the port, subject to reasonable Japanese laws. Choice (A) is covered in Article VI of the treaty, Choice (B) in Articles II and X, Choice (D) in Article I, and Choice (E) in Article IX.

306. (B) In 1833, Oberlin became the first U.S. college at which a woman student could earn the same four-year degree as a man. Oberlin became racially integrated only two years later.

307. (A) The potato famine of the 1840s caused many impoverished Irishmen and women to cross the Atlantic to the United States. They were not warmly welcomed in a society where people of British descent still held most of the power in both politics and society; the Protestant British traditionally despised the Roman Catholic Irish. However, the Irish were tenacious and determined to succeed despite the discrimination they faced on arrival. By the 1880s this immigrant group had become a powerful political force.

308. (A) The Mormons first established themselves in northeastern Ohio. They quickly wore out their welcome among non-Mormons for their unorthodox beliefs and their habit of favoring Mormon clients and customers over all others. Even Mormons themselves drew the line at polygamy (first practiced 14 years after the denomination had been founded), and many objected to founder Joseph Smith's autocratic ways. No disagreement was tolerated among the Mormons; Smith and his followers smashed the printing presses of the dissenting group. The Mormon community had to move several times to escape non-Mormon hostility.

309. (E) Temperance advocates wanted men to limit or cease their consumption of alcohol. (The movement did specifically target men because respectable women did not drink in public at this time and place.) They argued that the all-male saloon or bar was destructive to the institution of the family. It encouraged men to behave irresponsibly, gamble, get drunk, and spend their time with prostitutes. The temperance movement hoped to shut down all the saloons, believing that men would then behave responsibly, use their wages to support their wives and children, and spend their spare time at home with their families.

310. (A) Macpherson was a temperance advocate. The missing name from the list of five organizers of the Seneca Falls Convention is Jane Hunt (1812–1889), a native of Philadelphia and the wife of a prominent New York Quaker. Hunt, McClintock, Mott, and Wright were all Quakers—a faith that allowed women to preach on equal terms with men. Having grown up in a tradition that practiced gender equality no doubt influenced these women to support women's rights on a national scale.

311. (D) The American Colonization Society was a group of reformers who wanted to end slavery. The idea behind it was to establish a free African colony in Africa, so that free Africans and freed slaves could return to the continent of their ancestors. The colony of Monrovia, named for President James Monroe, was duly established in West Africa in 1822 (today its name is Liberia). Most Africans, however, did not want to resettle in what they regarded as a foreign country; what they wanted was full equality, freedom, and civil rights in the United States, which was their native country and their home.

312. (B) David Walker (c. 1785–1830), a free African-American, can be considered the spearhead of the abolitionist movement in the United States. *Freedom's Journal* was the nation's first black newspaper. The *Appeal* was among the most fiery abolitionist documents of the time; it urged armed rebellion in print, thus alarming white southerners. In the *Appeal,* Walker quoted from the Declaration of Independence, stressing language about equality and liberty. The Massachusetts General Colored Association was a forerunner of the NAACP; its purpose was to promote and protect African-American rights and interests.

313. (A) The purpose of the Seneca Falls Convention was to call for legal and social reform throughout the United States. It was not simply a fight for the right to vote; in fact, this suggestion seemed so revolutionary that few people supported it at the time. Women were fighting for many civil and social rights: attending college, owning property, controlling their own earnings, and so on. The Seneca Falls Convention was the first of many such national meetings; collectively, these meetings were responsible for converting tens of thousands of people to the cause.

314. (C) Turner's rebellion did not lead to a wave of similar uprisings. The other four choices all describe what happened during or after the rebellion. William Lloyd Garrison, the author and publisher of *The Liberator*, would probably have been lynched had he ventured into the South at this time.

315. (C) Choice (C) does not represent Mann's ideas. The other four choices explain why he played such an important role in the development of the American public school system. As head of the Board of Education of Massachusetts, Mann was in a highly influential position, and most other states adopted the reforms he instituted in Massachusetts.

316. (B) The exclusively male state legislatures had no reasonable grounds on which to support their insistence on denying women the right to vote; they could only justify it by tradition. Choice (A) is too sweeping; free women were second-class citizens at best, but they did enjoy greater civil and legal rights than slaves. Choice (C) is wrong because there are no constitutional grounds for inequality; the Constitution uses the word *person*, not *man*, in its description of the qualifications for high office, and nowhere does it suggest that women have fewer rights than men. Choice (D) is obviously wrong because denying women the right to vote means insisting on a government that is NOT consented to by half the governed. Choice (E) is wrong because the majority of American women were literate, and many were very well-educated.

317. (E) Wilde (1854–1900) did visit the United States on a lecture tour, but he did not write a book about American society; his literary career postdates the Civil War. The other four choices provide a fascinating outside point of view of American customs, society, and government. *American Notes for General Circulation* describes Dickens's impressions of such institutions as the Lowell textile mills and Philadelphia's Eastern State Penitentiary. He toured the United States in 1842. Kemble was a British actress who married a southern plantation owner; her *Journals*, published in the 1830s, paint an unsparing picture of slavery. For Tocqueville's *Democracy in America*, see answer 325. Trollope was a prolific British novelist (as was her son Anthony); her nonfiction work *Domestic Manners of the Americans* (1832) savages American culture, society, and the national character. Trollope based the work on her short-term residency in the Midwest.

318. (B) The South did not have factories, businesses, or a mercantile economy; wealthy financiers and businessmen were strictly a northern social class at this period in U.S. history.

319. (C) Douglass (1817–1895) published an important autobiography about his experiences as a slave and his escape to freedom; he was also an outspoken abolitionist and an advocate of women's rights. Emerson (1803–1882) and Thoreau (1817–1862) were noted essayists. Whitman (1819–1892) was a newspaper editor and journalist as well as the author of the remarkable free-verse autobiography *Song of Myself*, part of his larger poetry collection *Leaves of Grass*. Henry James (1843–1916) was also a great American writer, but from a somewhat later period; the bulk of his novels and short stories appeared between 1871 and 1900.

320. (E) Truth (c. 1797–1883) was born and raised in upstate New York; as a northern slave, she never lived in the South and therefore did not help other slaves to escape on the Underground Railroad. She left slavery behind in her early 30s, and spent the rest of her long life actively engaged in the endeavors described in choices (A) through (D). Truth was also a noted itinerant preacher.

321. (B) *Leaves of Grass* is the work of Walt Whitman; he continued adding to this unique collection of free-verse poems until near the end of his life, publishing several new and expanded editions. Whitman is historically significant for writing a free-verse autobiography, *Song of Myself* (included in *Leaves of Grass*). He also worked as a journalist and later served as a hospital nurse during the Civil War. Emily Dickinson of Massachusetts wrote hundreds of lyric poems, as avant-garde in their own way as Whitman's free verse. Dickinson was a recluse who rarely ventured beyond her own garden gate; most of her poems were published posthumously.

322. (B) Francis Scott Key wrote the poem "Defense of Fort McHenry" during the War of 1812. Set to British tunes, Francis Scott Key's lyric poem "Defense of Fort McHenry" and Samuel Smith's lyric "My Country, 'Tis of Thee" were both popular patriotic songs of the 19th century. Key was an eyewitness to the battle of his poem's title, which took place in 1814. "The Star-Spangled Banner" became the national anthem in 1931.

323. (A) New Jersey's 1776 constitution granted women the right to vote if they owned the requisite amount of property, but this law was overturned in 1807. Women would not regain the right to vote until after the Civil War; several individual states granted them this right during the last quarter of the 19th century. In 1920, the Nineteenth Amendment granted all American women age 21 and over the right to vote. Note on choices (D) and (E): Single women, of course, could own and control their own property and wages, but they automatically lost that ownership and control to their husbands upon marriage. If a single woman lived with her parents, as many did, she would be expected to contribute her earnings to the household expenses and would not be likely to own property.

324. (D) The Morrill Act granted 17 million acres of federal land to the states, with the requirement that they sell the land to businesses or individuals and use the profits to found and build agricultural and engineering colleges. These land-grant colleges continue to flourish throughout the nation as the state university system. Today, they offer a high-quality education in dozens of disciplines, at a substantial discount for students who are residents of the state.

325. (E) Tocqueville (1805–1859) was a French political thinker who traveled to the United States in 1831; *Democracy in America* (1835–1840) was the product of his trip. Tocqueville examines the republican form of government, tracing its development from the earliest colonial days. He describes government at the local, state, and federal levels. He considers issues such as the freedom of the press and explains why and how the U.S. government truly does function only by the consent of the governed. He predicts challenges and difficulties that seemed likely to arise, given the social, economic, and political conditions he found on his journey. The book is a classic of its genre, not only for its clearly stated observations but also for the accuracy of its conclusions; many of Tocqueville's predictions have come to pass in the 170-odd years since its publication. Note: Choice (B) is contained within the book, but only as one aspect of choice (E), the book's main focus.

326. (E) Both small-scale and large-scale farmers benefited from the invention of the mechanical reaper. An individual farmer and his sons, with a few hired hands, could easily farm a vast number of acres by using the reaper.

327. (D) The steamboat was of great benefit to the southern economy because it greatly eased the process of shipping cotton upstream (i.e., against the current) to the northern textile mills. The other four answer choices all help to explain why the South did not experience any kind of industrial boom while the North and West did.

328. (C) Labor unions were still a little way in the future; the Lowell workers did not have a union. However, they did enjoy the highest salaries paid to any working women in the United States. Many soon had substantial bank accounts in their own names—an unusual measure of independence for an American woman at the time. (Note: The company actually saved money on the women, because their salaries were much lower than a man's would have been.) The "mill girls" had limited free time in which to enjoy the attractions of the city, to read and study, and even to publish their own newspaper, the *Lowell Offering*. They paid a small sum to live in the boardinghouses but were not required to cook or do housework. Of course, the work was backbreaking, the hours were long, the chaperonage was probably irksome to many, and the air in the mills was heavy with lint and fluff, causing breathing difficulties and ultimately lung damage.

329. (D) The boom of canal-building that lasted from about 1825 to 1850 did not cause the Panic of 1837; rather, canal projects were the victims of the panic. Some canal projects had to stop construction when the depression hit the nation; others were completed with private funding.

330. (E) Protective tariffs are taxes on imported goods, designed to encourage people to buy items produced in their own country. This supports the local economy. Clay's support for protective tariffs was obviously incompatible with the idea of a free-trade agreement with Britain.

331. (D) The development of viable steamboats by 1814 and the opening of the Erie Canal in the 1820s revolutionized trade within the United States. Vastly greater quantities of goods could now be transported long distances at very small cost; this meant the opening of new and profitable markets for all kinds of goods. As profits grew, so did towns and cities along major trade routes. Beginning in the 1830s, the railroad would continue the trend of economic expansion.

332. (A) In one day, the cotton gin could process as much cotton as a thousand slaves. Slavery had begun to prove so unprofitable that some state legislatures had begun to discuss phasing it out. With the invention of the cotton gin, profits soared again and all talk of gradual emancipation was silenced.

333. (C) At a little more than 360 miles in length, the Erie Canal made it possible for shiploads of goods to travel quickly and directly from the Great Lakes to the Hudson River, which, of course, gave direct access to the Atlantic Ocean. Its completion created new national and international markets for goods produced in the Great Lakes region.

334. (B) Because beavers spend a lot of time in and around the water, their pelts are naturally water-repellent. This, and the shortness of the hairs of the pelt, made beaver fur the perfect choice for hats in an era when men invariably wore hats outdoors and in most public places—the high demand for hats meant a high demand for beaver pelts. Beaver fur was also used for coats and trimming on various garments.

335. (A) The Colt revolver, developed in the 1830s, was a major breakthrough because it could fire six times without being reloaded. Earlier models had to be reloaded after each shot—a process that took a full minute, during which the soldier had his hands full and could not defend himself from attack. When the Texas Rangers introduced the revolvers into military combat during the Mexican War, they proved so effective that the U.S. government ordered a thousand of them, and Colt's fortune was made. The Colt revolver became standard equipment for westbound pioneers, cowboys, and miners.

336. (A) The South grew cotton and tobacco as cash crops. Wealthy planters earned enormous profits from both domestic sales and exports to Europe.

337. (D) In 1832, President Andrew Jackson vetoed a bill that would have renewed the charter of the Second Bank; therefore, its charter expired in 1836. (It remained open as an ordinary bank.) Land speculators found it easy to borrow capital from state banks. They used it to buy land that they resold at greatly inflated prices. With land prices soaring, all other prices rose too. When Jackson tried to stem the tide of inflation by ruling that land must be paid for in hard money—gold or silver, not paper—the crash came. People were much readier to borrow gold and silver from the state banks than they were to repay the loans; the banks soon failed, and the nation was plunged into an economic depression that lasted into the 1840s.

338. (B) The light bulb, patented by Lewis Latimer and Thomas Edison, did not make its appearance until 1879. It was part of the Second Industrial Revolution, a wave of technological and industrial breakthroughs that took place in the late 19th century.

339. (B) Congress began to fund a national network of roads and canals around 1815 and a national railroad about 1830. The roads and canals made trade easier and more efficient, and the railroad drastically cut down on travel time, not only for shipping goods but also for passengers. Far from increasing the division between North and South, the transportation network tended to create bonds, especially economic bonds, between the country's various regions.

340. (C) Invented by Eli Whitney in 1793, the cotton gin mechanized the process of separating the seeds from the fibers—a chore that slaves had previously done by hand. The cotton gin revolutionized the southern economy because it could process cotton a thousand times faster than a person.

341. (A) Choice (A) is much more sweeping than the very few child-labor regulations that began to appear in the 1830s and 1840s. The Fair Labor Standards Act of 1938 was the first federal law that established the age at which a child could be employed and the hours he or she could work. The other four choices accurately describe the lives of urban workers from the beginnings of industrialization until the era of labor unions and meaningful federal regulations.

342. (E) The Panic of 1819 devastated the West; the steep drop in prices for western produce and the new requirement that mortgages must be paid in cash combined to threaten many western farmers with eviction. The Land Law was designed to protect these people. It allowed them to postpone payment of their mortgages, ensured that they could keep whatever portion of their property they had already paid off, and retroactively reduced the purchase price of government land.

343. (D) The Mexican Revolution was a successful rebellion against Spanish rule. Once Mexico became independent, the high Spanish protective tariffs on U.S. exports were abolished. This benefited the U.S. economy because exports and profits rose.

344. (C) The southern states objected to the Tariff Acts of 1816 and 1828 because they believed tariffs benefited the North at the expense of the South. Several southern states claimed that the Tariff Act of 1828 was unconstitutional under the Tenth Amendment (the amendment reserving certain rights to the states) and, therefore, they did not have to obey it. This standoff is called the Nullification Crisis because the principle of refusing to obey an unconstitutional law is called the doctrine of nullification. The impasse was resolved with a compromise; the South would pay the tariff on the understanding that it would be reduced gradually over the course of 10 years.

345. (E) Construction of the Panama Canal did not begin until 1904, but people had envisioned a canal connecting the Atlantic and Pacific Oceans as early as the mid-1500s. Two likely locations for such a canal were across the narrow isthmus of Panama, or via the San Juan River in Nicaragua. The Clayton-Bulwer Treaty is an agreement between Britain and the United States to cooperate with one another on equal terms in the construction and use of a Nicaragua Canal, if such a plan should be developed. In actual fact, of course, the canal would be built through Panama, and construction would not begin until 1904.

346. (B) Roads and canals worked together as parts of a national transportation system. The success of the Erie Canal encouraged road-building because it encouraged settlement of the Great Lakes region and northwestern New York. Note on choice (E): Because the Erie Canal terminated at the Hudson River and the Hudson led to the Atlantic Ocean through the port of New York, all trade between the inland United States and Europe passed through New York. This explains why New York became the most important of the U.S. port cities.

347. (D) The railroads made the telegraph practical and necessary; in fact, the Pacific Railway Acts required construction of telegraph lines along with the construction of the railroad. The telegraph made it possible for stationmasters to communicate instantly, which was necessary in emergency situations. Of course, it was also of enormous benefit to ordinary people wanting to communicate instantly for business or personal reasons, and with the rapid settlement of the West this service was more and more in demand.

348. (D) Cyrus McCormick is the inventor of the mechanical reaper, which could cut six times as much grain as a human being in one day. The reaper was pulled by a team of horses, but its gears, blades, and wheels performed the mechanical tasks of gathering and cutting the grain and binding it into sheaves. McCormick patented his invention in 1834 and put it on the market in 1841; by the 1850s he was selling thousands of reapers a year. Elisha Otis is the inventor of the passenger elevator, which made possible the skyscraper revolution of the early 20th century.

349. (B) The largest single factor in the demise of the fur trade was that there was no more fur to trade in. Beaver in the northwestern region had been hunted so persistently and successfully that there were very few left to hunt. In addition to this, and perhaps because of it, clothing styles and consumers' tastes were changing, and beaver was no longer fashionable by 1840.

350. (A) The southern economy depended heavily on the cotton crop, much of which was exported to Britain and France. The southerners were afraid that if the United States taxed all British and French goods, those two nations would retaliate by placing their own protective tariffs on American cotton. This would drastically reduce southern profits.

351. (E) The first practical steam-powered boat made its debut in 1807. Before steam power, manual labor was what made the keelboats move. Natural forces (gravity and the current) meant that it was easy and therefore cheap to go downstream, but hard and therefore expensive to go upstream. Upstream loads had to be relatively light and small, and the keelboat could not move upstream very fast. Steam power all but eliminated these difficulties. As a result, loads of cargo became larger, trips became faster and more frequent, communication improved among the trading posts and towns along the route, shipping rates for upstream trips dropped dramatically, and profits soared all around.

352. (D) When Europe recovered from the Napoleonic Wars, its own agricultural production rose, which meant it imported less grain, corn, and other crops from the United States. The drop in demand led to lower prices and debt for the U.S. farmers. At the same time, the national bank, having its own financial troubles, began calling in loans from the states and also requiring that individual loans be repaid in actual currency—at a time of falling prices. All these factors combined to create a financial panic that was partially solved by the passage of the federal Land Law of 1820.

353. (E) The success of the Erie Canal meant that the Great Lakes and the Midwest became much more heavily settled. With a denser population, more large towns, and viable, cheap trade routes for goods, the Midwest shifted from an agricultural economy to a manufacturing and trading one. Cities such as Chicago, Cleveland, and Detroit were based on manufacturing and industry.

354. (C) A protective tariff is a tax on imported goods. Its purpose is to encourage people to buy domestic products by making the imports more expensive. The purchase of goods made in one's own country is good for the domestic economy; it means that American manufacturers and vendors earn greater profits and leads to the protection and creation of local jobs.

355. (A) People who lost their property and/or their savings in the panic fled westward in search of land and economic opportunity.

356. (A) The Comstock Lode is beside Lake Tahoe, at the angle of California's eastern border. Its discovery caused a new rush of prospectors into the region; a sparsely settled area acquired a population of several thousand almost overnight. The need to organize the territory and establish law and order was clear. The Nevada Territory was created from the western half of the Utah Territory in 1861.

Chapter 5: The 19th Century: Westward Expansion to 1865

357. (B) Fulton's steam-powered boats made it much easier for people to explore and settle the West, but Fulton himself was not an explorer. In 1807, fur trader Manuel Lisa and his party followed the Missouri and Yellowstone Rivers deep into Montana, where they established a trading post. In 1820, Stephen Long led the Yellowstone expedition, part of a government plan to build forts along the western frontier. In 1822, William Ashley recruited 100 men to follow him on an expedition to trace the Missouri River to its source; by 1825 he had pushed almost all the way west to Utah Lake. Jedediah Smith, one of Ashley's recruits, set out from Fort Kiowa in 1823 and crossed the Black Hills to Flathead Lake near the Canadian border.

358. (E) Mexicans had proved unwilling to settle northeastern Texas; it was, therefore, sparsely populated and a scene of continual Indian raids and conflict. It also left Mexico vulnerable to invasion, either by the United States or by another power. Mexicans were sure that if Americans settled Texas, they would quickly elect an effective government that would protect the settlers against the Indians. Mexico had twice refused to sell Texas to the United States.

359. (B) Major geographical obstacles separated Mexico and the Spanish province of New Mexico from the Spanish missions and settlements in southern California. These included mountain ranges to the south and east of the settlements, as well as the Mojave and Yuma Deserts. Trading ships sailed up and down the California coast, however, and the Spanish settlers of California soon developed a prosperous economy—miniature in scale, however, compared to the boom that would come in 1848.

360. (A) Choice (A) applies equally well to both the West and Texas; in the days before swift long-distance communication, geographical distance from the central government meant a great deal of practical independence. Choice (B) is wrong because land in Texas cost one-tenth the price of land in the western territories. (This changed after 1862 with the passage of the Homestead Act.) Choices (C) and (E) are wrong because Mexico did grant special privileges to the American settlers, in the hope that this would make them oppose U.S. annexation. Choice (D) is wrong because in the West, a homestead was no more than 160 acres, but in Texas it could be as large as 4,605 acres.

361. (D) The Great Migration was a flow of westward movement that resulted in the settling of the Midwest/Great Lakes region. Choices (A), (B), (C), and (E) describe four important causes of the Great Migration. Choice (D) is not valid because Spain owned no territory in this region and because the United States had long held title to the Northwest Territory.

362. (D) Spaniards were the first to bring horses to North America. Although the Spaniards had domesticated the animals, using them for transport and hauling, some inevitably broke away and quickly adapted themselves to wild herd life in the Great Plains and the West. The Indians of the region quickly mastered horses and found that it was much easier to hunt buffalo on horseback. Mastering horses enabled the Plains tribes to live as nomads, following the buffalo herds on which they depended for food.

363. (E) The whaling industry was responsible for the first contact between U.S. citizens and the Spanish settlers of Monterey and San Francisco. Whaling ships from New England put in at the California ports to stock up supplies for their long voyages eastward. Other trading ships exchanged a variety of U.S. goods for California's leather and tallow—by-products of its growing livestock industry. These early contacts date from the first decade of the 19th century; U.S. citizens first began to acquire land and settle in California in 1814.

364. (B) The Illinois militia repeatedly fired on the Sac and Fox after the tribe raised the flag of truce. This clear violation of the terms of war resulted in the murder of many innocent women and children, and prolonged the Black Hawk War because it forced the Indians to counterattack when they only wanted to surrender. However, the U.S. government never apologized for the crimes committed by the Illinois militia. Black Hawk was universally acknowledged as a hero for fighting against such great odds, even though the rebellion was a failure.

365. (C) The British had their own fur-trading industry in the region—the Hudson's Bay Company. Therefore, they had an interest in hindering the Americans' attempts to establish their own foothold in the region. The U.S. government suspected that the British were behind a series of raids by the Blackfeet, Arikara, and Assinboine tribes in the region. However, the British played no role in the battle on August 9, which resulted in a cease-fire and an agreement that there would be no more raids. Edward Rose, a disgruntled American who felt that the treaty let the Indians off too lightly, is believed to have burned the Arikara village out of spite after the treaty was agreed to.

366. (D) The Santa Fe Trail began at Independence and ended at Santa Fe. It was established in the 1820s. Choice (B) describes the Gila Trail. It might be said that both trails actually began at St. Louis, but the journey from St. Louis to Independence was accomplished by boat. The Santa Fe and Gila Trails were overland routes.

367. (A) Jackson was born in a log cabin on the western frontier of South Carolina, so he had known conflict with local Indians from his earliest days. Not surprisingly, he shared the frontiersman's point of view that the Indians were a threat. Although he gave lip service to the notion of protecting the Indians from the settlers, his support for forced relocation had the opposite effect.

368. (B) Illinois developed a plan to end slavery quickly but not all at once. Illinois slave-holders might keep any slaves they already had when the territory became a state, but as of that date, no one not already a slave could ever become one. When a slave gave birth to a child, the child was automatically free.

369. (C) The greatest attraction of Texas was the price of the land, which was one-tenth the price of land in U.S. territories west of the Mississippi. To people who had lost everything they had during the Panic of 1819, this was a heaven-sent opportunity for a fresh start at a price they could afford.

370. (D) President James Monroe was determined to establish a Permanent Indian Frontier. His idea was to draw a line around territory that was to belong exclusively and permanently to the Indians. This land was not to be settled by U.S. citizens. The leaders of Michigan and Missouri met leaders of the Winnebago, Sac and Fox, Potawatomie, and Chippewa Nations at Prairie du Chien (in present-day Wisconsin) in 1825 to discuss terms. The Permanent Indian Frontier followed the Mississippi River in the north; the line then turned west, following the northern border of Missouri. At the Missouri River it turned south again, following the western borders of Missouri and Arkansas to the Red River, which was then the border between the United States and the Mexican state of Texas.

371. (B) Tecumseh believed that the lands that later became Indiana, Illinois, and the eastern Dakotas belonged collectively to all the nations in the region—Shawnee, Kaskaskia, Sac and Fox, and so on. He hoped to create a state in which several Indian nations would enjoy equal rights and freedoms. Around 1811, the British agreed to help Tecumseh because they saw advantages to his plan—it would create a buffer state between Canada and the United States (the two nations had not yet made peace).

372. (E) The "Great American Desert" was bounded by the Rocky Mountains on the west and the Missouri River on the east. Despite being crossed by the Red, Arkansas, Canadian, Platte, and Yellowstone Rivers, it was a dry and barren-appearing region, completely lacking trees and experiencing very little rainfall. This region approximates the present-day states of Kansas, Oklahoma, and eastern Colorado. The invention of the McCormick reaper would eventually convert the Great American Desert into the breadbasket of the nation.

373. (D) Pittsburgh is 15–20 miles north of the National Road, which is present-day U.S. Route 40. Note on choice (E): Wheeling is in West Virginia, but at the time the National Road was completed, there was no West Virginia. The western counties of Virginia seceded from the state in 1863, to become the Union state of West Virginia.

374. (D) The Black Hawk Purchase was a 50-mile-wide swath of land bordered by the Mississippi River and Illinois on the west, Missouri on the south, and Indian Country to the west. Its northernmost point was the boundary of Prairie du Chien in Michigan Territory (present-day Wisconsin). Since 1846, this land has been the eastern section of the state of Iowa.

375. (D) Calhoun developed his plan in the years following the War of 1812. Under the plan, Major Stephen C. Long began leading expeditions through the frontier territory in 1817. Choice (D) was the reason for the preliminary expeditions, not for building the forts; it was necessary to gather this information before the best locations for the forts could be chosen. Choices (A) through (C) describe the main reasons for Calhoun's plan. Choice (E) was never any part of the U.S. government's plan at any time in history. Expansion to the Pacific Ocean was described in some of the original colonial charters, and the government never abandoned this plan despite its many disingenuous treaties with the Indians.

376. (A) Black Hawk led the Sac and Fox in the Black Hawk War of 1832. From President Andrew Jackson on down, Americans acknowledged him as a hero, but, of course, the Sac and Fox could do nothing against the U.S. troops. The rebellion failed in its goal of retaining the original Sac and Fox lands.

377. (D) Mexico had thrown off Spanish rule in the 1820s. Under the Mexican constitution of 1824, the nation was a republic, and Texas was one section of the state or province of Coahuila-Texas. In 1835, Santa Anna overthrew the Mexican republic and established himself as a dictator. Texans claimed that Mexico had repeatedly refused to consider their application for statehood and also expressed their refusal to live under a dictatorship. The latter was the formal excuse for the revolution that resulted in the 1836 declaration of the Republic of Texas. Note on choice (E): Many Whigs at the time, and many historians today, believe that the settlement of Texas was part of a Democratic Party scheme to annex the state and thus expand the southern slaveholding power base in Congress. However, this was not openly acknowledged at the time nor did Texan officials claim that this was any part of their motive for the rebellion.

378. (B) The Alamo was a fort. In their rebellion against Mexico, the Texan troops occupied the fort. General Santa Anna and the Mexican troops laid siege to the fort, taking it over from the Texans on March 6, 1836. Soon after, the Texans defeated the Mexicans at the San Jacinto River and forced Mexico to grant Texas its independence.

379. (E) The men of Pike's Peak Country created their own territorial government in 1859, choosing the name "Territory of Jefferson." Congress refused to recognize the self-proclaimed territory, but by February 1861 had agreed to its organization as the Territory of Colorado.

380. (A) The chief concern of the U.S. government was to make sure that the flow of westward migration could continue. In fact, there had been very little trouble between westbound pioneers and Plains tribes; the Sioux and other tribes had no objection to the wagon trains passing through, as long as they did not stop and claim Indian land. However, it seemed best to the federal government to separate the two groups permanently. Therefore the tribes accepted promises of financial aid in exchange for settling in the Dakotas, Rockies, and Oklahoma.

381. (B) Magazine editor John O'Sullivan coined the term *manifest destiny* (see answer 398). This phrase almost certainly helped create public enthusiasm for the war, but O'Sullivan had no direct involvement in it. Polk was the U.S. president during the war. Scott and Taylor commanded the U.S. Army. Santa Anna was a former president and dictator of Mexico who commanded the Mexican troops and first suggested selling the territory that became known as the Mexican Cession.

382. (C) The Gadsden Purchase comprised the last acres of land (except for Alaska and the Hawaiian Islands) that would eventually become part of the United States of America. This purchase was completed in 1853; it included the southern portions of New Mexico and Arizona.

383. (A) The purpose of the Homestead Act was to settle the West. Farmers could acquire up to 160 acres of land for free in return for agreeing to live on and cultivate it for their own exclusive use for five years. When the five years were up, the farmer could prove his or her claim and would then own the property outright. Only once the claim was proved could the owner rent or resell the land. If the farmer wanted to own the land in six months instead of waiting five years, he or she could pay the nominal price of $1.25 per acre instead. A woman was fully entitled to claim land under the Homestead Act as long as she was either 21 years old or the head of a family.

384. (E) The fur traders were the first non-Indians to discover viable overland routes from western Missouri to the Pacific coast. The traders were looking for the most efficient ways possible to bring supplies westward and send furs back east. Various combinations of river routes were possible, but beginning in 1825, traders such as Jedediah Smith and Nathaniel Wyeth were also exploring the overland routes.

385. (D) Today, blue jeans are the most commonly worn garment in the United States, suitable for any social occasion at which formal dress is not required. American blue jeans got their start during the Gold Rush, when Levi Strauss earned a fortune selling them to the early California prospectors and miners. The reason jeans were so popular among the "forty-niners" was the twill fabric, in which threads are woven not only across and down, but also diagonally. The extra diagonal layer of threads makes the fabric hold up better to hard use and wear—thus it was ideal for prospecting, ranching, mining, and other heavy outdoor work in the mid-19th-century West.

386. (C) Part of the U.S. government process of relocating the Plains tribes was to separate them from U.S. citizens who were settling the Kansas and Nebraska Territories, which were then being organized for annexation as new states.

387. (E) Anti-Mormon sentiment in Illinois, where the Mormons established a stronghold in the 1840s, resulted in criminal charges against Mormon founder Joseph Smith and his brother Hyrum; both men were murdered in jail. The Mormons then followed their new leader, Brigham Young, to the Great Basin, where they hoped to live in isolation outside the reach of U.S. law. As it turned out, the area was settled much faster than they expected, due in large part to the California Gold Rush, which took place just after the Mormons' westward pilgrimage.

388. (D) Kearney was a Mexican War general. Congressman John Floyd of Virginia proposed several pieces of legislation regarding Oregon, all intended to encourage its settlement and future admission to the United States as a new state. Kelley imagined a permanent Oregon settlement along the lines of the farming villages of his home region, New England. His efforts inspired early commercial ventures into Oregon and the establishment of the first settlers. McLoughlin worked for the British Hudson's Bay Company, and was instrumental in making Oregon economically self-sufficient. In 1835, Narcissa Whitman and Eliza Spalding became the first white women to cross the Rockies and settle in Oregon, with their husbands. Their success encouraged more easterners to make the trip to the Pacific.

389. (C) Future citizenship was no part of the Laramie treaty. The other four choices describe the terms to which the Plains tribes agreed. To compensate the tribes for their concessions, the U.S. government agreed to pay each tribe $50,000 worth of food and tools annually for 50 years.

390. (E) Polk sent special envoy John Slidell to Mexico in the hope of achieving a peaceful resolution to the tension between the two nations. Choices (A) through (D) describe the terms Slidell was empowered to offer President Herrera. Public opinion in Mexico was strongly against the offer. When Herrera was deposed in favor of General Mariano Paredes, peaceful negotiation became an impossibility.

391. (A) The Gadsden Purchase of 1853 secured the last of the continental United States between the Mexican and Canadian borders and the Atlantic and Pacific Oceans. (Alaska is on the northwestern border of Canada, geographically far northwest of Washington State.) The United States acquired a relatively small parcel of land in the Gadsden Purchase; it forms the southern portion of both Arizona and New Mexico.

392. (D) The increase in population and diversity went hand in hand: African-Americans, Chinese, Mexicans, and easterners of all ethnic backgrounds flocked to California in search of gold. Violence was endemic in this almost exclusively male society; there were no professional police, and vigilante justice ruled. Levi Strauss is just one example of an entrepreneur who made a fortune in the West by filling a niche—in his case, providing sturdy denim work trousers to the miners and railroad workers. California never established slavery at any time; when it applied for statehood, it refused to consider admission to the Union except as a free state.

393. (A) The Mexican state of Texas had successfully rebelled against Mexico in 1836. Texas was ruled as an independent republic until it applied for statehood in 1845. Mexico had never accepted Texan independence and considered the U.S. annexation of Texas an act of war.

394. (B) The Pike's Peak Gold Rush centered around the front range of the Rocky Mountains and Boulder, Cherry, Clear, and Fountain Creeks. In 1859, this area was part of Kansas Territory; with the surge in population, Pike's Peak Country and the surrounding area were reorganized as the Territory of Colorado. It would become a state in 1876.

395. (D) The Great Plains had been set aside for the Sioux, Comanche, Shoshone, Crow, and other tribes. With the U.S. victory in the Mexican War and the discovery of gold in California, massive westbound traffic became a fact of life in the region. The heavily traveled Oregon Trail had a major impact on the tribal way of life for the reasons described in choices (A), (B), (C), and (E). The pioneers hunted and killed buffalo at a faster pace than the animals could reproduce. The livestock the pioneers took westward competed with the buffalo for grass; this caused the buffalo herds to seek out new lands, and the Indians had to follow the herds. When they did so, they encroached on the traditional territory of other tribes, and warfare was the result.

396. (C) The Mexican Cession—territory Mexico sold to the United States for $15 million after the Mexican War—included all of California, Nevada, and Utah, and parts of Arizona, Colorado, New Mexico, and Wyoming. Oklahoma, called Indian Territory at the time, had belonged to the United States since the Louisiana Purchase.

397. (A) Nebraska Territory was much larger than the present-day state of Nebraska. The territory was bordered on the west by the Missouri River and did not include any part of Iowa. It did include all or parts of the other four states listed, as well as parts of what would later become Colorado, Wyoming, and Idaho.

398. (D) In 1845, an editorial in the periodical *Democratic Review* referred to the United States' "manifest destiny to overspread and possess the whole of the continent which Providence has given to us for the great experiment of liberty." Editor John O'Sullivan became famous for this phrase. He continued to urge his support for westward expansion and for the United States to annex all the territory between the borders of Mexico and Canada.

399. (B) Frémont (1813–1890) never invented or patented anything along the lines of the cotton gin, the Franklin stove, or the McCormick reaper. He was a notable American in many other fields, though. Frémont led troops in California during the Mexican War and was a controversial commander in the Union Army during the Civil War. He served California and later Arizona as territorial governor and was an unsuccessful Republican (i.e., antislavery) candidate for president of the United States. During the 1830s, he carried out several major land surveys and explorations of the West. Frémont was also a noted botanist, and the author of an autobiography of his eventful career.

400. (C) Abolitionists in Congress tried to pass the Wilmot Proviso, which would have banned slavery throughout the Mexican Cession, but it was defeated. It turned out to be unnecessary. The people and the leaders in California and the Southwest showed no interest in acquiring slaves. They did not consider it in their economic interest, and besides, the time in history for slaveowning was past. The United States was the last slaveowning nation in the Western world.

401. (A) The Missouri Compromise line is at 36°30′, exactly even with the northern border of Texas below the Oklahoma panhandle. As a slaveholding state, Texas could not extend north of the Missouri Compromise line. This explains the existence of the Oklahoma panhandle—a 30-mile-wide zone between the borders of Texas and western Kansas.

402. **(C)** The trail led northwest from Independence, Missouri; the wagons had to cross Nebraska to get from Kansas to Wyoming and then across Idaho and Oregon nearly to the Pacific coast. Montana lies well to the north of the Oregon Trail.

403. **(B)** By 1856, the Mormons had thoroughly entrenched themselves in the Great Basin. The Mormon community did not recognize non-Mormon authorities, including the federal judges in the region. When the U.S. government sent troops west to support the judges, the Mormons fired on the troops.

404. **(D)** The terms agreed at the conclusion of the Laramie Conference were highly favorable to the U.S. government. With their agreement to remain within designated territories only, the Plains tribes lost not only their hunting culture, but their means of survival—hunting buffalo. Therefore, they were now entirely dependent on federal handouts. The United States agreed to pay each tribe $50,000 a year in food and trade goods until 1901, by which time the government assumed the Indians would have become self-sufficient farmers. This assumption was based on a serious cultural misunderstanding.

405. **(B)** Construction of the Union Pacific—the western end of the railroad, which began in California—would not begin until 1863. The other four choices all help to explain why California was a violent and dangerous society after the discovery of the gold. The forty-niners were boys and young men without the restraints of parents, wives, or children; they all carried guns; they did not hesitate to rob and even kill one another; and the Chinese, Mexican, Indian, and American populations had difficulty communicating. With no police or courts, the quickest way to solve a quarrel was to shoot someone.

406. **(E)** The Railway Act makes no reference to slave labor or free labor. This topic was not an issue for several reasons. First, the railroad covered by the act began at Omaha and traveled westward; it was entirely within free states and territories, where there was never any question of hiring slave labor. Second, by 1862 the Civil War was well under way, and the government that passed the Pacific Railway Act was a Union government with no slave-holding interests.

407. **(A)** The Pony Express carried the U.S. mail from Missouri to California. Since a single horse could run much faster than a team pulling a stagecoach, the Pony Express delivered the mail in half the usual time. When the telegraph wires between Nebraska and California were connected, there was no longer any demand for express-mail service; a person could send a telegraph that would arrive instantly, for much less money than the cost of a Pony Express letter.

408. **(A)** Choice (A) is an accurate statement, but has nothing to do with the U.S. takeover of California. The takeover was the result of the series of military actions described in choices (B) through (D).

409. (E) There were very few instances of hostility between Plains tribes and westbound pioneers. The other four choices accurately describe the most serious hazards of the journey. Giving birth in the open, with no trained medical assistance, was often fatal to new mothers, and it was a challenge for a new baby to survive without its mother. There was always danger from the weather; even in summer, the wagon trains were vulnerable to storms, hail, tornadoes, or sweltering heat and drought. Because families stuck close together for security, any illness spread swiftly through the entire wagon train. Supplies could only be restocked if the pioneers encountered Indians who were willing to trade or at one of the very few settlements along the trail.

410. (D) The federal government paid for the westbound U.S. mail to be shipped to Panama, carried across the isthmus, and then shipped north to San Francisco. For eastbound mail, the route was reversed. This process was so slow that the government was easily persuaded to subsidize an overland stagecoach route, which became a reality in 1858. The coaches carried passengers and mail from St. Louis to San Francisco via Texas, and from Independence to Sacramento via Denver. The Civil War, the completion of the transcontinental telegraph wires, and the development of the railway all contributed to the demise of the stagecoach mail service.

411. (B) As soon as people developed the proper farm implements for the soil of the Great American Desert and realized that the soil and climate were perfect for growing wheat, they flocked to the region. Railroads gave the wheat farmers the ability to ship their crops to distant markets, and also carried a variety of tools and products to the region. The presence of the buffalo herds proved that the grasslands were perfect for livestock, who could roam and graze to their hearts' content. It would take more time for the total removal of the Indians from free lands; the process had begun, but was not completed until after the Civil War.

Chapter 6: The War Between the States

412. (A) Anthony considered women's suffrage a far more important cause than abolition; in fact, she deeply resented the passage of the Fifteenth Amendment. Lifelong abolitionist John Brown led the Potowatomie Massacre and the raid at Harpers Ferry. Frederick Douglass's famous autobiography describes his experiences as a slave and his dramatic and successful escape; he became a powerful speaker against slavery. Garrison was the editor and almost the sole author of the abolitionist newspaper *The Liberator* from 1833 to 1863, when his last article celebrated the issue of the Emancipation Proclamation. Escaped slave Harriet Tubman led countless slaves north to freedom on the Underground Railroad.

413. (D) The preachers of the Second Great Awakening spoke out against slavery on the grounds that it was sinful to hold another human being against his or her will. They urged their converts not only to free their own slaves, but to persuade other people to free their slaves as well.

414. (E) The Underground Railroad was not a literal railroad with engines that ran on tracks. It was a secret network of people who helped runaway slaves escape to Canada, Mexico, or free states and territories. Some people provided food and shelter along the route; others guided groups of slaves through dangerous areas where they might be recaptured. Still others helped the runaways once they arrived on free soil, providing them with money and jobs and helping them establish themselves in the community.

415. (C) Congress agreed to assume liability for all debts owed by the former Republic of Texas.

416. (E) Between 1847 and 1860, dramatic narratives of the lives and escapes of Brown; Craft and his wife, Ellen; Jacobs; and Truth appeared in print. All four narratives sold tens of thousands of copies and helped to fuel the abolitionist movement in the North. Booker T. Washington was only nine years old when the Civil War ended; his autobiography *Up from Slavery* (1901) is not a slave narrative per se, but the success story of an African-American in what was still a two-tier society.

417. (B) The big issue of uncertainty regarding the territories was whether slaveholding would be permitted in any or all of them. Southern states argued for it, while those in the North and West argued against it. The Compromise of 1850 stated that California would be admitted as a free state, and that popular sovereignty would determine the slaveholding or free status of Utah and New Mexico Territories. Since northerners felt sure that the people of these territories would vote against slavery, they accepted this offer and signed the new Fugitive Slave Act (see answer 418).

418. (A) The 1850 Fugitive Slave Act did not ban slavery in the capital; President Lincoln would issue such a ban during his first term in office. The Fugitive Slave Act greatly stacked the odds in favor of the slaveowners. One provision of the act not listed among the answer choices is that the officials of the special courts were paid more money if they found in favor of the slaveowner's claim than if they did not. The Fugitive Slave Act was so obviously unjust that it created a powerful backlash of sympathy for the fugitives, particularly in the North.

419. (D) The Free-Soil campaign slogan was "Free Soil, Free Speech, Free Labor, and Free Men." The Free-Soil Party won no electoral votes, but it did swing the election from Democratic candidate Lewis Cass to Whig candidate Zachary Taylor.

420. (A) Free-Soil Party candidates for president garnered about 10 percent of the popular vote and swung the election to the Whig candidate, Zachary Taylor, who was not an abolitionist but who did oppose the Compromise of 1850. The Free-Soilers also won several seats in Congress. Thus, support for abolition now had a much stronger national voice than before. Note on choice (E): All U.S. presidents (although not all presidential candidates) supported the preservation of the Union; they must swear or affirm this support when they take the oath of office.

421. (B) As of 1845, the United States had an equal balance of free and slaveholding states. The annexation of Texas gave the slaveholding states a majority. Congress therefore agreed to extend the Missouri Compromise line westward. This line was the northern boundary of slaveholding territory (except Missouri); therefore, extending the line was a guarantee of freedom for all western territory north of that line.

422. (E) Congress included several factions in the 1840s. Northern Whigs and northern antislavery Democrats supported the Wilmot Proviso, described in choice (D). Moderate southerners supported the extension of the Missouri Compromise line. Northern and southern moderates recommended leaving the decision to the Supreme Court. Westerners, and some northerners, argued in favor of popular sovereignty as described in choice (C). All delegates were agreed that the president had no constitutional power to make any ruling on the issue.

423. (B) The Underground Railroad had no measurable effect on the Civil War. The other four choices help to explain its importance in U.S. history.

424. (D) *My Bondage and My Freedom* is the title of the second (1855) edition of Douglass's autobiography, called *Narrative of the Life of Frederick Douglass* in its first edition. The other four are major abolitionist newspapers, published by David Walker, choice (B); William Lloyd Garrison, choice (C); Douglass, choice (E); and Douglass and Gerrit Smith, choice (A).

425. (A) The Mason-Dixon Line defines the Maryland-Pennsylvania and Maryland-Delaware borders. Surveyors Charles Mason and Jeremiah Dixon first established the line in the 1760s to resolve a land dispute between the colonies of Pennsylvania and Maryland. Choice (E) is wrong because Maryland was not part of the Confederacy. Around the time of the Missouri Compromise, people began to use the term *Mason-Dixon Line* to refer to the cultural divide between the free North and the slaveholding South. The South's nickname "Dixie" is derived from the border name.

426. (A) Lincoln's name did not even appear on the ballot in the Deep South, where the voters were split between Democrat John Breckinridge and Constitutional Party candidate John Bell. All other regions of the country voted for Lincoln, who won a huge electoral majority of 180 to Breckinridge's 72.

427. (C) Choice (C) would not account for the fact that low-income southerners supported slavery. The other four choices all help to explain why they went along with a system that brought them only limited benefits. Overseers were few in number but highly paid. As in any society, the wealthy people could make things very difficult for the poor people who opposed their interests. Poor white southerners could and did collect economic rewards by informing on runaway slaves; those who were better educated could earn money as agents or bounty hunters. Class snobbery was also a significant force; every disadvantaged class in history likes to feel there is someone even worse off.

428. (B) In *Uncle Tom's Cabin*, Harriet Beecher Stowe portrays all types of characters—old and young, black and white, enslaved and free, northern and southern, educated and ignorant. The novel uses a dramatic, eventful story to make the point that the system of slavery is based on the belief that Africans are not fully human—and thus this system corrupts everyone it touches, however good and admirable they are in other ways. Southerners were alone in their disgust for the novel; it outsold every book except the Bible in the years leading up to the Civil War.

429. (E) In December 1860, in an attempt to preserve the Union and prevent secession, Senator John J. Crittenden of Kentucky proposed a package of constitutional amendments to Congress. Choice (A) sums up Article I. Choice (B) sums up Article II. Choice (C) sums up Article III. Choice (D) sums up Article VI, Section 4. The Crittenden Compromise did not call for what is described in choice (E). It satisfied southern Democrats, but dismayed Republicans and thus failed to pass.

430. (B) Southerners had threatened to secede over the Wilmot Proviso; since it was defeated, they took no action. They made no similar threats over the Kansas-Nebraska Act. The other four choices all describe historically important consequences of the passage of the act.

431. (A) The Republican Party of 1856 was the first in U.S. history that specifically represented a region (or rather, regions)—the North and the West. Republicans did not even campaign in the South in 1856; the party had absolutely no southern support except in border areas such as western Virginia.

432. (D) The violence in Kansas inspired Sumner to give a ringing antislavery speech that provoked Brooks into attacking and nearly beating him to death in the Senate chamber. The violent behavior of the proslavers angered abolitionist John Brown into leading a brutal massacre of five of them at Potawatomie Creek. The Reverend Beecher was only one of several northern ministers who urged the arming of the Free-Soilers in order to even the odds. Atchison was a slaveholding senator from Missouri who undertook criminal measures to influence Kansas politics when he was not even a resident of the territory.

433. (E) If the abolitionist movement had a particular stronghold, it was in the North. Influential abolitionist newspapers were published in the North, and the majority of runaway slaves who became active in the movement fled north. Choices (A) through (D) help to explain why the West supported the Republican Party. The West and the North were closely connected in business, economics, and politics, and the spread of slavery was bad for both regions in all three areas. Moral and humanitarian considerations also played a part, of course; tens of thousands of U.S. citizens outside the South—not to mention all enslaved people in the South—despised the institution of slavery.

434. (B) Kansas was admitted as a free state in January 1861. Immigration had taken care of the conflict; by 1858, so many Free-Soilers had settled in Kansas that they constituted a clear majority in the electorate and were able to outvote the proslavers.

435. (A) Taney believed that the Constitution did not apply to the slaves; their legal status was that of property, not free people. The Constitution was very clear in its protection of property rights. However, Africans *outside* the United States clearly were free people according to U.S. law, and it would have been illegal to take them into custody as slaves. The United States had outlawed the transatlantic slave trade soon after the ratification of the Constitution. Southerners accepted this ruling because the existing slave population sustained itself by new births. No one openly supported the slave trade; however, it did continue illegally for a surprisingly long time after it was banned in 1808.

436. (B) As of 1860, the Republican Party was not publicly advocating the abolition of slavery, but only of its prohibition in the territories. Lincoln had spoken out publicly on the issue many times, most famously in his series of debates with Stephen Douglas. He always took the position that as president, he would not have the constitutional right to abolish slavery in states where it already existed. As a newcomer to national politics, Lincoln had not made political enemies. Seward's home state of New York was also crucial to a Republican victory, but it was considered a safe Republican state while Illinois might swing either way. Lincoln's Kentucky log-cabin background appealed to westerners and the common people, and his great ability as a debater impressed educated voters.

437. (C) *Popular sovereignty* means literally "the rule of the people." During the antebellum era, it referred specifically to each territory's right to decide for itself whether it would allow slavery. Popular sovereignty meant that the citizens of each territory could vote for their representatives, and the freely elected legislature would then vote on the slavery issue. The citizens did not actually get to vote directly for or against slavery; instead, they voted for candidates who promised to support or oppose slavery.

438. (C) Fillmore was no longer president when Kansas held its first ill-fated election in 1854. Senator Atchison of Missouri is famous as the organizer and leader of the Border Ruffians. John Brown stirred up public outrage by playing the leading role in the Potawatomie Massacre. James Lane was a leader of the Jayhawkers, a militant Free-Soil group. William Shannon served as territorial governor from 1855 to 1856, finally resigning when he realized it would be impossible to maintain even an uneasy peace between factions.

439. (B) Douglas was considered a moderate in an era when his own party, the Democrats, despised moderation. In the years leading to the Civil War, the South refused to consider any limitations on slavery; even when legislation such as the Missouri Compromise was passed, southerners found a way to overturn it. Choices (A), (C), (D), and (E) describe the point of view of someone who was willing to work with the Republicans and to accept and support a Republican president; the white southern leadership could not tolerate such a point of view.

440. (E) The Republican Party was founded with the specific goal of halting any further expansion of slavery. The immediate causes are listed in choices (B) and (D); choice (C) is part of choice (B) because the Kansas-Nebraska Act overturned the Missouri Compromise. Choice (A) was a more indirect cause; the Compromise of 1850 had made the sectional tension simmer down at the time, but it was bound to cause trouble in the end because it did not address the root of the problem. Choice (E) is not a contributing cause because John Brown's raid on Harpers Ferry happened after the Republican Party was founded.

441. (C) Slaves were not the target audience of slave narratives; rather, these autobiographies were aimed at white readers who were in a position to change the laws. They helped to bring about the desired change by increasing awareness of the nightmare existence of slaves in the South. These narratives also provided the powerless slaves with their own voice in national affairs. The authors of slave narratives became powerful spokesmen (and women) for their own people.

442. (B) The famous Lincoln-Douglas debates took place in 1858, during the campaign for Douglas's Senate seat. The debates are important because they gave voters the opportunity to hear the candidates speak, at length and without high emotions, of the Kansas-Nebraska Act, popular sovereignty, abolition, and the potential spread of slavery into the western territories. Douglas narrowly won reelection, but he lost the support of most proslavers who considered his positions too moderate. Choice (D) is wrong because the positions Douglass supported were compromises. Choice (E) is wrong because of the two candidates, the winner was the southern sympathizer.

443. (E) California gained statehood in 1850. Texas had been admitted as a slaveholding state in 1845. Nevada was never a slaveholding state. The Missouri Compromise would not be overturned until the passage of the Kansas-Nebraska Act in 1854. The Wilmot Proviso had been defeated by vote in Congress in 1846. The Fugitive Slave Act of 1850 introduced extremely harsh measures against runaway slaves—so harsh that it had the effect of bringing thousands of formerly neutral Americans firmly into the abolitionist camp.

444. (A) Buchanan believed that no individual state should try to influence another state's policies; therefore, he opposed northern efforts to abolish slavery in the South. He became president in 1856, when *Dred Scott v. Sanford* was due to be decided, and his position was that the president must abide by the Supreme Court's ruling on the legality of slavery. He opposed secession but took no official action on the issue, apart from urging the passage of new constitutional amendments to address the crisis—a stance that found no support on either side. Buchanan was less than four months from the end of his term when the southern states seceded; he left all decisions on the issue to President-elect Lincoln.

445. (D) Presidents Franklin Pierce and James Buchanan were southern sympathizers who refused to support the Kansas Free-Soilers. Congress took its cue from the White House and held up the Kansas application for free statehood for two years. It did not go through until after Abraham Lincoln took office.

446. (B) The *Dred Scott* decision was based on a clause in the Fifth Amendment that stated: "No person shall . . . be deprived of life, liberty, or property, without due process of law." Chief Justice Roger Taney, writing the opinion for the majority of the justices, argued that since slaves were property, any law abolishing or banning slavery violated the Fifth Amendment and was therefore unconstitutional. Choice (B) describes the effect of the decision. Millions of people, from Supreme Court justices on down, disagreed with this logic; it helped contribute to the nation's sectional division.

447. (E) Senator Stephen Douglas of Illinois, who proposed the Kansas-Nebraska Act, thought that Congress had no right to decide the future of the territories. He believed the matter should be decided democratically, by the people who lived in the territories. The principle he invoked is known as *popular sovereignty*. (See answer 437.)

448. (B) On October 16, 1859, abolitionist John Brown led a small group of followers in a raid on the federal arsenal at Harpers Ferry in western Virginia. The uprising was immediately put down by federal troops. Many of Brown's men were killed; he himself was tried and executed for treason. Brown had concluded that nothing but the force of arms would ever put an end to the institution of slavery, which he wholeheartedly despised. He intended to raise an African-American army and lead it against the United States, with the object of emancipating the slaves. He attracted many followers, but during the months it took to prepare and arrange the attack, most of them faded away. The small group that was left had no chance of success against the U.S. troops.

449. (C) Choice (C) describes an earlier incident: Senator Henry Foote of Mississippi threatened to shoot Senator Thomas Hart Benton of Missouri during debate over California's admission to the United States. The other four choices (chronologically they would be ordered E, A, D, B) all describe the Brooks-Sumner incident. Because it was a criminal assault on a member of Congress by another member of Congress, it made national headlines and became a central theme of the 1856 election campaign. Sumner was so seriously injured that he did not return to his duties for three years. When the House recommendation for Brooks's expulsion failed to carry, Brooks resigned in protest; he was promptly re-elected.

450. (D) The ruling in *Dred Scott v. Sanford* stated that any U.S. or state law against slavery was unconstitutional. This clearly implied that northern states could do nothing to prevent slavery from spreading back into the North—obviously an alarming situation for a region that had existed without slavery since the Revolution. Choices (A), (B), and (E) are wrong because they are too sweeping, and choice (C) describes a Supreme Court decision from much later in U.S. history.

451. (B) The Federalist Party died out many years before 1854, the year in which the Republican Party was founded. The other four groups joined forces because they supported the abolition of slavery. The antislavery factions in the Whig and Know-Nothing Parties were not strong enough on their own or even combined to get an abolitionist president elected; together, though, members of all four parties were able to build a strong coalition, carrying Abraham Lincoln to victory in the election of 1860.

452. (E) There were many prominent Union supporters in Virginia, and the state even called for a national peace conference in a last hope that representatives of South and North could settle their differences without going to war. Support for secession grew slowly in the state, which seceded in mid-April, two days after the war began and 10 weeks after the last of the original seven seceding states had created the Confederacy.

453. (D) The Border Ruffians were Missouri frontiersmen. With the full encouragement and active leadership of Senator David Atchison, they stormed across the border into Kansas in November 1854, when the territory was holding an election to choose a delegate to Congress. They cast their own illegal votes in favor of a proslavery candidate, and used terrorist tactics to prevent antislavery Kansans from voting. Another group of Border Ruffians did the same thing in March 1855, when Kansas was ready to elect its legislature.

454. (B) If anything, the Fugitive Slave Act made slavery less profitable. It encouraged more slaves to escape, to take more care not to get caught, and to travel beyond the reach of U.S. law to Canada or Europe. Hiring agents to pursue the runaways was an expensive proposition for slaveowners. The Fugitive Slave Act went too far and thus helped to destroy the system it was intended to preserve.

455. (C) Proslavers knew that they would not succeed in spreading slavery throughout the West. There were two reasons for this. First, the pioneers likely to settle the West under a homestead bill had no sympathy with slavery; it was against their own economic interests to support a system of unpaid labor. Second, the western climate did not support the kind of labor-intensive, large-scale agriculture that made slavery economically viable. The proslavers knew, therefore, that the West would develop as free territory; this meant that the proslavery faction in Congress would become a minority. Therefore, they opposed any legislation designed to encourage settlement of the West.

456. (A) If anything, the Democratic Party was inclined toward imperialism at this time in history; Buchanan supported the annexation of Cuba in a proposal called the Ostend Manifesto. Foreign affairs, however, were very unimportant in the national consciousness in 1856; the main issue on everyone's mind was the fight over abolition.

457. (D) In the North, most people opposed the institution of slavery, but there were many southern sympathizers at all levels of northern society, from the White House staff on down. Right up to the outbreak of war, when support for the Confederacy became treason, northern newspapers still printed opinions on both sides of the issue, and both officials and ordinary citizens expressed their opinions openly. The difference is best summed up by saying that in the North, a southern sympathizer risked a noisy argument; in the South, a Union supporter risked being murdered by a mob.

458. (B) South Carolina seceded from the United States within days after Lincoln's election; it was quickly followed by six other southern states. Four more would secede somewhat later, bringing the total to 11.

459. (A) Northerners and westerners viewed the Kansas-Nebraska Act from a mix of economic, political, and humanitarian standpoints. Choice (A) describes the economic motive for many of them to oppose the act, which seemed likely to spread slavery into Kansas. Westerners wanted to compete on a level playing field; they wanted opportunities for everyone to earn fair wages for a day's work. If slaves were forced to work without payment, this would destroy the prospect of free workers finding jobs and thus supporting themselves and their families.

460. (D) Slavery was by far the most volatile political issue of the day. It was not only a matter of moral outrage on the part of the abolitionists, or economic concerns on the part of the proslavery faction. Each side wanted more senators and representatives to vote its way on any issue that came up, and congressmen from slaveholding states always voted together as a bloc.

461. (C) The Union troops won the battle because they were able to establish and maintain command of the high ground. The battle was hard fought over three full days, and both sides suffered heavy losses; the total casualties were more than 50,000.

462. (D) The Declaration of Independence is the most emotionally resonant document in the history of the United States. Americans celebrate the anniversary of its signing as their national holiday, and one of the original printed copies of the document is enshrined in a central display location in the National Archives of the United States. During the 19th century, American schoolchildren were required to memorize it as a matter of course. Its most famous phrase, "all men are created equal," occurs in two of the best-known and most important speeches in U.S. history: the Gettysburg Address by Abraham Lincoln and "I Have a Dream" by Martin Luther King, Jr.

463. (E) The Confederate generals were greatly superior to the Union generals. In fact, Lincoln had originally hoped that Robert E. Lee would command the Union Army. It was a difficult decision for Lee to make, but his primary loyalty lay with Virginia rather than the United States as a whole.

464. (D) Many northerners opposed the war, believing that the South and North should part peacefully without loss of life. These southern sympathizers did not hesitate to invoke their right to free speech, urging their opposition to the war in print, in the taverns and saloons, and elsewhere. They did not support the aims of the Confederacy as much as they simply did not agree that secession was cause for going to war. Once the war actually broke out, much of the northern opposition to it died down.

465. (E) New Orleans and Charleston were major port cities for the South. The navy, however, was loyal to the Union and blockaded the southern ports. Ships from Europe could not get through the blockade; this created a state of siege in the South.

466. (A) It was the Confederacy, not the Union, that hoped for an alliance with Britain and France, which were major buyers of southern cotton.

467. (C) The Union defeated the Confederacy at Antietam in September 1862, at Gettysburg and Vicksburg in July 1863, and at Shiloh in April 1862. The Confederacy won First (1861) and Second (1862) Manassas, also known as First and Second Bull Run after the name of the nearby creek.

468. (B) The Confederate Army never got any farther north than Pennsylvania. Most of the Civil War was fought in the Confederate states, although there were also battles in Pennsylvania and Maryland.

469. (C) Lincoln notified the Confederacy that he was sending supplies to relieve the troops at Fort Sumter. The southern troops fired on the fort. The Union considered this to be a declaration of war.

470. (A) The Confederate generals were at a disadvantage from the beginning. They believed that their best hope was to force the enemy to attack, in the hope that the North would wear out its considerable resources. Both men led attacks only when conditions provided an excellent opportunity for a swift victory. Lee's invasion of the North in 1863 was largely forced on him by circumstance.

471. (D) The Union naval blockade of the South was in place well before the naval attack on New Orleans, which took place in February 1862. Some Union ships were ordered to leave the blockade in order to participate in the attack. The Union was already attacking the Confederacy from the west and north; by taking New Orleans, the Union could now attack from within the Confederacy as well.

472. (C) The victory at First Manassas made the South complacent; many troops, believing the war was all but won, went back home with the idea that their contribution was not necessary. For months after the battle, the Confederate Army found it very difficult to recruit new troops.

473. (B) There was never any question of the Confederates abandoning their home base in the old South. The other four answer choices all help to explain the advantages the Confederates saw in their strategy of carrying the war into the West. Confederate troops from Texas and the New Mexico Territory fought Union troops from Colorado and California through the summer of 1862, when the Confederates conceded defeat. This ended the war in the West.

474. (A) Pinkerton was neither an African-American nor a spy. He ran a famous private-detective agency in Chicago. During the war, he employed and trained spies and secret agents, both black and white, for the Union. Scobell, a former Mississippi slave whose owner had granted him his freedom, was the best known of the black Pinkertons; he spent most of the war gathering intelligence behind enemy lines. Touvestre stole the blueprints for the Confederate ironclad ship *Virginia* and fled with them to Washington, D.C.; the Union soon completed construction of its own ironclad, the *Monitor*. Scott found his way from a Virginia plantation to the Union army camp at Fort Monroe; he shared crucial details of Confederate fortifications and troop movements. Tubman is best known for her success as a conductor on the Underground Railroad, but she also served the Union government as a spy.

475. (E) After the stunning victory at Second Manassas, General Robert E. Lee decided to push north and take the war into Union territory. The Union troops met the Confederates at Antietam; the ensuing battle pushed back the planned invasion. Note on choice (B): McClellan was relieved of his command after Antietam, on the grounds of repeated failure to take decisive military action when he was handed obvious opportunities to do so.

476. (D) Sections 8 and 9 of Article I of the Constitution suggest that the actions described in choices (A), (C), and (E) are reserved to Congress, not the president. However, Lincoln took office during a time of dire national emergency. The Constitution names the president as commander in chief, but does not specify the extent of his or her war powers. Faced with a civil war, Lincoln interpreted his powers broadly. He was determined to respect the spirit of the Constitution; on the other hand, he recognized that the emergency required decisive action, and he considered the preservation of the Union to be the president's highest duty. Note on choice (A): The suspension of the writ of habeas corpus means that the Union military commanders had special powers to arrest anyone they believed to be a spy or an enemy agent, without a warrant, and that such a suspect could be held in custody almost indefinitely. The Constitution states that it is legal to suspend the writ in case of rebellion, for public safety. Note on choice (B): According to federal law, volunteers could only be called up for 90 days; Lincoln defied that law by extending the term to three years.

477. (C) Vicksburg was situated on 200-foot-high cliffs overlooking the Mississippi River for miles in both directions. Its great height above sea level meant that whoever controlled Vicksburg could position cannons on the cliffs and easily prevent the enemy from using the river. When the Union forces took Vicksburg in July 1863, they achieved control of the Mississippi and blocked all communication between the eastern and western states of the Confederacy.

478. (B) By freeing the slaves, the Emancipation Proclamation naturally changed their hope for a Union victory into a positive commitment to aid the Union side. About five-sixths of the black soldiers who would fight for the Union came from the Confederacy and the border slaveholding states. This meant that the Union gained, while the Confederacy lost, considerably more than 100,000 viable soldiers—a crucial difference in the outcome, given that the Confederate Army was already vastly outnumbered. Although the Emancipation Proclamation did affect the war's outcome, fighting would continue for another two years and four months.

479. (A) It was clear to Lee that Vicksburg, besieged by General Grant and Union troops, was bound to surrender; it was only a matter of time. The loss of Vicksburg, and with it the complete Union control over the Mississippi, meant that the Confederacy was driven into a corner. Lee would have to stake everything on a bold throw of the dice. Lee's decision was to invade the North; this led to the Battle of Gettysburg (Pennsylvania), which is considered the turning point of the entire war.

480. (D) Chickamauga was right outside the city of Chattanooga, on the Tennessee-Alabama border and in a natural geographical passageway through the mountains into the heart of the South. By holding off the Union forces at Chickamauga, the Confederates blocked that access—for the time being.

481. (E) African-Americans took part on both sides throughout the Civil War. They were able to enlist in the Union Army as of January 1, 1863, and in the Confederate Army as of 1865 (too late to help the Confederate cause). Before enlistment, they served regiments on both sides as cooks, personal servants, teamsters, ditch-diggers, and couriers. Many served the Union as spies and secret agents. (For details of African-American contributions to the war, see answers 474 and 491.)

482. (B) *New York Tribune* editor Greely (1811–1872) was a prominent Republican and an outspoken abolitionist. His editorial urged the president not to bow to any pressure from the border states or southern sympathizers, but to enforce the Confiscation Act, emancipate slaves, and ensure that the Union military welcomed and protected runaway slaves who sought their protection on the field. The Confiscation Act, Greeley's widely read editorial, and Lincoln's published reply to it (stating that his primary goal was to preserve the Union, not necessarily to free the slaves) all helped to lay the groundwork for the Emancipation Proclamation.

483. (D) Georgia is not on the Mississippi River; both Alabama and Mississippi lie in between the two. The other four choices all help to explain why General William T. Sherman decided that his best course was to march on Atlanta. With General Grant's recent defeat at Cold Harbor and President Lincoln running for reelection in the North, the Union badly needed to strike a decisive blow against the Confederacy.

484. (E) The western region of Virginia, including Harpers Ferry, seceded from Virginia because its people did not sympathize with slavery and did not want to end up on the losing side of the war. The new state of West Virginia officially joined the Union in 1863.

485. (B) In the Fort Laramie Treaty, the U.S. government had promised regular and substantial annual payments to the Sioux and other Indian nations. In reality, the payments were often late. They were also much smaller than the promised amounts, because unscrupulous U.S. officials found it all too easy to skim off large sums of the money into their own pockets. When the Sioux complained to the government about the delayed payments or pleaded for relief after a poor harvest, the government turned a deaf ear. All these factors combined in 1862 and pushed the Sioux past the breaking point into open rebellion.

486. (C) Stonewall Jackson was a Confederate general; it was a terrible blow to the South when one of his own men accidentally and fatally shot him during the Battle of Chancellorsville. Admiral Farragut presided over the taking of New Orleans and later Mobile Bay. Grant began the war by capturing western Tennessee; his leadership was so effective that he was soon made the head of the entire Union Army. Sherman won the Battle of Atlanta, which he used as a base to begin his long march through Georgia. Sheridan commanded troops in Virginia.

487. (E) General William T. Sherman ordered the evacuation of Atlanta to give its citizens the chance to remove to a place of safety before his troops destroyed the railroads, factories, shops, and telegraph lines, and commandeered all the eatables in the city for themselves. The Union troops were under orders to spare private property as much as possible.

488. (B) Britain and France were the major buyers of the southern cotton crop. The Confederate leaders hoped that these two nations would want to protect their interest in that crop by joining the war on the side of the South.

489. (A) Grant struck the Confederacy a severe blow with his victories at Forts Henry and Donelson, which gained the Union forces an important base of power in western Tennessee. The Union victory at Shiloh, which took place less than two months after the fall of Fort Donelson, drove the Confederate troops south into Alabama. The power base in Tennessee was important to the Union for two reasons. First, it was an ideal place from which to invade the South and cut the Confederacy in two by taking control of the Mississippi River. Second, the presence of the Union Army protected and defended the western region of the state, which was not sympathetic to the Confederate side in the war.

490. (D) Mathew Brady organized and managed a sizeable crew of photographers who used the cumbersome, although fairly efficient, glass-plate negative process of the time to document the Civil War. Although Brady himself took photographs, his chief role during the war was in supervising his photographers and collecting, preserving, and printing their photographs. His work has provided students with a matchless collection of dramatic and highly detailed images of officers, soldiers, camps, fortifications, ships, and battles. The Civil War was the first war in history to be visually recorded in this way and to this extent. Brady is also noted for his sensitive portrait photographs of Abraham Lincoln.

491. (A) The Battle of Fort Henry took place in February 1862, before the Union Army had mustered any black regiments or passed laws enabling African-Americans to enlist. (There was, of course, black participation in the Battle of Fort Henry; the Confederates employed slaves to build the fortifications.) The other four choices describe actions that involved the 54th Massachusetts Infantry, the 1st Kansas Colored Regiment, and the 1st and 3rd Louisiana Native Guard (under the command of Captain André Cailloux, a free black officer).

492. (E) Lincoln invokes choice (A) in the final sentence of the Gettysburg Address: "government of the people, by the people, for the people, shall not perish from the earth." He invokes choice (B) by saying that the United States was "conceived in liberty, and dedicated to the proposition that all men are created equal." He invokes choice (C) by saying that the soldiers "gave their lives that the nation might live" and that their sacrifice consecrated the battlefield as holy ground. He invokes choice (D) by saying that Americans must "highly resolve . . . that this nation, under God, shall have a new birth of freedom." The speech makes no reference to outsiders joining in the fight.

493. (D) Washington was the capital of the Union. After Bull Run, the Union troops retreated toward Washington. Historians believe that if Confederate troops had pursued them, they might easily have taken the capital city and thus brought the war to an early conclusion. However, the early victory made the South complacent, suggesting that there was no urgent need to invade the Union capital in a war they believed they had already won.

494. (A) The Emancipation Proclamation (January 1863) was legal because of provisions established in the Confiscation Act (July 1862). The Confiscation Act gave the U.S. government the right to emancipate all slaves owned by traitors—traitors being Confederates, people in rebellion against the Union. It also gave the president the right to employ "persons of African descent" in the suppression of the rebellion. The Emancipation Act includes both provisions.

495. (B) The Union Army never captured General Lee. The other four choices all help to explain why the victory at Antietam was a welcome recovery for Union forces after they lost Second Manassas. Probably the most important result was the blocking of the Confederates' first attempt to invade Union territory.

496. (C) Fort Henry is on the Tennessee River and Fort Donelson on the Cumberland River; the Mississippi River lies about a hundred miles to the west. These two forts on the Tennessee-Kentucky border were taken one after the other in the same military engagement in February 1862. This early Union victory was important for the reasons described in choices (A), (B), (D), and (E).

497. (A) Gettysburg ended in such a severe defeat for the Confederates that they would never again penetrate into the North. Vicksburg surrendered to Grant and the Union forces on the same day that the Battle of Gettysburg was won; this made a Confederate loss inevitable.

498. (D) Free Africans were able to vote if they were residents in most of the states north of Maryland, but emancipated slaves were all residents of the Confederate and border states and did not have voting rights in 1864. Those who had left the Confederacy to join the Union Army most likely had no opportunity to vote; they would not have been able to establish residency yet in a free state. The other four choices all help to explain why Lincoln won the election, particularly choice (B). A string of Union military victories in the late summer and early fall gave the voters new confidence in the administration.

499. (B) The Emancipation Proclamation stated that all slaves in any state in rebellion against the United States were free as of January 1, 1863. The phrase "in rebellion" shows that it did not affect the status of slaves in slaveholding states that had remained within the Union, such as Maryland.

500. (B) Washington, D.C., is bordered on three sides by Maryland and on one side by Virginia. Virginia had already seceded. With its capital surrounded, the Union would be in grave danger of losing the war.